Dedication

This book is dedicated to my Aunt Linda. As long as I can remember, Aunt Linda has brought joy into my life. As a child, Christmas didn't start until she arrived with her Volkswagen bug packed with gifts for my two sisters and me. She was the first person to take me to the beach. Every birthday she asked me what I wanted to do for my special day, being one of the first adults to give me a choice. When I was eight it was Disneyland, as I got older I was much more greedy, asking to go snow skiing for a weekend. I will never forget the time we drove late into the night to get to our ski resort. It was freezing cold with two feet of snow on the ground. Driving up the snow-covered mountain in her tiny bug without snow chains, we were sliding around on the icy roads. I remember that I wasn't afraid because she wasn't afraid. After all, she was the adult. Then, Aunt Linda calmly told me to take off my seat belt and open the door to be prepared to jump out of the car if it started to slide off the hill. The next night we put on our swimsuits and ran in our bare feet through the snow to soak in the Jacuzzi. The weekend was a teenage girl's dream and memories were made.

My aunt always lived in unique homes. The first apartment that I remember was in Culver City, California. It was in the style of an old ship right in the middle of LA. It was the coolest apartment I have ever seen. The furniture was built into the walls and the doors had latches, no handles. The entire living area was made out of dark wood with windows up high as if you were living on an old ship. When she bought her first home in Laurel Canyon, it was 100 steps up and looked much like a treehouse. She decorated it beautifully only to have her dog, which she rescued from the dog pound, eat one entire side of her brand-new sofa. No, she didn't complain about that or anything else. After that, she moved to Manhattan Beach then to Arrowhead where paved roads didn't go. Today she lives in Seaside Oregon.

When Lorrin got sick there was a lot of madness. I, of course, did not have the tools to deal with this kind of chronic traumatic experience. Aunt Linda was a nurse practitioner. She got it! I mean she really got what I was going through. Her respectful, loving ways that served me as a child were still intact as she became my rock during the darkest days of my life. She never judged me or tried to fix me or Lorrin. She just loved us the way we were, broken. Auntie Linda always saw perfection.

The fact that she was there for me wasn't a surprise because she spent her entire life helping others. She was a big sister to many at-risk youths. She wanted to adopt an AIDS baby way back before we understood AIDS. She fed the homeless, worked at Meals on Wheels and food shelters for many years. After a failed attempt at adopting an at-risk boy, she adopted a daughter and is now a wonderful grandmother of two boys.

When Lorrin almost died on her third birthday, Auntie Linda drove her Volkswagen Bus to Cedars-Sinai from Oregon with her two large dogs and lived in her car for two weeks, while I lived in ICU. She came every morning with her coffee cup in hand and would just sit and hold Lorrin, stroking her hair, telling her how beautiful she was, while holding my hand and my heart. Later she quit her job and came to live with me to help take care of Lorrin. It didn't work out exactly how it was planned. Her two big dogs were snacking on my nurse's dog and actually bit one nurse on the foot. Aunt Linda said, "Well who puts their foot into a dog's mouth?" We all have our ways of looking at things. But it was just too much for everyone. The fact that she loved us so much that she would do anything for Lorrin and me was something that I had never experienced.

My aunt is always full of love and laughter. When Lorrin and I lived in California we drove at least once a year to visit her. We spent hours walking the beach, me crying as the waves crashed in from the stormy ocean. It was always a release for me to be with her. She listened, held my hand, and let me cry always telling me how amazing I was. One time I lost Lorrin's brand-new 400-dollar glasses. I had to report every dime I spent to the court and was worried that I would get in trouble for being so careless. My Aunt said, "All the things that you are responsible for, I think you do amazingly. Don't beat yourself up." I never felt that way or thought that way. I was always trying harder to stay one step ahead of disaster. Never feeling enough and always afraid of attack.

I will never forget the months before Lorrin's death. She drove 1,000 miles to be with Lorrin and me. She brought huge chocolate cakes from her local bakery for Lorrin. She knew Lorrin was a chocoholic. At the time Lorrin was on the Keto-Genetic diet and chocolate was not on it. But at that point, who cared? My daughter was dying. Lorrin would eat the cake and I would get out the Ativan to stop the seizures. It was worth the joy it brought the household and the big smile Lorrin had when she ate it. Aunt Linda was sitting next to me the night Lorrin died. I held Lorrin in my arms as her spirit left her body. My aunt said to me, "Did you see that?" I could not speak I was so afraid of what was to come next. We both knew in that moment Lorrin was gone. We laid her down and went to the kitchen and had a glass of wine together. My aunt doesn't drink, *ever*! We were both traumatized and numb. The next day she got into her car and drove home. I would have never asked her to go through such an experience, but she would have it no other way.

Today my aunt lives on coffee, eating chocolate, and the best pork enchilada The Stand in Seaside Oregon makes. She drives to the ocean every day, usually more than once, to look at the waves. I can never pay her back for all the times that she held space for me and my journey, and the love that she had for Lorrin.

I want to say to all those people who go above and beyond to help families with unique children, please know that it does make a difference. You may never know just how much your support helps keep sanity in the midst of chaos. I love you, Auntie Linda, and thank you!

Mascot Books
560 Herndon Parkway #120
Herndon, VA 20170
info@mascotbooks.com

PRBVG0314A

Library of Congress Control Number: 2014931898

ISBN-10: 1620866218
ISBN-13: 9781620866214

Printed in the United States

www.mascotbooks.com

A **UNIQUE** LIFE FULLY LIVED

A Personal Journey of
Love, Hope, and Courage

To: Amelee, Kylea,
keep your parents
reminded after you!
love you all,
Karen Kain

LORRIN & KAREN KAIN

Table of Contents

Foreword

I met Karen Kain at the Autism One Conference in May of 2011. A truly desperate mom looking for answers for my vaccine-injured child, I wandered into the large conference room where she held court.

In truth I was tired and overwhelmed; I'd seen a lot of doctors present that day and my mind drifted a bit. However, in moments she snapped me right back to center as the large screen behind her podium flashed a short film of her precious daughter, Lorrin, as an infant, seizing over and over again. Karen's sweet, motherly voice in the background repeated, "You're okay, you're okay, baby." A palpable terror beneath the smoothness of her voice told me, even before I knew the whole story, it did not turn out okay.

At the time, my son was still a toddler, and the wretchedness of watching a baby suffer so needlessly brought on immediate fits of sobs. Much like the autism spectrum, as it is termed today, vaccine injury casts a wide net of illnesses, disorders, and diseases. Seizures of this violent nature were not a part of our journey to date.

How can she stand there and present this information so matter-of-factly? I thought as I leaned in with a fist full of tissues, reluctantly willing myself to hear her story to the end.

Many people in my row got up and left, unable to process the callousness of The Department of Justice, a system that claims to protect and honor children, while secretly paying out large sums of taxpayer dollars to American parents for their child's life-long medical care as the direct result of vaccines.

She can tell it because she lived it for fifteen years. I concluded as her presentation came to an end.

"I saw this mom present today. She won her case in vaccine court. They killed her child! It took fifteen years, but they killed her baby, Lorrin. You have no idea what this woman's life was like, what she endured…and she's not selling anything. She is doing this to spare other kids and educate people about the Department of Justice. She's doing this to honor her daughter!" I exclaimed to my husband Dave, who was up in the hotel room trying to catch some sleep between presentations. Parents of vaccine-injured children can never get enough sleep.

My husband wiped his eyes and asked if I'd met her.

Thankfully, that moment came the next day in the hotel elevator. As Karen addresses so beautifully in this book, there are no accidents! People, situations, and signs manifest themselves just when they are needed. We need to pay attention.

Much like the feeling of seeing an old friend from childhood or beloved family member, a sense of home sparked between us. She knew I was the person crying in the audience. I knew she knew that we were the same, fighters for our children, to the end and after.

Over the years, I have come to know Karen Kain as person of extraordinary purpose and character. If you are reading this book, the same can be said of you. Many people walk away because the truth about what is happening to the children of this country is so incredibly hard to face. Like Karen and me, you will be forever changed.

But, you will also have the glorious honor of being captivated by Lorrin, her choices, her journey, her beautiful yet broken body, her limitless spirit and love for us all. You will grow in respect and admiration for Karen as she shows us what it really means to sacrifice, love, live a full life as a caregiver, but very much remain human, a woman who still has dreams in the midst of navigating an unpredictable life she did not choose.

Most laudable about this extraordinary telling of their lives are the lessons we can learn as parents facing incredible challenges. Karen, in the midst of her suffering and pain, educated everyone who crossed her path. Doctors, nurses, educators, and administrators all benefited from her remarkable tenacity and courage. In her efforts to create a life for Lorrin, a life as remarkable as Lorrin herself, Karen discovered herself and began her lifelong work as a tireless advocate for all our children. It is my sincere hope and prayer every American citizen will make their way through the pages of this book. This incredibly important chronicling of Karen and Lorrin's lives should fundamentally change us all—and by extension cause radical reformation of vaccination practices and patient care for those who cannot speak for themselves.

Lisa Joyce Goes

Co-author, The Thinking Moms' Revolution

Co-founder, The Thinking Moms' Revolution, LLC.

Contributing Editor, Age of Autism

Human Rights Panelist, The Academy of Excellence in Learning

Vaccine Safety Advocate

Autism Activist

Acknowledgements

Thank you, Dr. Kundell, for putting up with me for all those years. Lorrin would have never lived so long without your great care, and I surely would not have made it. Thank you, Larry Sulham, for being the best male role model a girl could have, for Lorrin and me both! I love you, Debbie Hessler. Because of you, Lorrin met her school friends. Your love and care is like no other. Thank you, Mr. Saute, for giving Lorrin a chance in your class. Karissa Boyce for joining our lives and being that awesome best friend to Lorrin and me. All my gratitude to Sarah Rivera, you are an angel sent from heaven. I know you and Lorrin are soul mates, but what you have given to me makes my heart as full and as happy as a human being could ask. There are no words. Thank you, Kelsy, Ariel, Merin, Angie, Taylor, Kelsey, Jennifer, Dylan, both Laurens, and all of Lorrin's friends. Thank you to The Hummingbird and The Honey Bee, previously The Akashic Record Bookshop in Thousand Oaks, for supporting spiritual growth. If not for my teacher, Pat Rouleau, I know I would have never gotten through the dark night of the soul and become the parent that I was to Lorrin. Pat taught me how to survive myself. Loye Barton, I will never forget the day I met you and thank you for your love, guidance, and friendship. Thank you to those who supported me in many ways: Cheryl Gooss, Kelsey Liddle, Dawna Shuman, and Sarah Laucks. Thanks to my lifelong friends Shelley Mager, Barbara Naomi Ortiz-Monson, Robert and Ellen Rohan, and my dear sister Stephanie Baumgardner for loving me through all of this.

Thank you to Lorrin's caregivers, Elizabeth, Denni, Merrianne, and Rosa. You lived the story with me.

Thank you to the 911 responders, the ICU doctors, nurses, and hospital staff. Sharon Cooper, Tessie Hernandez, Julie Edwards, Liz, Maureen, and all my friends at Cedars-Sinai for making unbearable hospital admits livable and fun.

Thank you to my intuitive friends who channeled Lorrin; Robin Devine,

Ed Rote, Megan Assaf, Libby Kimbrough, and Candace Calloway. Stacy Parker for being such a great friend and teacher. Thank you, Meg Blackburn Losey for listening to our children. Ed and Teri Arranga, Lisa Joyce Goes, and *all* the parents out there who stand up for their children. Thank God we found each other.

Thank you to my family for putting up with me. I am so proud of my nieces and nephew for making smart choices. Thank you, James, for listening when I told you to come and when I asked you to stay. I am so glad that you and Lorrin shared such wonderful memories. Thank you for melting that ice around my heart. I know I am a pain in the arse but I also know you love me more than any man ever has. Thank you to James' parents for accepting and loving me from day one.

Thank you, Barbara Jo Fleming, Barbara Glassman, and Sarah Sutton for your edits and, of course, friendships. Thank you, Christopher Trela for first edits.

Thank you, Island Dolphin Care, Jr. Blind of America, and Canine Companions for Independence. Thank you to The Abilities Expo for allowing me to share my story and connect with families.

Thank you, Todd Civin and Mascot Books, for getting this book completed.

Thank you to my brave and beautiful Lorrin. I am in awe of your courage and undying love of life. Thank you to all the children who have come here to teach us. We are listening.

Introduction

This is my story. I am a woman who gave birth to a tiny soul. A beautiful girl named Lorrin Danielle Kain. My journey starts here. I am just like you—I wanted to live a simple life full of hopes and dreams. My greatest dream was to be a mother, a wife and have a family.

The pages following are my story. You may find it difficult to read or you may see a beautiful story of love and commitment. My daughter Lorrin was like the Grand Canyon. "Some people come to the edge and see a huge hole and others witness one of God's wonders." Lorrin was a miracle and an angel. She was a teacher and my greatest love. It is my belief that Lorrin chose this life, chose me as her mother, and chose the vessel of a broken body to teach. She captured many hearts during her fifteen years of life. Two weeks after Lorrin's death, two thousand people went to her website. Lorrin's essence was full of love. She made everyone feel special no matter who they were. She reminded us that we have a maker who loves us. She exuded love to all she met. I have been told by many that Lorrin transformed their lives.

At first glance, many saw her as a person without any abilities. Lorrin never walked or talked. She didn't have movie star capacities. Lorrin's body made many people uncomfortable, so uncomfortable they would leave the room. My story is about the brave and loving ones who showed up in Lorrin's life and took the opportunity to see the world through different eyes. Lorrin only saw love. If you spent any time with her, she would convince you that she had a secret love and faith in God. She lived a lifetime full of peace.

This is my journey as Lorrin's mother. I have lost everything in my life that I thought was important. I have cried and screamed at God. I would never have chosen the life I have experienced. I endured rejection, rage, fear, and destitution. I had no idea how to care for and love my daughter. In my attempt to survive, I kept journals. I brought the best life I could to my daughter. I was privileged to be the one who witnessed her strength first hand. I brought life to Lorrin as she taught me my toughest life lessons. I am the lucky one. I have lived, really lived. She is my strength. It is for her that I try to be the best person I can, and it is for her I tell our story.

I see Lorrin everywhere there is love. I see her in the eyes of her best friend, Sarah. I see and feel her in all that is beautiful.

Chapter 1

~ *The Beginning* ~
Six weeks old

There is so much I will never understand. There is fate, destiny, and sometimes there are just plain accidents that change our lives forever.

My daughter, Lorrin Danielle Kain, received her DPT shot on April 27, 1994, at six weeks old. After the doctor administered the vaccine, she fell fast asleep. I woke her not long after to give her Tylenol as recommended, and she went back to sleep. On the way home from the pediatrician's office, I stopped to visit my girlfriend, Shannon. At her house, two hours after the vaccination, Lorrin woke up screaming and crying. Little did I know, our lives were about to drastically change forever.

I ran to Lorrin and found her arms extended stiffly out in front of her. Her hands were repeatedly clenching and opening, her eyes were blinking rapidly, and from her mouth came a high-pitched screaming. I held her as far from me as I could and I watched. I was afraid to touch my own daughter. My job as a mother was to protect her, but I didn't know how.

With her body twitching, I held her at arm's distance, and my mind flashed to the special I'd seen on television just the night before about vaccine injuries. My stomach dropped. Was that what was wrong with her? Was my baby having a reaction to her vaccination?

Lorrin's body softened back into the baby I knew. Her screaming quieted and my mind returned to the present. I thrust Lorrin into Shannon's hands, ran to the bathroom, and vomited. I held on to the bathroom wall to hold myself up. Fear overwhelmed me. My body trembled, and sweat drenched me. I knew in my gut that something was terribly wrong. For several minutes, I hid in the bathroom while my mind raced. Babies just do not scream and shake for no reason.

When I came out, Shannon kept saying, "This isn't right. This isn't right!"

I phoned the pediatrician's office to find my doctor was at lunch. Her receptionist told me to bring Lorrin in at two o'clock. I couldn't breathe. I was so upset, I went directly there. I waited outside a locked door, sitting on the ground with Lorrin asleep in a stupor, my arms locked around her.

By the time the doctor returned, the waiting room was full of mothers with babies resting comfortably in their arms. I felt detached. Everything was a blur. I was unable to connect to the other mothers, to my baby, or even to my own fears.

The doctor saw us first and laid Lorrin on the examining table. Lorrin started shaking and crying. I waited in dreadful anticipation for the doctor to do something. But she just stood over Lorrin and stared. We watched Lorrin shake, scream, and cry. Lorrin did this for five minutes. I found myself backed up against a wall. "Make it stop!" I yelled at the doctor. "Make it stop!"

The doctor said Lorrin was having a seizure. She was calm and started the necessary arrangements. Her staff walked in and out with telephone numbers. They called the hospital and other doctors. Then the doctor turned to me. "Take Lorrin to the hospital," she said. That was it. No explanation, no assuring words, nothing. Just take her to the hospital.

I stood there in disbelief.

By this time, I was afraid of Lorrin. I dreaded driving with her in my car. I was terrified she would have another episode; I was in no state to drive at all. I didn't even know where the hospital was. Panic threatened to swallow me. Even if someone gave me directions, I doubted I could find the hospital. My hands trembled so violently I wasn't sure I could hold onto the steering wheel.

I think I went into shock. My body was sweaty and shaking. I could hear the doctor talking, but I wasn't able to respond. I felt incapable of handling anything. I was completely alone. My husband, Tom, was out of town on business. I'm not sure why I didn't call him. I don't know if it was due to fear or shame. I wanted to be the perfect mother. Maybe it was pride that kept me from calling him—I should've been able to handle whatever happened with my child. But possibly it was something else that kept me from telling him. If I didn't say the words—if I didn't say them aloud—maybe this wasn't real. Maybe this horrific nightmare wasn't really happening.

Somehow I put Lorrin in my car and drove her to the hospital. Looking back now, I don't know why 911 wasn't called. This was truly an emergency. My six-week-old baby was acting like the exorcist. I was afraid of her.

The hospital admitted Lorrin, and we stayed for three days. My only previous hospital experience had been during Lorrin's delivery, so I had no idea what to expect. I did know enough to understand that this was serious. We were in the intensive care unit (ICU), and my baby was getting lots of attention. During the first twenty-four hours in the ICU, the doctors did urine metabolic tests, a CT scan and a spinal tap. I listened to every word they said and followed every direction. Anything they wanted to do and any test they wanted to run, I agreed to.

At six p.m. on that first brutal day, I was told to take a break—go home and come back to the ICU later, at 7 p.m., after the nurses gave their reports. I had no idea how familiar this routine would become to me.

It took fifteen minutes to drive home, and I found myself with less than an hour to kill. I sat in my living room. Too distraught to make any phone calls, I wanted to hide this awful news. I wasn't about to give it words. In the silence of my empty house, my thoughts twisted and careened from the unknowable future to the past.

Even though I was the middle girl of three, I was the last in my family to have a child. At the time I delivered Lorrin, I believed I had just given birth to the last grandbaby in our family. This was my second marriage. Being divorced once made me feel like a huge failure. I wanted to put my life right. This was my greatest dream. The responsibility and honor of being a parent was something I was very proud of. But now my life spiraled out of control. Even though I had done nothing wrong, I felt responsible for what was happening.

Looking back, I can see the pressure I put on myself was pointless. But, at that moment, I was not about to call my family and tell them that my daughter, my contribution to our family, was in the hospital having seizures.

As the sun set, I felt numb and alone in my quiet home. I didn't turn on the lights; I sank into the couch while tears pooled in my eyes. There was nothing I could do. The full weight of the day's events hit me. I sobbed and trembled uncontrollably. My worst fear had been realized.

This next statement may sound peculiar, but I had always felt sure my baby would not be healthy. I cannot explain that dark certainty, whether premonition or fear; I just felt it. I never talked about it to anyone. When, at sixteen weeks along, I saw the sonogram of my healthy baby girl, I was surprised and elated. My world felt complete. The sonogram dispelled my qualms. But, sitting now in my living room, all the fear came rushing back.

As I counted the minutes until I could return to the hospital, a new reality overtook the feelings of elation I had experienced since the birth of my baby. The dream of being a happily married woman living in a sweet little condo in Orange County with a beautiful and healthy baby faded away.

Just that morning, I had sat in the same spot on the sofa, holding Lorrin and watching her every breath, waiting for her to move. Being a new mom, I spent hours just watching her tiny body take each breath. She was so beautiful. She was mine. Only hours earlier, I had cradled her on my thigh with her head in my hands and her feet resting on my stomach. She looked up at me and gave me her first smile. All I saw were gums.

This image is still vivid, as if it had just happened yesterday. I'll never forget it. My daughter was a miracle. That smile would be the last I would see from her for a long time.

The first night I stayed with Lorrin in the ICU. The next night we were moved to a floor and I slept on a cot, which had to be put in a certain place. I tried to follow the hospital rules, even though half of them made no sense. The rules, along with constant intrusions and the worry of not knowing what was happening to my baby, exhausted me. The lab technician came before six a.m. He held Lorrin's tiny arms and legs, and jabbed her little arm over and over, trying to get a needle into a vein. She cried as he poked. I cried as he poked. It made me crazy watching her delicate, sweet body being pricked with needles. I felt I could not bear any more.

Lorrin didn't have another seizure during that initial hospital stay, and the doctors assured me that many newborns who have seizures while so young never have them again. I held on tightly to those words. That was the only prognosis I had at this point, and "seizures" were the only diagnosis. We went home and tried to pretend it had never happened.

Fourteen days after her first seizure, while Tom and I were going through our nightly routine of dinner and television, Lorrin started to scream and shake. I knew immediately what was happening.

We held Lorrin's body protectively while she shrieked, trembled and blinked unseeing blue eyes. This was Tom's first time witnessing Lorrin seize.

Tom kept repeating, "You're okay, Baby. You're okay." It went on and on. For five endless, eternal minutes, we watched our baby jerk in my arms as the entire room was filled with her screams. I called 911, but by the time the ambulance came, the seizure had stopped.

The paramedics seemed very nervous. I was hoping for some support when they arrived, but the look on their faces scared me. They were afraid of my baby.

We went back to the hospital. The same neurologist who had seen Lorrin when she was in the ICU came to see her in the ER. He suggested we check her vitamin B levels since babies with low levels of vitamin B sometimes have seizures. Since seizures didn't run in either of our families, the doctor reassured us that our baby was going to be just fine.

We wanted to believe that.

Results for the vitamin B levels took longer than the other blood tests, so the doctor suggested we give Lorrin vitamin B supplements. And just in case a vitamin B deficiency was not the cause, the doctor also recommended we put her on Phenobarbital, which is the traditional medicine used to treat seizures.

When we took Lorrin home from the hospital that night, we felt confident this ordeal would not progress further. Tom had a different attitude and approach than I did. He was adamant that our daughter was going to be fine. I know he was afraid too, but he didn't show it. So I piggy-backed on his bravado; I would never tell him of the deep fear in my gut. I hoped that if I didn't speak of my ill thoughts, they wouldn't come true.

Chapter 2

~ *Diagnosis* ~
Three Months

"I'm so happy she chose us as family. I remember visiting her in the hospital, but I was just so young. I didn't understand what everyone was going through at the time. Mom would just say, 'She's sick. The doctors are helping her feel better.' As a kid, I just pictured her in there with the flu. If only I'd have been able to comprehend."

~ Mackenzie, Lorrin's cousin

The end of May, 1994, Lorrin had nine grand mal seizures—episodes lasting five minutes or longer—in just one day. I was afraid to leave her alone for even a moment, and the constant vigilance wore me to a frazzle. She was already taking one anti-seizure medication. It seemed to be doing nothing. What else could be done to make them stop?

It had been six weeks since Lorrin's first seizure; the doctors had still not offered a conclusive diagnosis of her condition. I don't know if the delay in diagnosis was due to the medical profession's reticence to tie her injuries to the vaccinations, or because it was difficult to pinpoint the cause of the seizures. But I wanted to know why this was happening. I phoned the doctor every time she had a seizure. I was not about to just sit at home and watch this take place. If I was uncomfortable, I was going to make everyone uncomfortable until I got answers. I am sure he was sick of my repeated calls. Yet, I was starting to panic. He finally told me to bring Lorrin to see him.

My best friend from high school, Barbara, offered to meet us at the appointment. I don't know why she volunteered to come with me that day. We met in the parking lot. I couldn't speak. I was lost in worry and caring for my baby. I was no longer caring for myself. I'm sure I looked a wreck. I wasn't wearing makeup or paying attention to my hair or hygiene. I was clean, but that was about it.

At first glance, seeing Barbara's beauty reminded me briefly what was happening to me. I had no humbleness left in me. I was losing myself in fear and desperation. I could tell she was afraid for me. She always looked so beautiful and pulled together. I could see in her eyes the shock she felt at the state I was in. But it was a huge relief to have her at my side. I had felt so alone these past weeks. Barb and I hugged and went inside.

The neurologist's office was decorated in an attempt to provide an at-home coziness, with overstuffed couches, carpeting, and children's toys in the corner. But how comfortable can you feel in a pediatric neurologist's office? As we waited, I realized that I had not yet eaten that day. Barb tried to comfort me while I fidgeted with anxiety, holding Lorrin tightly in my arms.

"Doesn't it make you crazy," she asked, "that all of these pictures on the wall are crooked?" The walls were covered with black-and-white framed photographs of varying sizes. Yes, the pictures were crooked, but I didn't care in the slightest. I looked at Barb and said sharply, "No."

With my dreadfully wrong child in my lap, I was near panic and filled with fear about our uncertain future. I loved that Barb was with me that day and I would've given her a courtesy laugh—if I'd had it in me. But Lorrin's condition was terrifying. I could see no evidence of the child that I had given birth to. Her three-month-old body, draped limply across my legs, left me mute.

Lorrin was admitted to the Children's Hospital of Orange County later that day. I expected them to stop the seizures because that is what I thought hospitals were for. During the hospital stay, we saw the neurologist every day. Different tests were given. On the seventh day of our hospital stay, I noticed a change in Lorrin. I told the neurologist I thought Lorrin must be bored because she wasn't looking at me anymore. I explained to him how the night before, Lorrin, her father, and I walked around the colorful hospital. We were showing her beautiful, bright shapes and she had smiled and responded to us and to her surroundings.

"But today," I told the doctor, "she is just gazing. She isn't really looking at me."

I could never have prepared myself for what happened next.

The neurologist stood up, walked over to the hospital crib, and picked up a brightly colored toy. He waved it over Lorrin's face above her eyes to see if she visually tracked the object he held. He moved it from one side to another quickly as if he already knew the answer.

"Mrs. Kain, your baby is retarded."

Time stopped. His words slapped me. Before I could comprehend them, he continued.

"Look at her fists and the way her hands are clenched. Look at the way her back is arched. Your baby is retarded!"

My baby was retarded.

I'll never forget that moment. My baby was retarded.

The neurologist and the "white coats" in training at this teaching hospital must have been talking about Lorrin's case for days. But I was completely unprepared. No one had mentioned that her seizures were causing brain damage. No one had mentioned that my baby was retarded.

I could not believe a doctor would blurt out that information so thoughtlessly. He had just labeled my daughter with the most shameful diagnosis—the worst thing he could tell a parent. It felt like an accusation, a condemnation, as if he had said, "Mrs. Kain, you're fucked!"

I knew she was having seizures, but we had been in the hospital seven days and I thought we were fixing things. Until that day, the doctors had kept insisting that babies sometimes have seizures and they "grow out of them."

I doubt the interns crowded in the room were as surprised as I was, unless it was by the neurologist's callous delivery. Tears filled my eyes and streamed down my face. I'd never experienced such a deep pain. I'd been broken-hearted before, jilted by a boyfriend, but that was nothing compared to knowing my child's life was in jeopardy.

With her value being put into question by this diagnosis, my self-worth plummeted. My identity was completely vested in being Lorrin's mother. That life, as I had imagined it, was over. I couldn't grasp how I could live in this new world he had shoved me into, one in which my daughter was permanently defective and I was to blame because I was her mother.

The doctors left Lorrin's room as quickly as they had come in. It felt like they took all the oxygen with them; I couldn't breathe.

I called Tom, and his secretary answered. He never seemed to be available when I needed him. I tried to tell the secretary, but I was choked with tears and couldn't get the words out. Suddenly and awkwardly, I said, "The doctor says Lorrin's retarded!"

She fumbled with the phone before putting me on hold to find Tom.

By the time he came to the phone, I'd had time to reflect on what had just happened. The doctor's behavior angered and bewildered me.

Tom's response to the news was not what I expected. "Don't you let him say that about my baby!" he yelled, his anger evident. "He doesn't know what he's talking about. She's just a baby!"

My feelings quickly shifted. *Yeah! What does that doctor know? She's so beautiful and wonderful. She'll be okay.* As Tom reassured me, we took our first step towards denial, the only path we could embrace at that point, since all the realistic alternatives we could imagine looked hopelessly grim.

In spite of my newfound distrust and dislike for the neurologist, I came away with a new medication for Lorrin: Dilantin. So at three months old, when most babies are not yet eating solid foods, Lorrin was taking two anti-seizure medications in applesauce. The neurologist suggested we get a second opinion and gave us the name of a well-known and respected doctor in Los Angeles.

Chapter 3

~ *Specialists and the CDC* ~
Three Months Old

Knowing what I know now, if I could go back, I would stop reliving all the bad things that were happening in my life by sharing them with anyone who would listen. I was fueling the negative experiences and becoming a human disaster. I was lost. I had no spirit or any hope left inside me. I was fully consumed with my misery. I couldn't understand at the time that by holding my head up and focusing just a little, I could have possibly opened myself up to happier opportunities.

Despite the recent diagnosis, I was still filled with hope for Lorrin's recovery. Since Lorrin's first seizure, I had carried a piece of paper everywhere I went. I made notes of everything she ate, every seizure that she had, including the length and the time. I could not rely on my mind to recall the information, as the doctors asked so many questions. So I charted everything. Having this information aided me in many ways. I was not only able to respond to the doctors with accurate information and kept notes of all my questions, but this was also crucial information to have during our legal process.

Neither the doctors' opinions nor the way they delivered them supported my optimism. I was ignorant about dealing with hospital dynamics, and I had no idea how to extract the information I needed from medical professionals. In those early days, they offered very little, with one memorable exception.

During the first few days at the Children's Hospital, I bumped into a disease specialist, Dr. David Lang. He was doing rounds on the pediatric floor.

His approach towards me and Lorrin seemed different from that of other doctors.

He worked for the Centers for Disease Control (CDC), and he wanted to talk to me about something most doctors wouldn't discuss. He said some children do have reactions to their vaccines, and that Lorrin showed classic symptoms of a vaccine injury. Doctor David Lang, MD then explained the Vaccine Compensation Act to me. He gave me the information I needed to find an attorney and told me about the Vaccine Adverse Event Reporting System (VAERS).

I took what he said to heart that day because no other doctor had spoken to me with respect or honesty. I added it to my notes.

When I got home, I was fueled with anger and drive to prove those horrible aspersions that had been cast on my daughter's future to be false. I was referred to the Early Intervention Program for children who are at risk for normal development. I called to get Lorrin signed up for in-home therapy sessions. I understood that she would qualify for in-home therapies: physical; occupational; vision; speech and language. I wanted her to have every opportunity to get the best start.

When problems with newborns are identified before they leave the hospital, they are considered to be "at risk" and are immediately signed up for many services. Because Lorrin was born healthy and her seizures began at six weeks without a "known" cause, the doctors were slow to designate her as being "at risk."

I made my first call to the early intervention program. I held my head high. My daughter was the most important child on this earth. I soon learned that I was not alone and would become just another number in the system. Getting to talk to the actual caseworker involved first talking to an intake clerk and then waiting for the caseworker to call me back. Both of these positions were carefully guarded by a receptionist.

After several calls, I finally was referred to an intake clerk. She was not impressed and did not show much interest in my need to get my daughter on track. I am not saying she was rude—I just felt that I was becoming another parent of a child who was in need of a miracle.

I think this is where my fight for my daughter started. Once I gave the intake clerk all the information she needed—Lorrin's history, insurance, etc.—I still needed to talk to the case worker, who was guarded by a receptionist. I called five times that first day. I was polite and understood that the caseworker was busy, but I had every intention of getting my daughter these services.

I called the next morning at nine. I again told the receptionist who I was and why I was calling. I told her I would call every half hour until the caseworker returned my call. I did just that. The caseworker soon called me and we got Lorrin on schedule to be evaluated for services. I had every intention of getting Lorrin all the services that she qualified for. It became my mantra. "If she is not entitled to this service, please let me know. If this is an entitlement to her, I expect to receive it and I expect it to be the best quality available."

Tom was not used to having friends—much less strangers—in our home. While he went to work, I started my weekly sessions with Lorrin's new therapists. I remember meeting Suzanne, Lorrin's Physical Therapist (PT). She was one of the first angels that were sent to us. Her mother, brother and sister were blind and deaf, so living with disabilities was commonplace to her. She was not affected by my tears, my fear, or even my rejection of my new life. She brought me an article about going on a vacation to Italy but ending up in Switzerland instead. It talks about how you expected to take a trip to Italy and see Rome and Venice and all the things Italy has to offer. But if you dwell on the fact that you ended up someplace else you will never see all the beautiful things to be seen in Switzerland. The Alps and the chateaus. The cheese and chocolate. All that would be swept away, disregarded.

I read the article, but I resisted the point it wanted to make. I was not okay with Lorrin being compromised. I didn't want a kid who was screwed up. I wanted a healthy child and all the experiences that came with raising a healthy child. I was damned if I wasn't going to get one. I was not going to Switzerland!

Another beautiful gift she gave me was that she was not affected by or afraid of my daughter. She showed me and taught me things that helped me to become a good parent to Lorrin. One of the most powerful things she told me was to decorate Lorrin's crib. Bring the world to her. Vision is learned. Sensory and tactile experiences were critical for Lorrin at this early stage.

I went to the store and bought big buckets that Lorrin's tiny body could fit into. I filled them with pinto beans, rice, and flour. We would put Lorrin's naked body into the buckets and let her feel the different textures. I would marvel any time her little hands would make an attempt to open and feel the textures. Sometimes she would scream bloody murder. Lorrin really didn't appreciate working hard. She cried many times in therapy, especially during physical therapy. Suzanne kept pushing and Lorrin cried harder.

We worked on different smells and visual stimuli. I would go to the store and buy different fabrics and lights and decorate her crib with them. The problem was that Lorrin was never in her crib. She didn't sleep much—only about four hours a night. She cried constantly. So I would stand in her room and watch her in her crib, hoping that she would connect with or be interested in the new visual enticements that were becoming part of her world.

Tom and I made a box out of plywood that Lorrin would lie in. It had three sides and a top. I would lay Lorrin on the floor and let the box surround her with all the new gadgets that I had found. I hung different toys and crinkle paper that would make a noise if she happened to hit them. Even if she by chance came into contact with something and it got her attention, she might hit it again with purpose.

Yet, she continued to have seizures. As they grew worse, I noticed long periods of complete lethargy. She would go through phases of learning hand and eye movements, and then lose it all. Then she would regain it all again. The question was, were her memory problems a result of the seizures or the medication? Or both?

What started as an attempt to stimulate her in any way possible became a tradition. In 1998, I rented my first home with Lorrin. While we were at a restaurant called Chuy's in Thousand Oaks, I noticed the ceiling had dangling things hanging from it. It was fun and playful. I watched Lorrin noticing the colors and how she seemed to enjoy the visuals. On that day I got an idea. I went to Home Depot and purchased some chicken wire. With a staple gun, I attached the chicken wire to the ceiling. I started hanging things over her bed in the living room and over her bed in the bedroom. This became part of Lorrin's world.

At Halloween, I hung scary lights, pumpkins, bats, ghosts and all kinds of black and orange objects. Christmas was full of huge snowflakes, lights and ornaments. Valentine's Day—well, you get the picture. It became an obsession and a passion. People would come into my home just to see what was hanging from my living room ceiling.

Right by Lorrin's bed was a small aquarium. I wanted to keep Lorrin interested and entertained. I wanted her to interact with life, not just lie in bed. We were active and went many places, but she definitely spent more time in her bed than most children.

When the holiday season was over, I put up a dolphin water scene. We also had a Harry Potter scene with a broom and quidditch balls. I kept changing things to keep her interest and it actually it helped me too. I enjoyed it as much as she did. We were creating our own environment.

My friends and family got involved and would bring things to hang up, and my mom made Lorrin special blankets. When we went to Hawaii, I made an entire Hawaiian scene, including a grass skirt bedspread in her bedroom.

Chapter 4

~ Second Opinion ~
Five Months Old

"The only thing worse than being blind is having sight but no vision."

~ Helen Keller

Tom took the day off and we drove to UCLA Hospital to see a well-respected specialist. In the waiting room, we felt both anxious but hopeful. Lorrin was colicky, fussing, uncomfortable, and gassy. She suddenly farted loudly, eliciting a blush and a cringe from Tom. He whispered to me, "No one would believe such a loud noise could come out of this beautiful baby. They all think it was me."

We laughed—for the last time that day.

The neurologist asked us many questions about Lorrin. I would later learn this interrogation was the usual protocol. "Did you deliver full-term? What was her Apgar score? Is there any history of seizures in your family?"

The doctor was tall and had a crazy, unkempt beard. He leaned over to me, took Lorrin out of my arms, put her on the table, and examined her carefully. She was only four months old at the time, but he held her up and moved her as if she were walking. Her feet dragged across the table as his large hands moved her hips from side to side.

He laid her down on the table and turned to us. "At least she will be a pretty retard."

I could not believe my ears. "What did you say?" I asked.

He glanced up at me, then back at Lorrin. He shrugged. "At least she will be a pretty retard; she won't look like this." He then held up his arms, one straight out and the other bent, his hand opening towards his face while he made a shaking, uncontrolled movement.

I was dumbstruck by his ghastly impersonation of what a retarded person looked like. My whole body fell back against the wall of his examination room. I don't remember anything else that was said in his office. I think my soul left my body at that time. I can only remember silence between Tom and me.

This time, Tom did not seem as confident that the doctor was wrong, and we left reeling from our second opinion.

Rain poured down as we drove home. The miserable driving conditions on the unfamiliar LA freeways heightened the tension between Tom and me. I mumbled to Tom, suggesting a family suicide pact. I'd never been more serious. Tom didn't respond. He must have been in his own hell, while I imagined us driving off a cliff. How could I continue to live? How could we live with this as a family? My desire for normalcy, a regular family, a typical child, and a happily-ever-after marriage was as overpowering as it was impossible. Now, I was going to be the parent of a retarded baby—but at least she was pretty.

Even worse than enduring another devastating diagnosis was the duty of calling my family. Everyone waited anxiously for the results of our second opinion. I phoned my mom to give her the update. I felt as though I were about to vomit as the words came out. "They think she is going to be retarded," I said. I asked her to contact the rest of the family for us.

She answered with uncomfortable platitudes. After all, what could she say? How could anyone know how to respond?

I proceeded to do what I think anyone would in our situation. I went out and got a third opinion. Doing so involved a new hospital and another well-respected neurologist with a big name. Again, it was a teaching hospital, but this time, the neurologist never even touched her. He came into the room and went over Lorrin's medical records while his students examined her. He then advised me to go home and prepare for the worst.

What does that mean? Go home and prepare for the worst. In my mind, that meant death. Lorrin was four months old. I didn't want to go home and wait for her to die. I wanted to know exactly what he meant, so I turned and asked the doctor a dangerous question.

"When will I know?" I asked nervously. Even though I clearly understood what he was saying, I still had hope that he was wrong. And I wanted to know when I should give up all hope that she would start progressing. At four months old she was not doing anything that "normal" babies were doing, but I still had a mother's hope she could catch up.

At least this doctor showed compassion. Kindness crinkled his eyes as he replied, "When she's a year old."

Both fear and hope shot through my mind. I was afraid of what she might be doing or not doing at one year of age—and I also thought that I had eight months to get her caught up. This was another life-changing comment that weighed on my mind every day until she turned one. I pulled myself together because I had to walk back through the crowded waiting room with Lorrin in my arms.

A pediatric neurology office is no picnic. Leaving, I came face to face with a room full of children with all kinds of disabilities. There were wheelchairs everywhere. There were kids with helmets on to protect them from injuring themselves from falling while having seizures. My future. There I was again—crying uncontrollably. Tears ran down my face as I went to the front desk to pay the bill. I couldn't make eye contact with anyone, but it seemed they all knew I was the defective one. Lorrin was still too beautiful and too young for others to notice anything wrong with her.

As I asked the receptionist if I owed any money, I sobbed and wiped tears on my sleeve. I clung to the counter for support and asked for a cigarette. I hadn't smoked for years, but as my life fell apart, I craved something to dull the pain. The poor girl asked the rest of the staff if anyone had a smoke, and someone gave me two. Then I asked for matches. "Because, you see, I don't smoke."

The girl handed me her lighter—anything to get me out of there. As I walked to the car, I coughed through my cigarette. I quickly lit the second one. Smoking made me sick to my stomach, but at least that was a distraction from the pain I was feeling inside.

Chapter 5

~ *Passing Judgment* ~
During The First Year

"If you help just one person, it makes a huge explosion in the universe."

~ unknown

One of our first stays at the Children's Hospital of Orange County, we met another family just across the hall from our room, creating a powerful opportunity to learn an unexpected lesson. Lorrin was not yet a year old when we were admitted to treat her uncontrolled seizures. As I sat in our room, I watched the family across the hall and tried to figure out the dynamics of their situation. Watching other people was a way for me to gain perspective for what was happening in my own life, especially since the hospital experience was so new to me. My pastime also allowed me not to feel so desperately alone.

I sat watching what I guessed was a forty-something woman with a fourteen-year-old girl, an eight-year-old boy, and a ten-month-old baby boy. The fourteen-year-old was constantly taking care of the baby. She would climb up into the crib to cradle and coo at the infant. I loved the way the young teen simply chose not to follow proper hospital "etiquette." She just wanted to be with that little baby.

The woman also took care of the infant, and they all stayed in the hospital. It was not often that I saw an entire family spending the night, but it was obvious the baby was loved so much by all of them. With my limited knowledge of their situation, I thought the woman was too old to have a baby and that the fourteen-year-old must have been the mother. From where I sat, I couldn't tell the magnitude of the child's illness. He did have a feeding tube, but otherwise, he looked pretty healthy to me. I was taken with all of them, especially their loving warmth and connection as a family. Without meaning to, I was passing judgment.

One day, I finally got the opportunity to meet them. It was the young teenager who first started speaking to me. She asked me questions about Lorrin. She then told me her story. The older woman was not the biological parent of any of the children. She had first adopted the fourteen-year-old girl from a drug addict. She then adopted the girl's brother because she didn't want the siblings to be apart. When the drug-addicted woman gave birth to yet another baby, she adopted him too.

The strength of this woman amazed me! She had now adopted three children from a drug-addict who continued to give birth to unwanted children. She was doing all she could to keep together the children who had come innocently into the world to a mother who could not possibly take care of them. Though she seemed in over her head, this amazingly loving woman spoke to me about how lucky she was to have been blessed with such remarkable children.

I was ashamed of myself when I remembered my ignorant judgment of them. But I learned my lesson that day: things are not always how they might appear. It was another humbling experience that I have Lorrin to thank for.

It is my belief that along this journey of life, it is important to understand the power of not passing judgment on others. I will never forget the many hours I spent at UCLA Hospital. Not only did I need to take care of my child and exist in unlivable conditions, I was put into contact with people I would not normally get a chance to meet. I was stripped of my armor and I couldn't hide behind my clothes or my makeup. The "real me" came out—and so did the "real me" of the others who lived like I did.

I watched the mother of five children live in the cancer ward of the hospital to take care of her dying son. Her other children and her husband were trying to cope without them. Unfortunately, her husband turned to Internet pornography, and her children desperately needed her. I met another mother who had to leave her son's bedside in the ICU while she was treated in the ER for a miscarriage. I could go on and on, but one woman in particular won my heart with her bravery.

The woman's son had just turned a year old, but had never left the hospital. He lived in the ICU, and his mother took the bus to see him every day. She brought her daughter with her on weekdays and her husband on weekends. I had no idea how far they traveled, nor the true struggle this entire family went through. But every day, the boy's mom would show up, sit by his side, and hold him the entire day. On her son's first birthday, she brought in a huge cake to share with the nurses and doctors who had grown to love this little boy. He broke many hearts on the day he died. I will never forget her face at her son's funeral.

I attended the funeral because the woman and I spent so much time together. She spoke Spanish and I spoke English, and I am not sure we ever exchanged more than a simple hello. But I had so much respect for her, as did the many nurses who came to the funeral as well. I had been to many children's funerals that year—this one was the fifth. But I will never get over the look on this woman's face as she held her head low and sobbed uncontrollably. It is almost as if her son's passing away was a surprise to her, even though he had never even made it home from the hospital. She was living proof that no one can ever be prepared for a child's death.

It was another warning to me how precious every day with Lorrin was.

Chapter 6

~ Seizures ~
One Year Old

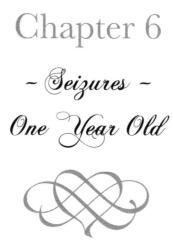

"God often uses those considered unimportant in the world's eyes to reveal His will."

~ Florentine: Lives of the Saints/Our Lady of Guadalupe

I was a dutiful parent. I followed all the doctors' orders to a "T." Lorrin still continued to have seizures constantly. We would try one medication, taking weeks to get to a therapeutic level, and it would do nothing. Then we would try another while tapering her off the previous drug. This process took months. Lorrin was already behind. Nothing was working. It seemed as though nobody cared. Lorrin was just another baby who was having uncontrolled seizures that no one could stop. I felt abandoned by modern medicine. I am sure it's frustrating for doctors to treat patients who never get better or make any significant strides toward recovery.

Finally, neurologist Dr. John Menkes was referred to us. He was unique because he was unafraid to try alternative treatments in an effort to stop Lorrin's seizures. When we met for Lorrin's first visit, he impressed me because he spent time looking at all her records. He carried a black doctor's bag, which I thought was cute. He touched her and examined her, taking as much time as he needed. You could tell he was thorough and not in a rush to make a hasty decision.

I was not about to give up on my child. For the next ten years, I asked him every time I saw him, what can we do to help Lorrin? I wanted to know about new medications and any ideas he might have to help her. I was not about to give up on my girl.

Dr. Menkes agreed to try Intravenous Immunoglobulin Therapy (IVIG) with Lorrin during the summer of 1996. Vaccine injury is theorized to be, in part, an overzealous immune system response, and IVIG is thought to help normalize that. I found it very interesting that today this protocol is being used to treat children who have autism.

IVIG Therapy treats a compromised autoimmune system. The treatments are given during a short time period, and I hoped the therapy would answer my prayers. I would lay my hands on the IV bags and bless the treatments before we started. These days, I was praying and laying hands on Lorrin constantly; holy water was everywhere. I proceeded to document Lorrin's IVIG experience.

To compound the problems, Lorrin had begun teething. She was in her twos, but still not pushing teeth through. Because of the Dilantin she was taking for seizures, gum overgrowth delayed her tooth development. As a result, all of her teeth were coming in at once. Of course, teething can cause seizures.

I kept a diary during the treatment—a glimpse of our horrific daily ordeal.

Chapter 7

~ The Vaccine Compensation Act ~
Ages Nine Months to Four Years Old

What I understand now is that like attracts like. Energy is a magnet. The more I spoke of my destitute life and my feelings of complete despair, the more I brought negative energy into my life. We simply cannot have both darkness and light at the same time—it has to be one or the other.

Lorrin reacted adversely to her DPT vaccine, which is a combination of three vaccines used to guard against diphtheria, pertussis (whooping cough), and tetanus. She received the whole cell vaccine in 1994, which, as of 2002, is no longer administered in the United States.

In the 1960s, when it was first discovered that the whole cell vaccine could cause severe adverse reactions, drug companies decided to stop making the DPT vaccine, because they were being sued by the families of the children who were affected. It was also known at the time that the a-cellular vaccine, commonly known as DTap, would dramatically reduce the risk for brain injuries. The government stepped in to protect the drug companies that manufactured the vaccine and the doctors who administered it.

The Vaccine Compensation Act no longer allowed families to sue the manufacturer or the doctor directly for vaccination damages until the whole legal process, as specified by the law, had run its convoluted course. The government then set up a fund to help those children who were injured. So, instead of suing billion-dollar drug companies, families sue a fund that is managed by the government. The funds are generated by taxing the vaccine. The compensation expense is passed on to the consumer.

At the time, Tom and I were uneducated about vaccine injuries, but I researched and found information, even though the internet was only in its infancy stages in 1994. Today, vaccine information is more readily available.

Lorrin was administered a vaccine from what is called a "hot" lot. Her vaccine had thirty reports of seizure activity or worse symptoms, and the surrounding lots had ten deaths. The reports are made by the parent or doctor, though many reactions are not reported by either party. I would guess that the most common reason for not reporting is that the doctors deny the correlation and fail to inform the parents of the possibility that what their child is experiencing could be a vaccination injury. As a result, the statistics about vaccine injuries are unreliable.

The law has required doctors to report any suspected vaccination injury. At the time Lorrin was injured, I found that doctors didn't want to blame the vaccine, which was supposed to be preventing disease, and didn't want to be associated with vaccine injuries. This is still the case. Even though Lorrin's injuries were clearly the result of the vaccination by the close timing of the onset and the type of symptoms, many of her doctors still insisted there was no correlation between the two.

But let's take a step back. What is a "lot of vaccines"? Each vaccine has a number on it, and this number is called a lot. A lot is created when the person bottling the vaccination begins work, and when he or she takes a break, the lot is completed. The actual number of vaccine doses in a lot is unknown. One lot could have just two vaccines or thousands.

Furthermore, when a drug company mails a box of twenty vaccines to a doctor, that box will contain vaccines from twenty different lots. Scattering the lots ensures that one doctor will not witness multiple injuries in his or her practice. It also makes the most damaging lots difficult to assess or trace. Astonishingly, the drug company can continue to sell vaccines from a lot, even though multiple injuries have been reported from its use. Lorrin's lot injured children throughout the United States.

The doctor is required to keep track of which lot number is given to each child. However, drug companies are not required to disclose the number of vaccines in a lot. To protect these companies, this number is kept secret and the percentage of injuries in a certain lot can't be determined. Therefore, Lorrin's lot could have had only forty vaccines in it or a thousand. This information is crucial in determining how "hot" the lot is.

The question remains: if there were 250,000 vaccines in a lot and only one severe injury was reported, would this be an acceptable number?

A few key aspects of our experience with the Vaccine Compensation Act need to be disclosed. The drug company may only be sued once, when the entire financial trial is finished and the financial award is offered by the court. At that time, the amount awarded can be rejected by the petitioner, and only then can the drug company be sued. Usually, the trial is so drawn out that by the time an amount is awarded, the parents of the injured child have been beaten down financially, physically, and emotionally, leaving them no choice but to accept the government's offer. The financially powerful drug companies can out-litigate almost everyone.

To file a lawsuit, an attorney who knows the specific rules regarding the Vaccine Compensation Act must be hired. Lawyers willing to litigate cases against the government are rare. Nineteen years ago, when we needed an attorney, only one came recommended. Familiar with the tragedies caused by the vaccines, he took pleasure in fighting the government for just compensation.

However, he did fail us in one area. In our case, he did not request reimbursement for the Medi-Cal state benefits Lorrin was receiving from Medicare prior to our settlement. Once Lorrin received her compensation from the government, we had to pay Medicare $100,000. This was a devastating mistake on his part. After an ordeal such as this, you discover that you would have handled things much differently if you had been better informed.

In order to even petition for a case to be heard through the Vaccine Compensation Act, many requirements must be met. For example, a victim must have had a seizure in the first 24 hours after the vaccination and must incur over $1000 in out-of-pocket expenses within the first year after the injury (for which records must be provided). The government makes it as difficult as possible to qualify for compensation and they do everything in their power to avoid paying you.

Next, there are two necessary parts to winning a financial award from the government. First, it must be proven that the vaccine is the cause of the damage. It is my understanding that Lorrin's settlement was one of the largest because it was a rare case in which the government didn't argue the cause of the injury. This was due, I am sure, to the number of reported adverse events. Second, the petitioner must argue the financial obligation owed to the child, and the government then also manages the settlement.

The hardest part for me was trying to identify what expenses I might need for Lorrin during her lifetime. As parents, we always hope for the best possible outcome for our children, but in this situation, optimism can undermine the only means of getting compensation. That said, how can anyone possibly know the entire future of a child who is so young? Lorrin was so very sick, but I could never have imagined that her medical needs would be as demanding as they were through her lifetime. Though no one can really know for sure, a life-care planner can help put together a list of what a child might need.

Once the compensation is agreed upon, the funds go into a trust. The compensation, known as an annuity, is distributed every year. Every other year the court audits to ensure that I am spending Lorrin's trust appropriately.

According to the Vaccine Compensation Act, the court appoints a Special Master to preside over the case in place of a judge and jury. During the time we were litigating, only eleven Special Masters presided over vaccine injury cases throughout California. I was told that we were lucky to have a kind Special Master. Our proceedings were held at our attorney's office in Torrance, California. Lorrin had her attorney, a life-care planner, Tom, and me on her side. The government had a nurse named Miss Ratched, an attorney, and a doctor.

Chapter 8

~ Court Negotiations ~
Three Years Old

When Lorrin was only months old, she was diagnosed as cortically blind. Soon after, I was backing out of the driveway and I heard this sort of scraping sound against my car and a faint, "Hello. Hello." I looked out my window and saw a blind man with a cane. He had walked right into the car! I jumped out, hysterical. But he was unfazed by the incident. I wanted to tell him my daughter was blind too. As I drove away, all I could think about was how brave he was walking in the city by himself.

We met at Lorrin's attorney's office. The attendees included the Special Master, the stenographer, me, Tom, our life-care planner, and the government's attorney, nurse, and pediatrician. It was one of the worst days of my life. I had to sit with what looked like civilized people and discuss my daughter's future as if she were a burden on society.

Before we even started discussing compensation, the government representatives told us we had to place Lorrin in a home. We refused and the argument escalated from there. Our life-care planner had determined eighty-five essential items for which we asked compensation. It took three long days to go over the items in question. We asked for item number one, the government said no, and the process dragged on.

I expected devil horns to grow out of Nurse Ratched's head. She was rude and made it clear that Lorrin's life meant nothing, and because I was her mother, I was of no importance either. The room felt toxic. The repeated insults towards me from the nurse became so offensive at one time the Special Master became irritated and threatened to kick her out of the room. Nurse Ratched was getting paid $50 an hour in 1996 to dehumanize me and Lorrin. In the atmosphere of her constant abuse and ruthlessness, I was barely able to keep focused on the process of defending Lorrin's needs. How could I put a price on my baby?

At one point during the three days, we argued for twenty minutes about the reimbursement cost for baby wipes; I asked for Huggies brand wipes. Nurse Ratched insisted the government should reimburse only the cost of a generic brand of wipes, because they were two dollars cheaper. We argued back and forth; it was ridiculous. The Special Master became frustrated because we had argued so long over everything and lost on so many issues. But we held our ground on this one item. Nurse Ratched was trying to figure out how many times I changed Lorrin each day and how many wipes I used for each changing.

The Special Master got so upset that at one point she sternly asked, "Mrs. Kain, why do you use Huggies?"

"Your honor, because they are thicker."

The Judge accepted the cost for Huggies wipes. You can only imagine what we went through discussing the other eighty-four items in question. We asked for wheelchairs, computers, a special bed for Lorrin. It was exhausting and completely out of any realm that I could wrap my brain around. Lorrin was my baby, and I hoped she would never need a wheelchair or a hospital bed. At the end of each day, I had to go home and care for my baby whose body was brutalized by the seizures she had suffered that day.

After the litigation came a horrific but real part of pursuing Lorrin's case: the government delayed payment, anticipating that she would die. Her death was expected by all her doctors, and I'm sure that was written all over her medical files. Lorrin's prognosis was grim at best. She was just money being spent, so the government looked for every excuse to deny it.

When you choose to vaccinate your child, you must sign a document stating that you understand the risks associated with vaccines. The statistics said that one in 250,000 may suffer an injury. The documents states that if your child has an adverse reaction, the government will step in and support your family with compensation for medical expenses. As I mentioned, once our case was filed, the government immediately acknowledged that my child was injured by the vaccine. The fact that the government did not dispute this fact is a miracle in and of itself.

Yet trust me when I say that no one from the government came forward to support me. While in ICU we had our court-appointed meeting. I thought they were there to help me. As I stood there in my hospital sweats, they went directly to Lorrin and took off her diaper to see if she had bed sores. They were trying to prove I was a bad parent. We were an inconvenient tragedy to be swept aside and denied dignity. Never once did anyone encourage us with even the simplest words of comfort for our grief and loss. No one expressed regret for Lorrin's injuries, let alone offered the financial compensation she was due.

I was so nervous driving to our court hearings that I drove into a pillar in the parking lot. On another day, I walked into a glass wall of the fishbowl conference room where our trial was held. This ordeal taxed me beyond anything I had ever imagined and left me so distracted that I could barely function.

To Tom's credit, he handled many of the grueling legal matters of that period. He was very involved.

Chapter 9

~ The Pain of People Rejecting Us ~

When I told my friend Barb that I was considering donating Lorrin's organs, she suggested I should put Lorrin's eyes in a jar and keep them. "How dare you donate them—they're too beautiful!"

Lorrin's beauty has always drawn attention. She was a beautiful baby. She got away with so much because of her long eyelashes and big blue eyes. She had perfect skin and a smile that would stay imprinted in your mind forever. It was easier for the public to accept Lorrin when she was young, but as she came into her teenage years it was clear to me that she was not so cute anymore. Lorrin became the white elephant in the room. It was a huge adjustment for me, and I found myself feeling wounded and cried often. Some days I would wallow in my pity and feel full of despair. I would have crying spells that I couldn't stop. I would lay my head down and cry and cry until I couldn't breathe. I wished that she would die. I wished that I would die. I would fall asleep only to wake up to my living hell.

My body was surviving but my soul was broken. I had so much pain inside me. The grief was suffocating. I felt so alone. I tried to be brave, but society does not like brokenness. My daughter was beautiful, but she could shake up a room quicker than anything I have ever seen. We would go to the movies, and people would get up and move if we sat beside them. At restaurants, people would change tables if they were seated next to us.

Lorrin did not make any noise. She sat in her wheelchair without making a sound. There were times that children and even adults would stand in front of her wheelchair, forcing me to stop. They would gaze in disbelief and shake their heads as though they were looking at a monster.

Many children with medical needs like Lorrin's don't ever leave their homes because it is so hard to be stared at, pitied and rejected. It wears you down. It takes a ton of courage to show up in public, knowing that everyone in the room will stare at you. People get off elevators when we get on them, and even slam doors on us. It is really tough to push a wheelchair through a closed door. It's as though they are afraid they will catch what we have. Some are just afraid of looking at what others go through in life. I guess people don't want to be reminded of what could possibly happen to them.

Countless times in public, people would ignore us to the point that they would actually walk right into the wheelchair and look down at Lorrin as if wondering where she'd come from. My heart broke as I tried to hold my head high, knowing that people were constantly rejecting us and were even afraid of us.

If they had only known how vulnerable we were.

Chapter 10

~ Steroids ~

One Year Old

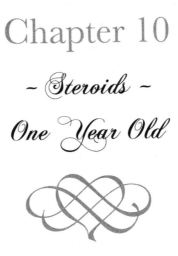

"With our minds, we create the world we live in."

~ Buddha

Once we realized that the drugs and IVIG treatments were not reducing Lorrin's seizures, Dr. Menkes decided to put Lorrin on steroids. Doctors don't understand why steroids sometimes work or even how they work for seizures. But they have been known to halt seizure activity or lessen the severity. Steroid treatment is usually given immediately after an injury. I am not sure how we missed that protocol. I have friends who have been successful with this treatment. Well, you know, Lorrin was different.

Gloria, a friend of mine whose six-year-old daughter Maxie had gone through the protocol, warned me what it entailed. She'd had no idea what to expect when Maxie went on steroids until they were in the hospital. They were admitted in the hospital when they started the series of steroid shots. But the doctor didn't inform Gloria until she was leaving the hospital that she would be responsible for injecting the steroids into her daughter's leg twice a day for the first week and then once a day for the second week.

Gloria responded frankly, "We'll not be leaving this hospital then."

With the chance that Lorrin might benefit from steroid treatment, I reluctantly learned how to give my bony, nineteen-pound daughter a steroid shot in her thigh. I didn't opt to make the hour-and-a-half drive to and from the hospital every day. After I was instructed briefly about the procedure, they make you practice and watch you give about two shots. Then the nurse from UCLA said, "The needle may break off in the bone. But don't worry; you'll get through it."

I didn't find comfort in his words.

Once home, I prepared to give Lorrin her first shot. I agonized for hours trying to muster the courage. Drenched in sweat and shaking, I was scared witless. My hand pointed the needle to jab her leg, but I pulled back at the last moment. But then I thought of her tiny body wracked with seizures and I just did it. The skin gave way and the denser muscle tissue resisted, but I kept pushing. While Lorrin cried out against the pain I was causing, my fingers fumbled with the plunger to empty the cortisone into her stringy thigh muscle. All the while my heart was breaking from the strain of hurting this vulnerable child I was supposed to protect. I withdrew the needle. A mix of relief and remorse washed over me. I had given her the first shot, the first of many.

When Lorrin continued to scream hysterically after the injection, I was grateful my pediatrician had warned me about the side effects of steroids. His wisdom and caring had supported me through many previous crises, several sleepless nights in the ER, and saved me and Lorrin too many times to count; I trusted him. He'd said that steroids can make a person feel psychotic. Without that piece of information, I never could've handled her reaction. When she didn't calm down after the shock of the shot wore off, I would've been sure I'd made some terrible mistake. The rest of the day and throughout the night, while she cried and had seizures, all I could do was hold her.

When the time came to give Lorrin another shot, I did that too, crying right along with her. Even compared to the major surgeries and the near-death illnesses we went through later, the steroid treatment was truly a nightmare. Worse yet, the treatment did nothing to stop or even lessen the severity of Lorrin's seizures.

She did, however, get a new nickname: Roarin' Lorrin. Maxie's mom called to check on me. As I picked up the phone, she said, "Never mind. I was just calling to see if Lorrin had stopped crying, but I can hear she hasn't."

Chapter 11

Spirituality and Alternative Treatments –
Four Months to a Year

People make choices every day that change the way we live. God gave us free will. I believe we make agreements before we come to this earth and that sometimes we abide by those decisions and other times we make a different choice.

I was so alone. My life was spiraling out of control. I couldn't relate to my friends or family. My family was so worried that I was going to crack. I stopped telling Tom about Lorrin's progress—there was no progress. It was unbearable to watch my child's life be destroyed in front of my eyes and not be able to do something. I didn't know anyone who had a child like mine. The doctors kept throwing medical terms at me. It was my job to go home and make some sense in what was becoming my worst nightmare. It was up to me to find resources and connections. I could not relate to anyone I knew because of Lorrin's unique situation—or, at least, it was unique to me.

As I spent time in the hospital I saw other babies that had seizures. Most of the parents didn't stay at the hospital. So I was unable to connect, meet, or speak to them. I spent countless nights with Lorrin in the hospital, sharing a room with infants that had seizures and no parent in sight. Before I met these children, I thought my Lorrin was unique, having seizures combined with cortical blindness. *Cortically blind* means that the eyes are okay, but the brain is not interpreting what the eyes see. What I was finding was that lots of the babies who had intractable seizures were blind. The doctors never told me nor warned me of this, but it seemed pretty obvious after meeting baby after baby with uncontrolled seizures who were also visually impaired. I felt confused and completely rejected by modern medicine; we were trying medications that were simply ineffective, and there was little hope that she could be "healed."

I was desperate to get information that would heal her—or at least explain what was happening to her. Of course, no one would talk to me about the vaccine having anything to do with my baby's problems.

During one of my doctor appointments with a brain surgeon at the Children's Hospital in Los Angeles, I was told there would never be a cure for what Lorrin had because no doctor would admit that it happens—and that no research would ever be done to reverse vaccine injuries. How could I argue with that? It didn't help my already lack of confidence in modern medicine.

I sent out over thirty-five letters to television stations and magazines, including *Oprah, Montel, 20/20, Parent Magazine*, and *Health Magazine*. You name it—I sent one to it! I called relentlessly to any doctor, healing practice, parent, or alternative treatment center I heard about. I also carried Lorrin door-to-door, holding her in my arms with great desperation, in my attempt to heal her. I looked for anyone who had any knowledge or any idea that might help my baby. Only a few responded to my cries for help. A handful of parents wrote to me and shared their vaccine story. I received letters with pictures of their children who were similar to Lorrin. Their support was important to my survival at that time.

I quickly learned that vaccine reactions were too much of a taboo for anyone to address. I also found that no one wanted to talk about a baby who was not going to get better. It was the first time I experienced rejection from modern medicine—and from our community. They wanted my broken baby story to be silenced—there was no interest in my story. I had a feeling that they just wanted us to go away.

I kept each reply I received. These were stories that bound complete strangers' hearts together. Reading each one made me realize that I was not alone. I received handwritten letters with pictures and words that inspired me to carry on. I learned how parents coped with their unique children. I received letters from other parents who had vaccine-injured children. There were children who were born with all kinds of situations. Those parents took the time to come forward to help me and give me a bit of emotional support.

Our hearts were the same but our children were unique. Ultimately, I was left to figure out the majority of the medical things on my own. I started talking with and focusing on those people who could give me some hope that Lorrin might get better. I connected with people who gave me hope that I could help Lorrin be the best she could be in her body.

My research quickly led to alternative treatments. Lorrin had been treated with vitamins, oils, massage, Reiki, cranial sacral therapy, chiropractic, acupuncture, energy healing, sweat lodges, hands-on healing, and homeopathic medicine. Lorrin had also ridden on specially trained horses (treatment known as *equestrian therapy*) and had dolphin therapy. For years Lorrin was fortunate enough to be treated by a famous Osteopath, Dr. Viola Frymann in San Diego. She is a gifted and wonderfully loving doctor.

When Lorrin started to eat foods, I tried juicing, a macrobiotic diet, and cooked all of Lorrin's food from scratch. I tried nut milk and wheat grass. You name it, I tried it. We had Lorrin's blood tested to see if she was allergic to the foods I was feeding her.

In the beginning, I had it in my mind that I could stop and/or control the seizures. It is natural and human to think cause and effect. I was determined to stop her body from constantly shaking. I stayed up nights preparing her food. She ate organic lamb, beef and chicken, green beans, asparagus, and loads of sweet potatoes. At one time the doctor asked me if she was orange. I said yes. She was eating so many carrots and sweet potatoes she actually turned orange. I wanted her to have the best organic food and the healthiest diet possible. I would do anything for Lorrin. I am not sure I would have done the same for myself, but for my kid, anything.

All my efforts for the first three years of Lorrin's life were focused on trying to fix and/or "heal" Lorrin. I also knew that the early years were crucial to her success. The window of opportunity was brief. Each day that she was alive was another day she fell behind.

Essentially, I tried every treatment available. Though I have experienced many controversial and alternative ways of making our lives work, I have learned so much and I have no regrets because one piece of information would always lead to another. I kept a filing cabinet with files filled with people I met, places I had been, and another for places I would still like to go. I have copies and documentation for everything we experienced. The way I saw it, why leave any stone unturned? I was determined to uncover the key to Lorrin's healing (and others like her). I saw the movie *Lorenzo's Oil*. The struggle that family went through. I felt as though a miracle was owed to me. I would find it!

In my desperate attempts to heal Lorrin, I had many positive experiences. We also had our fair share of bumps in the road. I once drove forty miles in Los Angeles traffic to meet with a man who was referred to me by my church. He was thought to have "gifted abilities." He prayed for Lorrin, then looked me straight in the eye and said, "Seizures are from the devil."

As I drove home, I felt confused and thought, *Was he saying something about me or about Lorrin? How am I supposed to take that? How is that even helpful?*

I have been taken advantage of financially countless times. In my desperate plea I tried all kinds of treatments that were "healing." I have learned much discernment over the years. I learned the hard way to trust my gut—not listen to everyone who had a new idea or healing technique, especially when it came with a hefty price.

I think it is important to mention that Lorrin cried all the time. She cried until she was five years old. I watched her poor body suffer countless seizures. Her stomach was permanently bloated with gas and her intestines forever constipated. I understand now that gut issues go hand-in-hand with vaccine injury. I wanted to make her comfortable. I was giving her so much medication for the seizures and a different medication to help her sleep. As an infant she only slept about four hours a night. In the beginning, I tried to go back to work. When she was awake, I was awake, and I started cooking our meals and her meals at two a.m. Lorrin would sleep from 10:00 p.m. until 2:00 a.m. She would wake up until 4:00 a.m. I would be up too, so I used that time to cook. What else was I supposed to do?

She was not like a normal infant. I had never been a parent before Lorrin and I had nothing to compare my experience of motherhood to, but I knew enough to know that babies were supposed to sleep. When she was awake, she cried. The doctors kept telling me to give her medication to help her sleep and warned me that if she didn't sleep, she would have more seizures. It was a crazy cycle of trying drug after drug and getting the same failed result. My entire body wanted to resist the drugs that everyone was telling me to give her. She was still having countless seizures and screaming all the time. I kept plying her full of medication. She would look at me and spit it out in my face. I would then panic. What did she get? What should I do? Should I give her more? She weighed only nineteen pounds on a good day. Worry plagued me.

Tom and I would frequently argue about the medications that Lorrin was on. He would get to go to work all day while I had to find a way to get this crap in her. I hated it. One time when he was out of town, I took her off all the medications she was on. I did it slowly. I felt as though we had tried everything else and it wasn't working.

One of the doctors that was treating her said to me, "If she were a dog she would go into the forest and die." I thought to myself, *Why doesn't she die?* How can this existence be worth it to her? Her tiny body was furious with rage and tears. Her tummy was hard all the time. She was constipated and uncomfortable. Of course the drugs made her constipated. So the doctors prescribed something for that!

After weeks of weaning her off the medication, I was sleeping in the bed one night next to her so I could watch her. I always left a tiny light on so if I fell asleep I could open my eyes to check on her without turning the light on. I never really slept. The bed would shake and I would open my eyes, knowing that her tiny body was having another seizure. Lorrin had long seizures that lasted five minutes or longer. Afterwards, her tiny body would lay limp. My attempt to take her off the medications wasn't working. I knew it. I tried my best and prayed my hardest, but her body was still convulsing. Heartbroken, I ended up in the ER, with Lorrin going into "status" seizures—seizures that wouldn't stop.

The doctor bumped her up on the Dilantin through an IV. I knew I was risking Lorrin's life, but what life did she have? I was glad I tried it. I knew the drugs were actually doing something. They were stopping the seizures from killing her. But the drugs were not fixing her. I was a desperate parent and I wanted to fix Lorrin!

As I continued to "network" and desperately search for answers, I started to hear similar stories and familiar threads with what was available through alternative treatments. I knew there were people who had a greater understanding about what I was experiencing. I met people who seemed to find peace in life even though they had adversity and suffering. I was drawn to others' pain and how they managed to survive. I could feel their acceptance and strength. I was still fighting and resisting what was happening to my baby. I knew I needed to change my thoughts that were based on ego and replace them with being at one with God. I always wanted to "speed up" my spiritual growth, and I was ready for change.

In the beginning of Lorrin's ordeal, one of my favorite doctors suggested I read the Book of Job. I didn't understand what I had read at the time, but I knew I didn't want to suffer as Job did. I was not able to come to peace with my suffering—I wanted it to go away. I wanted Lorrin to be healed.

I knew that although my problem was my sick kid, I needed and wanted to be able to control my emotions and change how I was reacting to the situation. Although I admired the doctor and I knew she was a gifted healer, I found her advice confusing. I did not want this life that I could not handle. The pain was much greater than any spiritual understanding I had. But I still wanted help because I knew it was wrong to fear life more than death.

I went to a support group for couples, alone. And I was in therapy. I tried all kinds of therapy. I preferred seeing therapists who were more spiritually-minded. I will never forget a session in which I talked about Lorrin's body. I explained how she would move, out of control, constantly. Her arms and legs would flail around. It was horrible to watch. She would literally slap herself with her own hands.

My therapist said, "You may just have to get used to this. Lorrin may be like this. Enjoy the moments when she is not flailing about."

My entire body cracked. I felt as though I was going to explode. I didn't want to hear those words. I sat there staring at her and hating her for what she said. Yet, all the while, I knew she could be right. I tried my best to focus on the good moments and let the painful, torturous moments go, always knowing that tomorrow would come and change was inevitable.

I began to write down my pain. At first, I believed that I needed to keep track of what was happening so when the miracle finally came, I would have documentation. I still wanted Lorrin to miraculously be healed. I was experiencing so much sadness, loss, and pain that I could not believe there was no reward at the end. I thought that maybe I was just in a bad phase that would end soon. If someone had told me how many years of hardship I was to face, I would never have believed it.

I now know that I was just fueling the madness, sadness, and despair. I was telling everyone about my story, my baby. Words are so powerful. I have learned the hard way that by constantly being the wounded victim and telling everyone about it, that I became the wounded victim. Who wouldn't get on board with my pain, my loss, my broken baby? I earned my story.

Knowing what I know now, if I could go back, I would stop reliving all the bad things that were happening in my life by sharing them with anyone who would listen. I was fueling the negative experiences and becoming a human disaster. I was lost. I had no spirit or any hope left inside me. I was fully consumed with my misery. I could not understand at the time that by holding my head up and focusing just a little, I could have possibly opened myself up to happier opportunities.

What I understand now is that like attracts like. Energy is a magnet. The more I spoke of my destitute life and my feelings of complete despair, the more I brought negative energy into my life. We simply cannot have both darkness and light at the same time—it has to be one or the other.

Though I was in a negative place, Lorrin always fueled me. Her tiny body in all of its brokenness was a huge light. Her eyes were filled with faith and hope. Her strength constantly fueled me. Her love was endless. Her spirit was powerful.

Looking at her, I couldn't believe that there wouldn't be a reward at the end. I was at a loss in the medical community, but I was counting on spiritual direction to lead me to her cure. Her healing. I tried to remedy and ease my pain by reading spiritual studies of acceptance and love. I would read and read, but I was unable to achieve that inner peace, her peace. I wanted to become strong. I pushed myself, always feeling that I was the weak link. I needed to get closer to God. I needed to have more faith. I had to let go of my mad ego mind and understand *source*. I needed to change my thoughts based on ego and loss to acceptance and love. My suffering was the impetus forcing me to open up to a higher awareness. I wanted to speed up my spiritual growth. I needed a huge leap in faith. I wanted peace!

I didn't, at the time, understand that it started with me.

Instead, my spiritual awareness seemed to come in waves. I would find temporary peace that would last for just a short while. The next step would enlighten me and I'd feel a greater sense of peace about Lorrin, which made me feel closer to God. After a while, the feeling seemed to stay. I felt safe in snip-its. I would move forward and then get shoved back. My constant drive was to move forward. I met people who lived in peace, yet they were without safety and health. I wanted to understand them and how they came to be.

The worst possible thing happened to me. My baby was suffering in my arms and I could not protect her.

In my journey towards finding some kind of inner peace, I was referred to a meditation group. The old adage is to "love yourself" and be at peace. It made absolutely zero sense to me at the time. I was just about at the end of my rope, my nerves shot. But something strange was happening. The universe started to answer my questions in a weird and wonderful way. It didn't happen as quickly as I would have liked, but when I asked a question, it was getting answered—I would receive some kind of answer out of nowhere.

I would ask a person in Thousand Oaks a question, and a total stranger that I met in Los Angeles would randomly answer it. I was learning to be open and to listen. Amongst the chaos some interesting spiritual stuff was going on. I was meeting all kinds of people who specialized in alternative healing, and they encouraged me to get some support. I joined a meditation group at the local bookstore in Thousand Oaks, The Humming Bird and The Honey Bee Bookshop and Center.

While I was waiting for a doctor's appointment in La Jolla, I shopped at a metaphysical shop and a young lady started to talk to me. We talked about Lorrin, and as fate would have it, we ended up having coffee. She told me something that stayed in my mind until this day.

She had a good friend who'd been in a horrible car accident. While he was in a coma, she prayed for him all the time and spent many hours mediating and talking to him. She was talking to his "higher self," as she put it. After many months, he came out of the coma. It was quite a miracle for the entire family. He returned to work. One day while she was laughing, he put down what he was doing, ran up to her, grabbed her by the arms, and said, "It was you!"

In that moment when he heard her laughter, he realized she had been the one who was talking to him. He said, "You were with me the whole time." He was amazed and they hugged and cried.

At the time, it was a sweet story for me to enjoy. I had so many reservations about Lorrin and her future. She was a powerful young being. I knew that for sure, and I had hope that I could communicate with her in a different way. This story really helped me later on in her life during the time we had to put her in the coma to stop her seizures. It was a powerful story that made me second-guess our spiritual and intuitive gifts. I wanted to work on mine.

During my journey towards finding God in a way I never knew God or love existed, I also found other spiritual places. Perhaps one of our more interesting experiences was when Lorrin was prayed over by Native American healers. First, I began studying with a Native American meditation group. I took part in sweat lodges, and studied crystals and native animal totems. I was able to deeply meditate with Lorrin, and I always felt the great pain of where I was, but I could finally also see a greater meaning to our journey.

I took Lorrin to Russian healers, a Polish healer, and numerous healers from Mexico who also helped give me hope during my deepest despair.

Chapter 12

~ 911 Your Family ~

I felt confused and told the doctor that he should call the pediatrician. Imagine my surprise when he told me he was the pediatrician. I slapped him on the arm and told him I thought he was the neurologist! All this time, I had been telling him about Lorrin's brain.

By now, Lorrin's uncontrolled seizure disorder was accepted as part of our lives. I even had friends whose kids also had seizures. We had tried at least thirteen different seizure medications with no success.

Note: once a drug of a certain class is administered and fails to work, the likelihood of a second drug in this class succeeding is only fifty percent. The next is only fifteen percent and so on.

As a result of the battery her body had endured, Lorrin had not made any significant developmental gains. She had no head or trunk control; she could not walk, talk, or hold a toy. She was still consuming a diet of mostly organic, pureed foods.

I remember one frantic call I made to Dr. Menkes. I asked him, "What is going to become of her?" He told me quite frankly that one day I would wake up and she would be dead. What else could he say? We had tried every seizure medication, every drug, and every homeopathic treatment I could get my hands on. Nothing worked. Period.

As if things were not already bad enough, Lorrin took a turn for the worse.

We were at a picnic in Los Angeles—a gathering for families with kids who'd had unique life experiences. I was holding Lorrin in my lap; she seemed more lethargic than usual that day. I sat cross legged, Indian style, while feeding her. She lay lifeless, draped across my legs and breathing very shallowly. Even though Lorrin didn't have head control, her limp body was concerning. I was worried about her, and I shared my concerns with my friends, but no one ever knew what to say.

There was definitely something different about her that day. In my gut, I could feel something bad was going to happen, so I took Lorrin to UCLA for blood tests. The results showed her Dilantin, the medication she was taking for seizures, level was forty-two when it should be fifteen to twenty. She was at twice the level she should have been. She was toxic.

I took her home that day, but the next day, I went to her pediatrician and then to the local hospital. We were admitted to the hospital. After one night's stay, I felt uncomfortable and agitated. We were used to staying in a much larger hospital, and I did not feel right about the treatment Lorrin was receiving. There was also no doctor during the night on our floor, meaning if something happened, the nurse would need to call the ER doctor from another floor. I called her pediatrician and told him I felt Lorrin was being misdiagnosed and that she was going to die if she stayed there. I cannot explain mother's intuition. I just knew there was something terribly wrong, I just did.

He tried to reassure me that Lorrin would be fine, but he trusted my judgment as her mother and caretaker. He said, "I always listen to the mother." He decided to have us transferred to Cedars-Sinai. While I felt relieved, another part of me knew the worst was yet to come.

We took an ambulance to Cedars-Sinai Hospital in Beverly Hills, and Dr. Menkes quickly met us in the emergency room. At that time, Dr. Menkes had recently become head of the Pediatric Department of Neurology. With a new hospital came all new faces. This was Lorrin's first admit to Cedars. As Dr. Menkes spoke, everyone listened. He spoke in detail about her seizures and about what was being done to treat them. An electroencephalogram—an EEG – where electrodes are placed on the brain to monitor brain wave activity—was ordered along with a chest x-ray and blood tests.

The EEG was performed on the pediatric floor inside Lorrin's hospital room. At the time, my sister was visiting. During the test, I was told to watch Lorrin's "saturation level," which was the amount of oxygen reaching her lungs. I was instructed to use an instrument called an Ambu bag, which would fill Lorrin's lungs with oxygen for her if she became unable to receive enough by breathing on her own.

During the test, I had Lorrin lying on a cot, which was going to be my bed for the night. I remember my sister, Stephanie, and me sitting on each end of the cot facing each other with Lorrin lying between us. We were talking and laughing and using the Ambu bag every time her stats went too low. We never truly realized at the time the magnitude of what was happening. We knew we were at a new hospital, and there were three cute, new doctors.

It was mid-afternoon when one of the doctors that had met us in the ER walked into the room and saw that we were giving Lorrin oxygen with the Ambu bag. He asked us what we were doing. I told him if we didn't give her the boosts of O2, her stats fell.

He was quite shocked and told us that Lorrin should not be lying on the cot, and the fact that we needed to keep boosting her with O2 was quite alarming. I'm not sure where the nurse was until now, but she was at Lorrin's side after his concerns were made. He quickly ordered a chest x-ray. Soon after, the doctor told me to 911 my family that Lorrin was dying.

I was confused and told him he should call her pediatrician. Imagine my surprise when he told me he *was* the pediatrician. I slapped him on the arm and asked him why I had been telling him about Lorrin's brain. "Because of the way you were talking with Dr. Menkes when I met you in the ER, I assumed you were on the neurology team."

Most of the conversation was about her injury and her seizures. I was new to Cedars and didn't understand at the time just how important and respected Doctor Menkes was. I soon found out that he was the doctor who wrote the books all the neurologists studied from. When he walked in the room, you could hear a pin drop.

The doctors told me they could put Lorrin on life support. She had double pneumonia, but with life support, the doctors believed they could clear up her lungs with aggressive respiratory treatments and IV antibiotics. I was also told there was a possibility that Lorrin would never get off life support or 'the vent.'

Even if they put on her life support, she may not make it. I already knew I would not agree to Lorrin living on constant life support. She was suffering, and I was only surviving by the grace of God. Was I helping Lorrin by agreeing to the vent, or was I prolonging her pain?

The doctor told me we did not have much time to make a decision. She was going to die if she was not intubated quickly (to place a tube into the larynx to allow for breathing). Minutes were passing, and somehow my parents got there before Tom. I asked my parents what they would do in my situation, to which they replied they could not make the choice for me. I knew Tom wanted all measures taken to keep her alive, but I wanted to give up. I stared at them, waiting for someone to agree with me that this was her fate and it was her time. She deserved a better existence than the one she had been given here on Earth.

Had Tom remotely agreed with me, Lorrin would have died that day. But we were still married and he was her father, even though for years we were just surviving while living a life of heartache. Tom told me again he wanted to try to save Lorrin. So we did, even though the doctors were very clear that Lorrin may die despite their best efforts. She was intubated and sent to the ICU.

All of my family was able to stay in the ICU, seeing how no one expected her to leave the hospital alive. The next day, the doctor explained that one lung had collapsed and suggested that we place a chest tube. Due to the large amount of medicines that Lorrin was taking and the anticipated length of her illness, he also suggested a PIC line for Lorrin. A PIC line is a central line (a permanent IV) giving medical staff quick access to draw blood and administer medications during an emergency. The good news was that Lorrin would no longer need to be continuously poked with needles during emergencies for IV lines. (On one occasion, the medical staff had to stick Lorrin twenty times before they could place her IV).

I will never forget how kind and patient our doctor was in our time of need, because my entire family was an emotional mess. Tom and I agreed to both the chest tube and the PIC line, and Lorrin made it through the night. I never left her side.

Chapter 13

~ *Lorrin Has a Life* ~
Three Years Old

Lorrin always looked her best. It wasn't easy getting her out of the house and often I was multi-tasking. On this day, I was feeding her through her g-tube a can of formula. I accidentally spilt quite a bit of it all over her stomach. I started laughing at the mess I'd just created. Lorrin took a deep breath and let out a long sigh—as if to say, "Not again!" Which only made me laugh harder.

I did not realize that the Cedars-Sinai ICU would become my home away from home. I more than just watched Lorrin. I stayed and stared at her. I stared at the doctors, then sat next to my daughter under a fog of emotional pain and exhaustion. Everyone worked on getting Lorrin's pneumonia under control. It seemed there were more lab tests, x-rays, and respiratory treatments than I could count. Lorrin had the ICU doctors at her beck and call, and she kept them busy! The team of doctors and support staff included the entire ICU staff, a neurologist, a gastrointestinal specialist, a nutritionist, a social worker, an ear-nose-and-throat specialist, and an orthopedist. I also called to have a minister say her last prayers.

On about the third day, I had Tom bring me clothes, a radio, some of Lorrin's cute blankets, and hair clips. I also asked him to bring pictures to hang on the wall. He brought photos of Lorrin at Disneyland with her cousins, another of her at school, and one of her making a pizza. In the pictures, Lorrin was surrounded by her cousins who loved her so much. I looked at her smile. I could see how much love was in her life and how important she was to us all. The pictures told her story of survival and of her life outside the hospital walls.

Later that afternoon, one of the respiratory therapists told me something I will never forget. He apologized to me. He said he initially felt anger towards me regarding my choice to keep Lorrin alive. "I didn't understand why you were keeping her alive. It appeared that she didn't have a life worth living." It was not until he saw pictures of Lorrin with her family and friends—having fun and experiencing life—that he could understand the decision to put her on life support. He thought I was hanging on to her because I could not move forward with my own life.

While he was explaining all this to me, I kept thinking of the irony. It was Tom's decision to keep her alive—not mine. I cared for Lorrin and I wanted her body to be at peace and go to heaven. Tom, however, did not want her to go and was able to make her life and death decisions for her, even though he was clearly unable to be truly present and involved in her life.

The respiratory therapist shared with me that he had a brother with special needs, and it was hard for him to watch his mother care for him. He also shared how his brother's life affected him as a sibling. But now he could see the magnitude of how much Lorrin filled our lives with happiness. He could understand how much we cared about her and enjoyed her.

Even though his words initially shocked me and hurt my feelings, I was grateful for his honesty, so much so that we became very close after that day, and I consider him to be one of the kindest, gentlest, and most loving people who has ever worked with Lorrin. Of course, we had many long days working side-by-side on Lorrin's lungs. In 1998 alone, we stayed in the ICU for 156 days over the course of nine months.

I learned that because of the pictures that were hung on the wall, all the staff seemed more connected and present with Lorrin. They could see she had a life too. She had things she liked, and she experienced things we all enjoy. They saw her as a person, not just another body to be saved by machinery, technology, and tubes. Her life mattered to many.

I learned from that experience in the ICU. Photographs of Lorrin's life made such a difference in how she was treated. After that, I brought them with us for every hospital stay. When we would get to our room in the ICU or on the floor, I would go through my routine. I taped our favorite, most recent pictures to the wall at Lorrin's bedside and placed her cutest blankets around her to brighten up the bed. I unpacked her snazziest pajamas, her nail polish, hair clips, and stick-on earrings. I always carried my CD player with music to relax or rock-out to. These items were the essentials. I knew I could get a razor and toothbrush at the hospital. With Lorrin's ambiance items, my sweat pants and purse in hand, I could survive the hospital.

We spent our hospital time holding hands and listening to music. I made the best I could of our days and nights indoors with our close friends, the hospital staff. While Lorrin slept, I prayed and begged for everything to be okay. Simple comforts were all I needed and all that I had.

Chapter 14

~ *Putting Lorrin into a Coma, Twice* ~
Three Years Old

"My half-sister has blue eyes and blond hair, and she is very cute. She has touched my life with a gift from heaven. She is the first person who touched my life. She inspires me to do my best, and all that I can do because I have a gift. She is the best sister I could ever have."

~ Louise Aagaard (age 11)

Lorrin's near-death experience in March 1997, accompanied by a seventeen-day ICU stay, did not prepare me for what was coming. August of that year brought us to another new low. Lorrin was admitted to the hospital for having uncontrolled seizures. The neurologist told me the latest test showed Lorrin was experiencing constant seizure activity. He suggested we put Lorrin in a coma to try to stop the seizures.

I remember this as though it were yesterday. It was a warm day—the sun was baking my skin through the windows. I was wearing a purple shirt, white pants, and sandals. The hospital chair I sat in reminded me of my school days—uncomfortable with filthy floors. I was holding onto my seat for support as I listened, trying to remain calm. I made what I thought was a great attempt at asking the appropriate questions one might ask before putting their child into a drug-induced coma. To say the magnitude of what was taking place was overwhelming for me is an understatement. I sat and tried to let it sink in, remembering that the doctor had her best interests at heart, right?

Once the doctor left the room, I did what I always do and proceeded to fall apart. I wanted to scream. I was shaking and started to cry. Things were getting out of control. I was pacing the floor and thinking to myself that we had just reached a new all-time low. I now had the pleasure of phoning my family. "Hello, Mom. They want to put your grandbaby into a coma." What was to become of her?

Life can be funny. While walking the halls as Lorrin lay in the ICU, I bumped into a very highly respected doctor I knew from UCLA. It was one of those random moments that makes life just a little better. When I told him what we were about to do, he simply reassured me. "Oh, yeah, they do that all the time. And if she wakes up and is still seizing, you put her back into a coma for another week." I believe our meeting was fate preparing me. His words really helped me through the next two weeks. I was experiencing all kinds of new medical procedures, and this one would be just that.

We put Lorrin into a coma. And, yes, after a week when they started to wake her up, she went into a seizure. So they put her under again.

Lorrin stayed in the ICU and I watched as the medical staff put her into a Pentobarb coma. I watched Lorrin being hooked up to electrical nodes to monitor her brain activity while the doctor drugged her brain into a flat-line—meaning that they gave her enough drugs that she had no brain activity at all. Throughout the course of the week, the doctor administered more drugs anytime Lorrin showed any sign of brain activity.

I worried every moment. I had horrible thoughts that Lorrin might not wake up or come out of the coma even worse than before. I prayed there would be a day when I would see her beautiful blue eyes again and her big fat-face smile.

I set myself up as comfortable as a parent could be to care for her and recalled the story about the boy who was in the coma and how he had heard that woman's prayers and voice. I knew I had to be as calm and as comforting towards Lorrin as possible. I brought healing music and aromatherapy. I sat by her side and did every soothing thing I could think of. I played classical music, decorated her bed, massaged her with essential oils, and read to her. I truly believed, as I still do, that a person can hear, smell, and be present, even while in a coma, because the soul knows.

Sometimes I felt silly when the nurses would stare, but I also felt I was making a positive difference in supporting my girl. I wanted her back—my daughter, my Lorrin.

After the first week, Lorrin was brought out of the coma and started to have seizures. While the doctor put her under again, I remained calm and confident. However, what I had never expected to happen, did. While I sat beside her twenty-four hours a day, every day, Lorrin was being injured. The electrodes that had been cemented to her head created huge open sores on her skull.

I was beyond upset with myself. I was her servant the entire time, making sure she was turned from side-to-side to prevent pressure sores, yet I completely missed the obvious.

We discovered the wounds on a Sunday, which is normally an easy day, meaning no doctors and no procedures. I felt I was handling everything so well, but I was devastated when I discovered her sores. This left huge scars on the back of her head—scars that could have and should have been avoided.

I felt like I was becoming a permanent fixture in this place—just like the pictures that hung on the hospital walls. We were living in the ICU and had begun a new journey of medical awareness. Lorrin's lungs were being referred to as a pulmonary toilet. It was a living nightmare. She was fighting one bout of pneumonia after another. The doctors suggested Lorrin undergo a tracheotomy, which involves cutting a small incision into her neck and placing a tube there to allow access to the lungs. At first I refused to have it. I secretly hoped she would leave her broken body before we got to that point; I was really struggling. She was constantly ill, and yet, unbelievably, still continued to have seizures.

To make things worse, Tom drank heavily while we were in the hospital and his visits became less frequent. I hated how he was coping, and he hated me for so many reasons. This was nothing new for us. But I was going crazy. Lorrin was out of the coma, and I needed to get out of the hospital. I told the doctors that we needed to go home. They were against it. I told them I had everything at home that I needed, and if I had to, I would bring her back. I reminded them that the longer she stayed in this germ-invested place, the sicker she would become. So, against the doctor's wishes, I took Lorrin home.

Ironically, once we got home, Lorrin went into a long seizure. When I hurried to the refrigerator to get her IV Ativan, I was shocked. The refrigerator was empty. I had been home one day. I didn't even notice it missing. Tom had drank at least ten boxes of the medication while we had been staying in the hospital. There was nothing left to give her to stop the seizures. I went into a bit of a panic.

I knew he had been taking her pills, so I hid them while we were away. Even when I hid them, I counted them to make sure he had not discovered my stash. He refused to listen to me when I told him to stay away from Lorrin's meds. But I never would have guessed he would take her IV Ativan, which should be administered directly into the bloodstream or rectally. I wound up giving Lorrin a pill, which takes longer to enter the system, but it was all I had.

I called the doctor and had him prescribe a new bottle of Ativan. I was really angry at Tom and exhausted with my life. We argued about his stealing her meds. It costs us $300 to replace the medication. I told him to stay away from it. I actually marked the bottle with a pen as one does to monitor a liquor bottle with teenagers. At this time, Tom and I were not really speaking to each other. A few days later I saw that the bottle was missing Ativan. I called Tom out on it. He got outraged. He was screaming at me and actually scaring me. He usually didn't scare me, but on this day, I was concerned. He kept denying that he had taken any Ativan. I showed him where I had marked the bottle, and his faced dropped. It wasn't that he was caught—it was that he didn't remember doing it.

I think on this day I knew our relationship was over. It was beyond repair. His out-of-control addictions were a distraction I didn't need while trying to care for Lorrin. He was drunk all the time and barely spoke to me. When he did, he didn't remember what he'd said.

During Lorrin's hip replacement, Tom went to the ER for anxiety. He thought he was having a heart attack. I pulled the doctor aside and told him about Tom stealing Lorrin's Ativan and that I had called Tom's doctor to tell him of his erratic behavior. The doctor said Tom was probably having withdrawal symptoms from the Ativan and the other drugs he was taking. That was that, as though it happens all the time.

Chapter 15

~ The PIC Line ~
Three Years Old

While at the grocery store, a woman whose face I didn't remember told me, "I saw you at the bank yesterday with your daughter. I loved the way you were talking to her and the two of you really left an impression on me. I think about you every day. I realized that I don't have anything to complain about. I'm going to try harder to be a happier person because of you."

Lorrin had a temporary PIC line placed during her horrible bout with pneumonia on her third birthday. This provided immediate access to IV medications. It was a huge convenience. Lorrin's tiny veins were all collapsing and blown. Sometimes the ER would try for an hour to get a line. Access to a good vein became increasingly important due to her prolonged and numerous hospitalizations. They would poke her and almost get it and her veins would collapse. At the local ER and at Cedars-Sinai, I knew the best nursing staff to call. Once a person would try twice, I would not let them keep poking my precious baby.

I knew exactly who to call, usually from the neonatal team. They would always manage to get a vein on the first try. The problem was that Lorrin was crashing on the floor and needed STAT medication so they could intubate her. This inability of getting a vein was seriously jeopardizing her life.

For this reason, a permanent PIC line was placed. To my surprise, there was a department called the PIC team. Their focus was to get IV access into patients. They were some of the nicest people I have ever met. Their department was full of patients being treated for cancer and kidney failure. They were the experts, the best of the best.

Even still, the PIC team took two hours just to find placement in Lorrin. They cut her in both upper legs, her left arm, her chest, and ended up placing it in her right arm. Lorrin hated it from day one. It is a very serious thing to have done and must have a sterile environment, because this line goes to her heart. After months of it being placed, the skin on Lorrin's arm was deteriorating due to the permanent tape that had to secure the line. It was really gross. Her arm also became scarred from the numerous times the line has been reattached to her skin. At first, Lorrin hated it and pulled it out so many times that her skin became raw.

The line went from Lorrin's right arm at her elbow directly to her heart, so it was critical the site be sterile. It is a nurse's responsibility to change the dressing for this very reason. Normally, cleaning the site and changing the dressing required two people, but I was stubborn and learned to change it myself at home without the help of any medical staff.

I learned that I could do a lot of things without any help. Caring for Lorrin by myself was difficult at times, to say the least. I remember one Christmas Day in particular when I was changing Lorrin's PIC bandage. As I carefully unwound the gauze, I noticed that her IV was pulled out—not completely, but far enough to be at risk for being totally lost. I was firmly holding Lorrin's arm and I needed to make a decision quickly because I knew the line was vital. I needed to call someone for help, but the phone was across the room. Of course, Lorrin would not stay still as I struggled to reach the phone.

I finally reached the phone and then dialed the PIC team at Cedars. The nurses and staff there had now become my friends. They knew Lorrin, and they knew me. I spent more time with the doctors, the nurses, the PIC team, the ambulance drivers, and the ER staff than I did with my own family. As I explained my situation, Dr. Nice chuckled and said that he was in the middle of barbequing a turkey for Christmas dinner and could hardly get to the phone.

I laughed awkwardly and tried to remember what a normal Christmas day was like. He told me to wrap Lorrin's arm tightly and to come in the next day.

Despite the difficult aspects of Lorrin's PIC line, the medical staff was always helpful and patient. One doctor told me that when patients had difficulty with IV lines, he puts two stars beside the name in his palm pilot. Lorrin's name had five stars.

Chapter 16

Another Near-Death Hospital Stay Leading
to my "Aha" Moment of Acceptance
Three Years Old

When Lorrin was only two years old, we were at Target with her cousins Baylee and MacKenzie, who were a few years older than Lorrin. I was used to people staring by this point, but the girls hadn't really experienced the stares and whispers that were part of Lorrin being out in the community. A young boy with his mom said, "What is wrong with her?" Baylee, who was about five years old, told him, "She has brain damage!" The poor mom grabbed her boy and ran fast out of our aisle. I just laughed.

I can't tell you how many times Lorrin nearly died in the hospital. That was Lorrin's thing. She would get pneumonia, and I would take her to the hospital. She would crash on the pediatric floor, and we would be rushed into the ICU. She would be intubated, and the fight for her life would begin. Doctors ran test after test, x-rays, blood work, sputum cultures. The respiratory team would work on her around the clock. They would give her treatments and pound on her chest to help clear up her lungs. They were the best. Her care was the best. The more tests they would run, the more they found wrong with her. I told them jokingly if they would quit looking, they wouldn't find so many things to treat. I would tell them they should just focus on the pneumonia. I never left her side. I slept down the hall when she was in ICU. When she was on the floor, I slept in a cot. In the morning, I would get my coffee and I knew the doctors would have a huge report of all the things they wanted to treat. Her blood count was too low and she needed a blood transfusion. She was deficient in this or that. It was crazy.

When I was home alone, I was forced to call 911. If I had a nurse who was willing, I would have her drive us to Cedars. There were many times when my nurse, Denni, would be in the back of the van with Lorrin lying on the floor. Denni would be "bagging" Lorrin the entire way to the hospital. Basically when you use an Ambu bag to help get oxygen into the lungs you are actually breathing for the patient. This is complete madness for any normal person. For Lorrin it was second nature. Bless Denni's heart. She worked for Lorrin for about 10 years. She became part of our family and we became part of hers. This was one of Lorrin's many blessings.

Lorrin was four years old just a few months before her trach was placed. I stood watching the nurses at Lorrin's bedside. Lorrin had her permanent IV, they were giving her meds and flushing her IV line. It is as clear to me as if it was yesterday. It was the summer of 1998. I can almost smell the tape on Lorrin's sweet skin. We were always in the hospital. On this particular stay I came to one of my many "aha" moments.

I was constantly exhausted. I tried my best to be present and focused. I looked at each drug they gave her. On one occasion, I witnessed Lorrin getting ten times too much medication. I was the one who caught it. I knew every detail about her care. I was making decisions on her life that no parent should ever have to make. It was my job to be on top of things. Human error happens all the time. Mistakes happen in the hospital. It just can be more dangerous when it comes to the massive amounts of drugs that Lorrin was being given. I watched everything that she took and asked questions about every procedure. I went to every test with her, holding her hand.

I found it ironic that I had spent the last three years doing everything alternative medicine had to offer to help Lorrin, and now I was living in the ICU. Technology was keeping her alive. Her father refused to allow her to be considered as a "do not resuscitate" (DNR). We, of course, fought about this. When I married Tom I knew we would have problems. I thought we might disagree on where to send Lorrin to school. I never in my wildest dreams thought that we would be arguing about what medical measures would be taken to keep Lorrin alive or when to let her go. Every time she was put on life support, we had a choice to make. How much does a parent intervene? When parents don't agree, who gets to decide?

I was the one who was Lorrin's caretaker. Tom went to work. When he came home, he sat outside and drank and smoked. He hated me for being able to live in the hospital. I hated him because he got to go to work and sleep in his own bed at night. He showered when he wanted to and he pooped when he wanted to. I took care of Lorrin. Everything I did was centered on her. We kept Lorrin alive at all costs. Sometimes I thought it was his way of hanging on to me. As long as I was consumed with her care, how could I do anything else? I would tell the doctors that Lorrin was a DNR. They would say they knew her father had other wishes. I knew all the hospital staff on the fourth floor, the ER, and in the ICU. They were my friends.

One day I decided I needed to make the best of my hospital experience. I could not fight it any more. We had spent 156 days in the ICU in 1998. It was becoming my life. If this was what my journey had become, I had better pay attention to the lessons I was being taught. I tried my best to take it for what it was. I truly felt I was there to be a witness to the gifts of modern medicine.

I thought that the sooner I learned my "lesson," the sooner we could go home. I allowed myself to be present with her. I told her of my love for her. I told her, as I had told her many times, "I will care for you if you stay, and I will be okay if you go." I wanted her to know that she was also making a choice. I was meant to witness her experience, our experience. I have never seen anything like her will to live and her love of life and people. I told her if this was her journey, I would help her. I would sit beside her while she went through this. But, I would no longer feel sorry for her. If she was in pain, she needed to pull herself out of her body. I would do all I could to make her comfortable. I would not pity her. I would stay by her side and love her and care for her.

In my heart and my mind, we made an agreement. It was our pact, our pinky swear, our soul commitment. It released me from feeling sorry for her, and, more importantly, I could no longer feel sorry for myself. It was a very powerful and beautiful gift when I could be present with Lorrin and sit beside her.

On that day, I became a very powerful partner and mother to Lorrin. I held her hand in a new way. I could better support her and be more in tune with what was going on around us. It took the fear away from me for the most part, and I was in a position of power for her. We were in agreement. We were spiritual partners. It is, in my opinion, one of the best things I did for her. Being present in her journey, not controlling it, and not feeling sorry for her and not feeling sorry for myself. It was a huge shift for me.

Chapter 17

~ *Documentation* ~
Four Years Old

"The most beautiful people I've known are those who have known trials, have known struggles, have known loss, and have found their way out of the depths."

~ *Elisabeth Kübler-Ross*

Many times during our doctors' visits, they would question if she was really having seizures at all. I quickly learned that occurrences that did not seem significant to me might be important to the doctor. Furthermore, it seemed that I was always under the gun during our appointments. By the time they got into the room and sat down, someone was always knocking on the door interrupting us with a phone call or page. When the doctor asked me questions, I had notes, facts, statistics, and quick answers. Being prepared, punctual, and to the point makes a world of difference.

I even videotaped Lorrin's seizures and carried the camcorder in my purse. In 1994, a camcorder was a large piece of equipment. Today, you would just use your phone. Each time we saw a new doctor, he would ask the same questions. What did the seizures look like? What part of the body was affected? How long did they last?

I just handed over the camera and hit "play" so the doctor could see that Lorrin was indeed having a seizure. By determining the part of the body being affected during the seizure, an appropriate medication could be prescribed. In

Lorrin's case, we needed to decide which medication to switch to.

In addition to taking notes, keeping a diary, and filming Lorrin's seizures, I started journaling. I did this to keep my sanity. I also wanted everyone to witness our life—the extremes we went through together on a daily basis. One day as I was bathing Lorrin, I laid her tiny body on a towel on the floor. She was about three at the time. I stared at her skinny little body squirming on the towel. Lorrin had had the gastric feeding tube (g-tube) placed just months before.

Before Lorrin's g-tube was placed, she weighed just nineteen pounds despite her healthy, completely organic diet. I fed her a more varied diet than most kids her age would have, including chicken, beef, lamb, pears, apples, dates, figs, oatmeal, carrots, beans, sweet potatoes, and squash. I pureed all of her food so it was easy for her to swallow and purchased her food from health food stores. I wanted her to have the best possible opportunity for healing, so she ate two fruit meals and two meat and veggie meals a day.

As with all the intrusive medical procedures suggested by her doctors, I fought the g-tube. I wanted to use more natural measures. In spite of everything I had tried, I felt that feeding Lorrin through a tube meant I had failed as her parent. Since Lorrin was having such difficulty eating and breathing on her own, I relented. After the tube was placed in a relatively simple surgery, I was able to give her more nutrition with greater ease. I could get any medicine that she needed in her and was able to give her an excess amount of water. I regretted having delayed the procedure to salve my tender ego.

Back to that day with Lorrin on the bathroom floor: as I stood over Lorrin's naked body, I could only focus on her g-tube. It looked as big as she did. On her stomach, she had developed a nasty-looking growth, known as a stoma, around the tube. I was caught up in the ugliness of it. Lorrin's doctor had been using silver nitrate to burn off the excess skin—this would become yet another lovely procedure I learned to do at home. Burning the stoma with silver nitrate left a black mess around the tube. I decided I wanted people to understand what my baby looked like and what I dealt with every day. I wanted people to know what my life was like. I shook my head in silence, playing over in my head everything we had been through. Looking forward, there seemed no hope in sight. We were just plugging the holes of a dam when it came to Lorrin's care. We would fix one thing and then move on to the next part of her body that wasn't working. Once I was educated on that, another crack would form and need attention.

I got my camera and took a picture of her stomach. The more I looked at it, the madder I got. I was furious by this time. I wanted to send the judge and all the people who represented the Vaccine Compensation Act a visual of my life.

This moment in the bathroom was the start of my filming Lorrin. I went on to hire a cameraman to document every part of our day. I wanted to have a record of it in hopes I could someday see something positive in retrospect. I wanted to capture the moment that I would always remember just how hard we fought to survive. I did not want to lose the magnitude of what we were going through.

When our lives refused to get easier, filming gave me an outlet. I could not possibly relay to other parents the struggle I lived each day, and I could not make sense of all the suffering Lorrin endured, but I could record it. I assembled twenty-seven forty-minute, mini-DVDs. I shot footage of Lorrin's teachers, Girl Scouts, and her bike riding. I captured what I went through to get her ready in the morning and her physical therapist helping her to exercise. The film reflects her courage and will to survive. She was not just a sick child, but rather a person who had a life full of hopes and desires like everyone else.

Dr. John Menkes, who came on board with Lorrin's treatment when she was two, was one of the only neurologists who would talk about the correlation between brain damage and the DPT vaccine. He was a light in the storm of Lorrin's ordeal. A brilliant, well-respected doctor, in fact, I heard rumors that when Dr. Menkes graduated from medical school he had to wait to become a doctor because he was too young. When he retired, he spent his time in Wales doing research and writing. Dr. Menkes died in 2009. I am grateful to have spent so much time with Dr. Menkes and to have had the opportunity to interview him on camera about children like Lorrin.

During my interview with Dr. Menkes, he told me something that came as a shock. He stated that Lorrin was one of the worst seizure cases he had ever treated. I tilted my head while trying to hide my surprise. I guess his statement should not have surprised me, but it did. I took a double take and felt like Scooby Doo for a moment, wanting to say, "Rut Ro."

I had nothing to compare our chaos to. I oftentimes forgot just how not right everything was.

Chapter 18

~ The Dreaded Trach ~
Four Years Old

"You never know how strong you are . . . until being strong is the only choice you have."

~ Cayla Mills

Lorrin started turning blue until she passed out at home. It is human nature when you watch someone stop breathing to bring them back to life, especially a child. I remember looking over and seeing Lorrin lying lifeless on the bed, her face blue and not breathing. I went over to shake her.

I would at times fantasize about what a normal life would look like. I walked out of the room countless times, fully expecting her to not be alive when I returned. Each time I saw her blue face, I jumped and grabbed her and shook her back to life.

It was at this time I hired someone to do my grocery shopping and my banking. I did not leave the house. I baked to show my appreciation to those who were so kind to us. This consisted mostly of the ER staff, ambulance drivers, doctors, and nurses. I was so grateful for their understanding and tenderness. My time at home was full of cooking and crafting. It was how I kept my sanity and helped make me feel useful and kept me busy. I started sewing and made Lorrin's clothes and blankets.

I longed for freedom from her demanding medical needs. It was a very confusing time. The days were full of surprises. I would start my morning thinking it would be a peaceful day, but then Lorrin would suddenly get sick. What I thought would be a regular day would end with her on oxygen, struggling to get a breath.

One day, she again struggled to breathe. It was impossible for me to drive her to the hospital in this condition. I phoned 911, and we were taken to Cedars. Lorrin crashed on the floor, and we rushed her into the ICU for another emergency intubation. It was about four a.m. when I laid down my head to sleep. I remember walking into the ICU the next day, searching for my child. I knew that if she had died during the night, they surely would have come down the hall and told me. I was both relieved and sad she had made it through another night.

The doctor who had been her ears, nose, and throat specialist walked right up to me, stood in front of me and blurted out, "We need to trach her!" I just looked at him and replied, "I know."

Secretly, I wanted Lorrin to die. I had no desire for her to have a trach. The thought of it grossed me out. I didn't think I could deal with it. I was scared and alone. I was exhausted. I knew the entire medical team was also drained from rushing around doing emergency intubations on Lorrin. It was horrible and damaging to her lungs and stressful for all involved. I understood that it was ultimately my decision, but if I wanted to continue having the Cedars team supporting Lorrin, I needed to be a cooperative parent and do what was obviously the next step.

It was a devastating time for me. There was no secret what was happening to Lorrin. Everyone knew, but somehow this was my intervention. I did not want my child to be trached. I had nothing left inside of me to fight. I crawled up in Lorrin's hospital bed, and we had a girl to girl chat.

I told her, "Lorrin, if you don't want to be trached, you are going to have to leave your body."

I talked to the team of doctors and asked them to check her heart and see if it was healthy. My logic told me that prolonging her body if her heart was failing seemed ridiculous. The cardiologist was so cute when he told me, "Her heart is strong." I was full of mixed emotions. If only her heart was weak, I wouldn't have to go through with this.

I scheduled the surgery and I explained to Lorrin that we were going to put a hole in her neck to help her breathe. I also told her that for the most part, her body was healthy. If she didn't want to have this done to her, she would have to stop her heart.

As her mother, this made perfect sense to me. We discussed things all the time. I knew she was listening and making choices.

A funny thing happened. Her heart started to fibrillate. It would go really fast and then slow down. This is a very bad sign, and the entire team of doctors in ICU stood at her bedside watching her. This alarmed me and somewhat frightened me. Did she have this amount of control over her body? Did she want to die? For the next hour we all stood and watched Lorrin's heart rate. They could not figure out what was going on. Then one nurse named Liz suggested they check the placement of Lorrin's pic line. Lorrin had a pic line in her right arm at the crook of her arm, and it was threaded up to her heart. This gave the doctors permanent IV access allowing them to draw medicine and take blood.

They took an x-ray and found out the IV line was actually tickling her heart and making her heart fibrillate. They pulled the IV back a bit and the problem was resolved. I went up to Liz and told her that Lorrin wanted to stop her heart and she had just screwed that up and had gone and saved her life. She was puzzled until I explained what I had told Lorrin.

Lorrin went into surgery November 4, 1999. This felt like the worst day of my life up to that point. The thought of Lorrin having a trach was completely devastating to me. When she came out of surgery, I could smell the familiar after-surgery smells of tape and skin Betadine. I walked up to Lorrin with much trepidation and saw that she was still my girl with a small change. Yes, she had a trach, but her neck was still beautiful, her skin still soft, and her eyelashes still long.

I bent over her hospital bed and kissed her, and in that moment, I knew we were both going to be okay.

The nurses came over to change her position. After surgery, I was always afraid of Lorrin. Especially while in the ICU. I let the nurses change her immediately after surgery. I was afraid to touch her for the simple fact I didn't want to cause her any more pain. Katie, the nurse on staff, went to change

Lorrin's position. Lorrin was still completely knocked out from the surgery. Katie asked for help from one of the other nurses. I took a few steps back, my eyes never leaving Lorrin.

Katie flipped her from one side to the other, keeping the weight off her hip to avoid bed sores. Katie said, "Her trach is out!" She said it loudly, as if asking for back up, and then she said, "It's back in."

I flatly said, "I am not taking her home!" I was trained for the next three days on how to suction my daughter. It scared the shit out of me. But I did it.

When we finally got home, I received ten huge boxes of medical supplies delivered to my door. No one came to the house to make sure I was doing things right or keeping things sterile. I just received a delivery of boxes of medical supplies that stacked up to the ceiling. It is shocking that I didn't kill her with my lack of understanding and direction for her care. I think I was just so relieved to be in my own home, I didn't actually think about the magnitude of care that my daughter now required.

Chapter 19

~ Mother or Caretaker? ~
Almost Five Years Old

"What matters is not the features of our character or the drives and instincts per se, but rather the stand we take toward them. And the capacity to take such a stand is what makes us human beings."

~ Victor Frankl, *The Will to Meaning*

It was 1998, and we finally settled with the Vaccine Compensation Act. Lorrin was four years old and now had an annuity to pay for her medical expenses. She was far more medically compromised than I ever imagined her to be. Her medical expenses were exceeding what we had asked for with the life-care plan, and the nursing costs were much higher than expected. So for the first six months after Lorrin's case was settled, I did everything on my own because I didn't want to waste her money on nursing care while I was not working.

It took time for me as a parent to understand the difference between being the parent of a typical child as compared to that of a child with a unique life. Make no mistake, the difference is huge. Because Lorrin was my one and only, I didn't have anything to compare my experience to. My plan to do everything by myself backfired and left me feeling hopelessly frustrated.

By January of 1999, I crashed emotionally and physically. I was unable to cope and make the medical decisions that were demanded by Lorrin. I suffered bouts of uncontrollable rage and tears, and was on the verge of a true breakdown.

We were in the midst of trying to make a decision about a surgery for Lorrin. Once the tracheotomy was placed, it made it easier to treat her constant pneumonias. We no longer had emergency intubations—access to her lungs was easy. But, the problem was that she was catching pneumonia over and over. Lorrin was swallowing her saliva and food into her lungs. She was unable to cough it out, and then it would grow bacteria. She was constantly sick. A nurse in Cedars ICU that had previously worked in Chicago recommended a surgery to me. She told me that it was done all the time for children like Lorrin. It is called a tracheal diversion. They cut the vocal cords and pouch the airway separating the lungs from the stomach. The research showed that 95% of the patients and caregivers were glad they did the surgery. Lorrin was not speaking and it didn't look as though she would ever become vocal.

Tom and I were separated and not exactly seeing eye to eye at this time. I was frustrated because my life was consumed with her care and living in the hospital. He would go to work and visit her on Sundays. I felt unsure if this surgery was actually going to help her or if it would simply prolong what I thought to be more suffering and a life of misery.

When I asked the pulmonary doctor about the surgery, he told me, "Most parents opt to let their children die."

But the problem was, she wasn't dying. She was existing. Every doctor told me that if I didn't care for her so well, she would be dead.

Tom and I started getting counseled by the doctor separately. I was living in the hospital at the time and was close to the entire team of pediatric doctors. The head of the pediatric team told me that he had a proposition for me. He said, "I will keep Lorrin here for a week if you agree to take that week and go somewhere alone and give yourself a break so that you can be strong and clear-minded, and then you can make this decision."

As I paced the hospital floor staring at Lorrin lying on the bed, the reality of our life came crashing down on me. It was impossible to comprehend the mess that I was in. How did this happen? How did we get here? He was right. I could not make any decisions. I could barely put my shoes on. I was exhausted and lifeless, confused and broken. This madness had been going on for five years now. I had not left Lorrin's side. There was no evidence left of the person I used to be. I was a robot, caregiver, nurse and somewhere deep inside me, a loving mother.

On the outside, I was a mess, trying my hardest to survive and make life decisions for my precious daughter.

I heard the doctor and respected him. I took Lorrin home and hired the nurses from the ICU to work in my home caring for Lorrin while I took a break. Taking a few days away from Lorrin was heart-wrenching and costly, but it was also critical for my survival.

I called Barb and told her it was time for my nineteenth nervous breakdown. "Are you in?" I asked.

We spent a night or two in Santa Barbara, and then I went on to Cambria alone. I was there for four days, desperately searching for answers about what I was supposed to do. I longed for companionship. I was wounded in many ways. On the fourth night, I had dinner by myself and came back to the room and went to bed. There was no clear evidence of the right decision. I woke up at four a.m., deep in thought and filled with enormous sadness. I got up and took a drive to the ocean.

Bundled up in my sweater, I sat in my car crying and praying for answers. My mind was a blur, full of worry and fear of what was ahead. Dark death and feelings of loss consumed me. Everyone kept telling me that if I didn't care so well for her she wouldn't be here. Was I keeping her alive for selfish reasons? What was I supposed to do? How much could God ask of me?

The sun started to rise over the ocean. Joggers appeared on the beach. There was a gentle peace that came over me as the rays of sun started to bounce on the ocean. The sound of the waves as they hit the sand calmed me. Suddenly, it came to me. It was clear and simple. I realized that I didn't have control over Lorrin's life. I could only care for her the best I could. My love for her was endless. I knew in my heart that if it were her time to go, that no matter what I did, she would go. Until then, I would do what I could to give her the best life possible. She would be the one to make the decision to live or die.

I was just not that powerful. This was between her and God.

I returned home and decided to do the tracheal diversion. It was one of the best decisions I made regarding her medical care. Lorrin started to heal after that and lived another ten long years. She was able to make peace with her body. Her personality started to shine through. For the first time in her life, she was not smothered with constant illness. We both got a chance to enjoy life.

Chapter 20

~ Cultivating Better Hospital Experiences ~
Ages Three to Seven

"The idea that some lives matter less is the root of all that is wrong with the world."

~ Dr. Paul Farmer

From ages three to five, Lorrin and I almost lived at the hospital. In 1998, we spent 170 days in ICU. Lorrin received a g-tube placement, a fundoplication, and a tracheotomy. She was also put in a coma twice to stop the seizures. Once Lorrin received her tracheotomy, she started to heal. Her body started to grow, and for the first time in her life, she was healthy.

Then the doctors told me she needed to have both hips replaced and a rod put into her spine because her spine was crooked, and that affected her heart and lungs.

During these hospital stays I would load up my van with strands of lights, stuffed animals, dolls and blankets for our long stays, sometimes three weeks at a stretch. I brought things to decorate Lorrin's bed, usually themed: heart blankets at Valentine's Day, ghosts at Halloween, Santa at Christmas time, and flowers for spring.

A hospital is a boring place for a child, full of painful procedures, sleepless nights, mind numbing with boredom and sameness. Her view of the hospital was from her bed, so I made the space above her a collage of color and meaning to stimulate her vision and her mind. Lorrin spent two birthdays and three Halloweens in the hospital.

The first Halloween she was a butterfly. I brought her Halloween costume and decorated her bed and decorated her wheelchair. We made the best of the day, walking around the halls and talking to all of our friends. The second Halloween was a bit more complicated. Lorrin was going to be Snow White. I was going to be the evil stepmother. I had spent a fortune on the costume and months getting ready. I spent hours painting bags and sprinkling them with glitter to attach to her chair to represent the coal mine. Tom, with the help of my nurse Denni, had brought everything down to the exact eyeliner and make-up for the costume. We managed to pull it off. It was one of the best costumes ever. We walked the halls with Lorrin hooked up to oxygen.

I will never forget that day. We spent about an hour talking to a male volunteer. He was so enamored with Lorrin and her beauty. He kept talking about her beautiful blue eyes. At the end of the conversation, he said, "I just realized she is wearing a wig." That was probably part of why Lorrin wanted to have black hair.

With each admission to Cedars, the nurses all came to visit. They would say, "I heard you were here, and I needed to come see what Miss Lorrin was wearing." They would give her a once over—check her nails to see what color they were painted. They would admire her hair and makeup. Or just stop by to say hi. They knew they were going to see something new and fashionable when Lorrin was admitted. And they wanted to hear about her latest adventure. Lorrin, even in her sickest state, would bat her beautiful blue eyes to acknowledge her visitors.

Lorrin communicated by blinking or by a "thumbs up!" She loved the male nurses and male doctors. She would give a huge smile at just the right moment that would get the whole room laughing. She said so much by the timing of her blink. Everyone would sit on her bedside, waiting for some kind of response. She always made an effort. She loved how kindly everyone treated her.

We would share our travels, our latest philosophy and spiritual studies, our trips to Oregon, or our swims with the dolphins. It seemed as though everyone enjoyed our upbeat attitude. I was sad and anxious, but I did my best not to be cranky, and I tried to never take it out on the nursing staff.

We seemed to have a special relationship with each person in a different way. Velma was a shopper, and we would talk about fashion and make up with her. She always threatened to steal Lorrin's latest bling.

Sharon and Tessie from ICU always made a point to come down the hall when Lorrin and I were on the floor. I can still hear Sharon saying, "I heard you girls were down here. What's going on?"

Liz had a son close to Lorrin's age. He had the biggest eyes. She would keep me updated on her family. Each person was close to us in their way. They were becoming my friends and my family. I spent more time at Cedars than I did anywhere else. Strangely, I felt comfort in our friendships. Home away from home!

Life was tough through these years. Tougher than I'd ever known. My heart was ripped out. But I learned that by cultivating my relationships with the hospital staff, they would come to care about Lorrin. They understood better than anyone what we were going through.

Outside the hospital, people looked at Lorrin as a freak, a terrifying mistake. People were afraid to acknowledge that something so terrible could happen, afraid to say the wrong thing, afraid of being inadequate, afraid of being contaminated. The hospital staff wasn't afraid of her and would treat her like the tender, aware, and courageous child she was. They saw her illness as normal. It was a hospital. They saw past her illness.

We became professional patients. I knew where the linens were. I knew exactly how many blankets it would take to make my cot bearable.

As I changed my attitude from resistance to acceptance, Tom reacted to me being at the hospital with anger or jealousy. He noticed that everyone at the hospital was nice to me, and he hated it. He didn't understand that they were returning courtesy. I was respectful and friendly to them. I cultivated relationships with the staff to make the hospital stays tolerable. He accused me of using Lorrin's hospitalization as social time and of taking her to the hospital when she wasn't sick at all.

It was true that I was becoming more accustomed to being there than anywhere else. My positive attitude confused him. If I wasn't miserable, he assumed I must be acting out of choice instead of necessity. But the only thing I could choose was my attitude.

He couldn't understand my ability to cope. I couldn't understand how he could stay away from Lorrin's bedside. He could only tolerate two hours at a time at the hospital. I would have rather he not come at all.

We weren't okay. He wasn't okay. His reaction to the situation was to anesthetize his feelings with alcohol. I was moving more towards meditation and spiritual studies to aid in my understanding of our journey. He began to hate me for that—and for many other reasons.

By this time, I was consumed in Lorrin's needs, support groups, and other families that had children who were unique. In the beginning, I would take Lorrin to prayer sessions with the Elders at the church down the street. I was reading all kinds of books about spirituality.

I think our marriage was in trouble long before Lorrin. When I was pregnant, I realized how much he drank. Now that Lorrin was obviously not going to be a "normal" child, I submerged myself into therapies, all the while doing medical treatments.

He got very angry with some of the alternative treatments that I arranged for Lorrin. I would take her to a doctor named Viola Frymann in La Jolla. She was a doctor of Osteopathic medicine. It took an entire day to travel there and was very expensive. It was the only hope I had. Tom hated it. I continued to see her.

I took her to another chiropractor for cranial sacral treatments three times a week, driving an hour each way.

I took her to a local acupuncturist twice a week. There was a huge gap in our conversations. Lorrin's health was always bad news. My beliefs, her treatments, and my desire to heal her consumed me. Tom did not agree with what I was doing. We became two completely separate people living in the same house. Our only bond was Lorrin.

Tom and I had nothing left in common. His drinking was out of control. I continued to go to my support groups. My favorite was at the Steven Weiss College. I met a group of parents that I am still friends with. The group was helpful for me. It was hard because most of the couples who were together went to the support group together. I didn't badger Tom about it. But I do think going to the group meetings helped me cope. It also made my heart heavy knowing that we could not share this burden as a couple. He did his thing, and I did mine. We both were in an enormous amount of pain.

I tried everything I could to help her. He was traditional and didn't appreciate me trying non-conventional treatments. I couldn't share my new ideas with him. He saw them as foolish and invalid. He told me many times, "Your whole family thinks you're crazy."

I stopped telling him about Lorrin's horrible symptoms. How could I say, "Hi, honey. Welcome home. Your daughter just had ten grand mal seizures. How was your day?"

I couldn't share with him, and we stopped talking. He drank, and I held Lorrin. It wasn't that he didn't love her; he did. It was just that we had different coping strategies and beliefs.

After Lorrin had her trach placed, she started to heal and became much more aware of her surroundings. During her surgeries, which involved lengthy hospital stays, I started bringing along her Easy Bake Oven and cotton candy maker. Needless to say, the hospital staff thought I was whacky—until we made s'mores that everyone gobbled up.

Many of the hospital visits became not only about Lorrin's recovery, but also about the people we met there. One of the many moving experiences I can recall, happened because of her Easy Bake Oven. At the time, Lorrin had both her hips replaced simultaneously. The surgery was difficult and the recovery awful.

While there, we met a young boy who was twelve years old. Although he seemed healthy, I had learned not to pass judgment, especially at the hospital. He had obviously been admitted before and knew the hospital staff. He stayed a few days on the same floor as us. His mom and I passed each other in the hall, dressed in sweats with hair a mess and with that familiar look: searching desperately for bad coffee, eating horrible hospital food, struggling to keep it together for our kids, and dealing with a severe lack of privacy.

The boy's mother, Francine, and I struck up a conversation. She told me her son, Kyle, had a brain tumor, but that after much treatment, he had been in remission. Some alarming symptoms cropped up, so they had just been re-admitted to the hospital. She had not yet told her son of the bad news. But the doctor had just come into her son's room and blurted out that the tumor had returned. I could feel her pain. Her otherwise healthy boy was possibly dying from brain cancer. My completely unhealthy child may live forever in her broken body or die tomorrow. Our children's fate was in question every day. As parents, we were so different, but our pain was so similar.

As she told me her story, I was at a loss for words. I tried to simply listen and empathize with her pain, which can oftentimes be the most powerful tool we have for coping with tragedy—just to listen. My whole body felt heavy and my heart ached for her and her son. She could see my sadness.

I tried to lift the mood by offering to share our Easy Bake Oven. Kyle had already become fond of it. He thought the little pink dessert machine was wonderful, and so I let them take it to their room. I left them with a half-serious warning about breaking hospital code by plugging in a foreign electrical device. I was constantly scolded for my electric lights, toys, and other crazy decorations.

The next day, Francine returned the oven with heartfelt thanks. She told me that Kyle had not eaten in days, and she was delighted to see him gobble up food he enjoyed, even if it had no nutritional value. I was privileged to be able to distract them from their ordeal for a moment and to share a small part of their journey.

I am sure at home, Kyle would not be caught dead near an Easy Bake Oven, a young boy's worst nightmare. But on that day, he baked and ate and had fun.

Chapter 21

– *Meditation Moments* –

To survive my caretaker role at home, I started country dancing. Every Thursday and Saturday, I would go to the local Borderline Bar and Grill and dance, even if that meant going by myself. My favorite dancer was Kevin. He was a great dancer and wonderful teacher. His dance card was always full. One night, I asked him to dance. He was obviously tired and a bit sweaty, not that I minded. I told him that he was dancing with me 'cause he was afraid that I was going to kill myself. He smiled a beautiful grin and said, "Honey, if you haven't killed yourself by now, it isn't going to happen!"

When Lorrin was about to have her first birthday, Tom made the choice to change jobs. We moved to the other side of Los Angeles to a town called Thousand Oaks. I resented him for taking me out of the only safe thing that was left in my life. All of Lorrin's doctors, therapists, friends, and family were in Orange County. You see that I put doctors and therapists first. That was my life. Friends were becoming far and few.

I returned to Orange County and was in Huntington Beach shopping at a health food store.

I had just read *The Celestine Prophecy*. That was my first spiritual book. Lorrin was not yet a year old, and my life was changing very quickly. I was desperately searching for guidance from anyone who might have a bit of hope for my baby. At that time, doctors were very grim about any hopes for normalcy for my Lorrin.

In a wonderful synchronicity, I started talking to a woman who had lived in Thousand Oaks for years. She told me I would have a hard time finding spiritual places in Thousand Oaks. She told me there was one store called The Hummingbird and The Honey Bee. She said I would love it, and whatever I needed, I would find at the The Hummingbird and The Honey Bee. We chatted for a bit and exchanged numbers. I left there with a new friend who shared similar interests. I also left with a bit of hope in finding some alternative support in Thousand Oaks.

The first time I went to The Hummingbird and The Honey Bee, I immediately felt a safe and comfortable energy. I started taking Tai Chi lessons, did hypnotherapy, and joined a meditation group. I felt so alone in my new community. It was very difficult meeting new friends.

When strangers meet, there is an immediate focus on what they have in common. When new moms connect, there are so many obvious topics—unless your child is becoming a living medical nightmare. My new motherhood journey was similar to the plague. I was broken; my marriage was a mess; and my daughter had the worst possible diagnosis. Who would want to get to know me? I was a train wreck in every way.

I found an enormous amount of comfort going to a weekly meditation group. I loved the teacher, Pat. It is my belief that Pat's love and guidance saved my life. She is the most gifted, powerful, gentle, and loving person. She is one of the few spiritual persons that I have met who never operates from her ego. Her talented meditations carried me through the week and gave me hope. She also did Tarot card readings.

Pat held space for me. She listened, loved, taught, and supported me. I realize that this is cliché and many students probably say this, but I feel as though Pat and I are connected in a deep way. She is an ancient teacher, but to me her energy is familiar. I did then and still do feel very close to her.

One time long ago in a Tarot reading, she said, "You have no idea how big you are going to be." She doesn't remember saying that to me, but I can promise you in my darkest nights and deepest pits of depression, I have remembered those words. They have carried me through some horrible times of despair that I never thought I would survive. Words are powerful.

I never missed Pat's class. It helped me in so many ways. I was doing meditations at home by myself daily. I would often ask Lorrin to join me in my meditations. I would quiet my mind so I could hear her spirit voice talk to me. I felt that she was always hearing me and my inner thoughts and feelings.

When I focused my attention on her inner voice during meditation, I felt that I would really understand her better. I was learning to follow my gut and ask her questions, later getting her to blink for confirmation that I was on the right track. The first meditation that Lorrin visited me when I had not invited her to was when she was about five years old.

It started out as a typical Wednesday evening at the The Hummingbird and The Honey Bee. There were about ten or twelve of us that regularly took Pat's class. Pat told us that we were going to take a guided journey. I loved when she did this. She would take us to an altered state and guide us in a meditation. She would narrate parts of it, and we would each have our own unique and individual experiences.

We made ourselves comfortable. I remember lying on the floor. Pat started the meditation off with a drum in her hand and music from a CD with nature sounds of the wind, water, thunder, and rain. Pat beat her drum.

We started off with deep breathing. Pat would help shift us into an altered state by changing our breathing patterns. We took slow, deep breaths. She was our guide. I felt safe. I was listening to Pat's voice as the vibration of the drumming was deepening my awareness. With each breath, I fell deeper and deeper into a trance.

The first part of the meditation started off with me sitting with my back up against a tree. I could smell wet grass. Pat guided me to walk towards the water. There was a canoe waiting, and I was told to get into the canoe. It was then Lorrin seemed to accompany me. This was the first time she had really entered my meditation without me asking her to. I was startled at first. I told her "no." This was my time alone, my meditation. I felt as though her presence was an intrusion, and I was looking forward to my own time. I was with her every day, 24-7. These Wednesday nights were my healing time—my only time away from her. I was there to get my spirit back so I could care for her. It was my selfish time.

But here I was, in the middle of the meditation, and I was bantering with

Lorrin. I was telling her to go, but her presence was so strong. I knew she had every intention of being in the meditation whether I wanted her to or not. I also realized that if I continued to argue with Lorrin, I would miss the journey.

I was familiar with Pat's journeys. It's funny, but many times I would know what she was going to say before she said it. It was so easy for me to go along with her every direction.

I dropped back into the meditation and focused on Pat's voice. I became a Native American woman. And as Lorrin would have it, she was in a papoose strapped to my back. I stepped into the canoe and paddled down the river. The water was doing most of the work. I could feel the wind in my hair. I could smell the water. It felt real. All of my senses were cooperating. I could feel the breeze on my face. I could feel myself wearing a leather dress with Lorrin tied to my back. I could smell the leather. I could sense her presence and feel the weight of her. The canoe came to an embankment. I was instructed to step out of the canoe, and as I did so, I looked down to see myself in moccasins.

I walked along the trail to an opening in the earth. It was a huge hole. At the bottom was a fire blazing. I was instructed to climb down this hole on a ladder. I felt alone but could sense that there were many others around me. Once I was at the bottom, I went to the fire. There were Native Americans dancing around the fire in ceremony. The fire was huge I could feel the heat of it on my face.

A Native American man appeared in front of me. I felt his presence. He was gentle, strong, and powerful. I felt as though he were very kind and I knew I was safe with him. He put his arm on mine as though he were guiding me to sit down. I sat cross-legged. There was a sense that Lorrin was still on my back, but I couldn't feel the weight of her as before.

The man sat in front of me, cross-legged with a bare chest. He wore leather pants and moccasins. His hair was in braids with a headband around his head. His face was full of lines and his dark eyes were tender. I felt a sense of great wisdom and an inner knowing came to me as I looked into his eyes. I spoke to the medicine man with my emotions. We were communicating without words. Our gaze was intense.

We were communicating, but our lips never moved. I could feel him, and I knew he was reading me. His energy comforted me as I sat, open to the experience. I felt vulnerable.

I suddenly became aware of all of the pain and the suffering that I had been living through since Lorrin was born. My heart was broken into a million pieces. I felt the burden of carrying the papoose, being Lorrin's mother. The devastating diagnosis of my baby was told to me over and over by numerous doctors. A mother's worst nightmare was my reality. My hope that Lorrin would be healthy was a long lost memory. I considered this to be a devastating fate for us both.

Our energies seemed to merge, and I felt a feeling of timelessness. He was wise. He was a teacher—my teacher. I felt as though I was being reminded of what I came here to do. I felt as though I had chosen long ago to make this difficult journey. As a child, I never felt like I wanted to live this life. Now the complete knowing and understanding of what I had agreed to do by being Lorrin's mother made so much sense.

I could feel our energies mesh. He felt strong. I felt so young and weak. Then I saw his face in a different light. He was wearing a White Buffalo skin. He started to shift. A very strange thing happened. I started merging with him, and we became one. I was suddenly wearing the White Buffalo cloak. I understood this immediately. I felt the weight of it on my back. The papoose was gone. I could feel the rough hair tickling my face and smell the fur. I was given a White Buffalo cloak. This was my medicine. It was my tool to use. I shape shifted, and we became one. It was so powerful. I will never forget the impact it had on me.

This was the first time I could say a sacred knowing came to me—an inner feeling that during everything in this lifetime, I would be okay. I was challenged, but I was not alone. In that pain was also the energy of the amazing gift that was taking place—the sacredness and mystery of the "White Buffalo." The pain was so raw, yet with it came the overwhelming knowing that what we were doing was important.

After the meditation, I could barely breathe. I was overtaken by love, pain, happiness, and sadness. I cried, even though I knew everything was perfect. I knew my Lorrin came to show me, to help me. She came to the meditation to remind me that I had agreed to this work. I had agreed to be her mother and to share our story to help other parents. This was a painful and wonderful journey, a commitment from long ago.

I felt so much respect for Lorrin. My body was aching, and I wanted to cry. I was completely overwhelmed by her amazing strength and courage. She could remember our agreement. I was too human to understand. I was so caught up in my so-called "life" and what was happening in it that I forgot our contract.

I could hear Pat's voice pulling us out of the journey and getting us back into the canoe and back to our physical bodies. I was somewhat sad to be coming back. I was returning to a physical body that was suffering. My heart was hurting. But my mind had just been reassured with a powerful spiritual message. The gift of White Buffalo's medicine was mine to use as a tool to help me along the way.

The powerful reality of my life and how it was transforming was overwhelming me. What a powerful and amazing experience my daughter had brought to me. I was obligated to her and committed to her. A soul commitment—our soul commitment.

As I came back into the room and back into my body, wide awake, I could not stop the tears from streaming down my face. I wanted to share with the class about my journey, but I could barely put words to what had just happened. It was so powerful. I wanted to get home and hold my Lorrin.

When I got home, I thought about the White Buffalo. So much was clarifying. When Lorrin was two, I fell in love with my first of many Native American masks. For Mother's Day, Tom bought me a mask made by an artist named Judy. It was a White Buffalo mask. He brought it to the hospital where Lorrin and I were staying at the UCLA pediatric ward. She was hospitalized for uncontrolled seizures.

Tom surprised me on that day. He was very against my alternative ways. They confused and threatened him. When he showed up at the hospital with this very expensive Native American mask, I was shocked but very happy. I did not understand at the time the meaning of the mask. I just knew that I was attracted to it. It was beautiful, magical, and very powerful.

That was the first of many masks that I purchased. I was falling in love with the artwork and the energy that the masks represented. I bought so many pieces of Judy's work that she gave me a "baby White Buffalo mask." Even after years of Pat's teaching and having three masks hanging on my wall, I never realized the White Buffalo was my animal guide.

The Native Americans believe that animals are messengers. Mother Earth is always communicating with us. For years in Pat's class, we would talk about the meaning of seeing an animal—especially if you see the same animal three times. That is a huge confirmation. There are many books written about animal messages and their meanings. My two favorites are Ted Andrews' *Animal Speak* and Steven Farmer's *Power Animals*. I think it's funny that it took me so long to identify with the White Buffalo as a totem for Lorrin and me.

I can be a slow learner and am thick in the head. Since I had that meditation, I think the White Buffalo message is one to be revisited. I am reminded to have courage when I don't feel any. There will be guides along the way who will help me stay on track. There is magic and mystery in life even when I feel alone and afraid. I was not given instructions with Lorrin. I had to look deep inside myself to find the tools that would help me be her mother. I paved our way with a commitment of love in an attempt to survive what I felt was killing me.

I write with an intention to help other families. I hope this encourages you to go within yourself and reach for answers, ask for help and go forward with your head high. All children are magical and mystical, no matter their looks, abilities, and/or intelligence. Each soul is here for a reason. They picked us, and we picked them long ago.

Our greatest teachers can show up in this life dressed in lion's clothes. I believe that Lorrin's father loved me so much before we came that he agreed to come and teach me to be strong by showing me what it was like to be alone. We battled constantly. But there were times when he did things that were very sensitive and caring, such as giving me the White Buffalo mask. What a beautiful gift that has become such a powerful message for me.

I know he agreed to be Lorrin's father. I know we all came here to aid Lorrin. Do I totally understand? No. I am lost and get angry often. I often wonder if Tom and I once had the free will to change our destiny and have another child together. If there is a parallel life that exists in which we are a family with Lorrin—perhaps with more children? Is there a parallel life that exists in which Lorrin is healthy? I don't have the answers to those questions, but I do know that we all agreed one time long ago to come into this world together.

I work to understand my purpose through my writing. I try to raise the vibration of this book. I have been calling out to the universe and asking the children to help me make the connections that I need to get my story out. I call on my spirit guide, Rose, who helps me write. Today I am reminded of the sacredness of White Buffalo.

Lorrin was so full of magic. She was a White Buffalo. She came here to teach. She came here to live in a unique body.

There have been many times in meditation when I've asked Lorrin to download her information, power, and wisdom into my third eye. She would often tell me that things are going to take off soon, and she'll remind me to keep my energy balanced and stay grounded. She also reminds me that I am to tell my story from a mother's viewpoint. I am not the master, healer, or guru. I am a mother, a student, a regular person. Lorrin is the White Buffalo. She is my master. She is sacred Native American medicine.

I am reminded to stay empowered and feed myself so that I can do this work that scares me.

A Tale Of Lorrin's Sadness And Meditation

I had just finished reading the third book of Harry Potter to Lorrin. I asked her if she wanted me to hold her. She said yes.

"Do you want us to do a meditation together?" She blinked yes. I have never been able to focus on a meditation while holding her. Yet, I knew when I woke up that morning I wanted to meditate with her. I have discovered that the more I meditate, the more I am drawn to do so.

As I held her in my arms, tears pooled in her eyes. I had noticed she had been crying more lately. She seemed especially sad on Sundays when she went with her father. His health was getting scary. I was at the point where I wanted to have Lorrin spend time with her father with the aid of a nurse. He refused. He was not behaving in a way that I felt was safe for her. Lorrin's medical needs were extreme. It would be unfair to any medically untrained person. But Tom had been showing many signs that he was slipping. I had not seen him drink during the day, but I knew how much he was drinking at night. He was not the same brilliant man I had married.

The more I meditated, the more I was becoming strangely numb to things. I was less reactive to Tom's drama and attacks. I was adjusting to Lorrin's shifts and constant medical needs. I was almost floating. I had a new sense of knowing that everything was going to be all right. In a very strange way, life was happening and I was becoming an observer, not operating as the reactor to everything as I was so used to doing. There were more times I felt at peace, and I was okay with what was ahead. I didn't need to rush anything. That was new for me. I was spiritually maturing. I was growing.

Lorrin's body was growing also. She was seven years old. She was not a baby anymore. There is a change when a healthy baby becomes a child. Lorrin, in her broken body that could not walk or talk, was also changing. She could still get away with being cute. She had made it to a vital age. In my limited experience, once children who struggle with medical needs as a baby reach the age of five, they seem to get strong and stay around for a while. I felt as though Lorrin was hitting a plateau in her health. Maybe I should say her health crisis. She still was tiny and weighed about 55 pounds. Her body draped over my lap. I held her as a mother holds her baby. She would lie in my arms gracefully, naturally, as she had for years.

I went into meditation. My intention was to open myself up to receive information from Lorrin. I started with slowing my breathing and grounding myself. The deeper I breathed, the deeper I sank into an altered state. I saw colors over my head, which spiraled down onto me. The colors—white, blue, gold, green, pink, purple, yellow and orange—coiled around me. In my mind, I had been thinking about pink. I was surprised to see so many different colors. It was beautiful.

Then I saw Lorrin; she didn't usually enter my meditations as a visual image. Today she stood in front of me like a typical seven-year-old would. The colors encircled us and a pyramid appeared above us. This image of a pyramid had been coming to me since hypnotherapy a week before. My hypnotherapist made mention that after Lorrin passed, I would travel to Egypt. I did end up going to Egypt, four months after her death.

I saw a detailed image of Lorrin and me at the museum in Chicago we had visited four years earlier. One of the exhibits was from Egypt. It had really felt very powerful to me then. But I was surprised that it was all coming to me now in mediation. Then I saw Lorrin and myself entombed, wrapped like mummies. Then the bandages came off us both.

My mind flashed to the "Judgment" card from the Tarot deck that I was reading. I had been doing Tarot card readings for seven years now. The Judgment card usually contains the image of mummies rising from caskets with bandages falling off, as a symbol of resurrection.

As I came out of this meditation, I sensed Lorrin and I had been resurrected. We had made it past her three-to-five year constant medical crises. She

Wendy Konick

had been so sick during those years. She had almost died too many times to count. She had just had her trach placed, a tracheal diversion, and her hips rebuilt, her spine straightened. We both had been through so much. I felt that we had made it past a threshold. We were done, leaving behind the past.

I felt a huge pull to go back into the meditation. So I continued to hold Lorrin and go back into a trance state. The meditation began with opening my third eye. This is the place on the center of my forehead. I envisioned Lorrin, and I connected with a tunnel between our foreheads. This was a new process for me. We also connected at the solar plexus. My throat opened with readiness to receive, but wasn't connected to Lorrin's throat chakra, perhaps because her vocal cords had been severed. As I held her, I contemplated what she had endured. I wondered if by cutting her vocal cords, we had affected her throat chakra area.

I watched as my throat expanded like a funnel. In a flash, it was as if the whole world entered and exited through my throat. Horses and other objects floated in the funnel like perhaps they would in a tornado.

I saw Lorrin and me connecting in many different forms. My arms held her as we sat, and I watched all of our chakras link. She shifted to the form of an angel, cherub-like, with tiny wings that lifted her. She was still joined to me at our chakras. Then she appeared, facing me as an adult woman. Her golden curls lay against a blue gown. She had huge wings that spread behind her; they were white and luminous. Then I transformed into an angel; I had the sense that I knew I would only be able to change after her process of transformation was complete. I felt reminded that I needed to accept the natural process of growth. I felt as though she was communicating with me, encoding me with her message.

The next time she came on a meditation with me was in January. She was gravely ill, and I thought she was close to or thinking about leaving her body. Another death scare. I had taken a lock of her hair and a drop of her blood and wrapped it in suede and made a medicine pouch with it. I did this in a kind of ceremony. I burned sage in the room and sat and drummed with her next to me. A few days earlier, a friend of mine told me that I would be receiving a gift. I had no idea what that meant.

I started to meditate without an agenda, only pure openness. I had become accustomed to doing journeys with Pat, so I was quick to go under. I started in an open field sitting next to a tree. I smelled dry grass and felt a cool breeze. The image is vivid in my mind as I write. It feels so real I can almost taste it. I saw my throat open up. I knew that my time was coming to do more writing and to speak about my experience as Lorrin's mother.

I returned to that familiar hole in the ground where the fire was blazing. I climbed down the ladder. I looked for Lorrin. I did not see her or feel her this time.

Once I climbed down the ladder, I was given my White Buffalo cloak. No words were spoken, but it was understood that when I am here, I am White

Buffalo medicine. I feel the head, horns, and weight of the fur on my shoulders. I become the medicine. I'm a man and a woman both at the same time.

I sat down on the damp earth in front of the medicine man. I could hear the fire crackling and feel the heat on my face. Other Native Americans danced around the fire, but they didn't interrupt us. As I sat across from the medicine man I looked into his eyes. I searched again for Lorrin. I couldn't see her. Then I became aware that the ancient man in front of me was Lorrin. He was tall, a century old. His long black and gray hair was gathered in two ponytails. First he wore only a dark suede piece covering his groin. Then he became wolf medicine. Then he was not a wolf. He transformed into a dark brown bear, into a hawk, then into an owl.

Suddenly tears came to my eyes. I felt an odd comfort and understanding of what this was about. There was no specific message for me, but I felt a mutual respect and honor and gratitude for our journey. My growth was being acknowledged. We didn't speak, but I knew we understood each other's pain. I felt an enormous sadness swelling in my heart, a lump in my throat. Lorrin never cried or complained unless she was in pain. It had never been obvious to me that she was sad. But today in our meditation, I felt a heaviness and sadness.

I wanted to stay open to receive all that was intended for me. I told Lorrin how thankful I was for all that she had taught me. It was weird, sitting in front of a Medicine man, feeling that he was Lorrin. If I thought too hard about what I was experiencing, I would have come out of the mediation right then.

I continued to thank her for all that she had done. Words couldn't convey the gratitude, grace, respect, admiration, courage, strength, and love that I had received from my child. My heart ached. I opened my heart to her so that she could see my gratefulness.

We both stood up and the medicine man took an arrowhead and cut into my chest. I was not sure what was happening. In this world I would describe it is a tattoo or an incision over my heart. I was now in the form of a man and my chest hard and tan. The cut was not painful. My mind flashed, and for a brief moment, I thought I needed a tattoo to show the work I had done. I quickly scanned my body for a place to put it, and wondered what image I would pick to symbolize our journey. I returned to the meditation, and the medicine man drove a stick into my incision. I felt that this was a badge of honor. I had earned this marking. I felt proud and thanked him.

I felt a weird sadness come over me. I felt that once I left here, I would not be returning. I asked him for a message. He said, "I will be there when you need me. You have all that you need." I was still afraid to leave, so I asked him if I could dance. I danced around the fire. I was a woman again, surrounded by other woman. We all danced together. We didn't speak, but I felt comfort in their presence, as if they were my sisters.

When I was ready to leave, I climbed up the ladder. I no longer had my Buffalo fur on. I was carrying a bag made of fur with a long strap that looped over my right shoulder. As I climbed, I put my hand on the bag as to reassure myself that it was there. As I touched it, I knew that I now carried the tools I needed. This was my gift. The bag opened and twinkling stars flew out. The tools were mine. I earned them and now I had to continue on my own.

All of a sudden excruciating pain sucked the breath from me. It was not only my pain, but pain shared by many.

Lorrin coughed and I came out of my meditation. What was supposed to happen next? What was to come? I felt elated with my secret gift and compelled to write.

Chapter 22

~ Healing, Fate, and Karma ~
Three to Five Years Old

"The more I see, the less I know."

- unknown

Somehow, throughout everything, I managed to keep Lorrin in the UCLA Early Intervention Program (EIP). The program allowed me to connect with other parents who were going through similar experiences with their young children. EIP also educated me on how to handle Lorrin's medical needs while we were at home. It probably saved my life—and hers—in more ways than one.

Though there were some other severe cases in her group, it seemed to me that Lorrin was always the most affected. It is only human to compare your child's challenges to those of others. Most all the other kids were doing more: hand-holding, expressing, using sign language or speech, walking, or working towards the goal of walking. I also noticed that the other mothers seemed to have better relationships with their husbands. By this time, Tom and I barely spoke, and I felt isolated in every area of my life.

In January of 1997, and after almost three years of craziness with no end in sight, I called my mother and my sisters with a desperate plea. I told them I needed someone to come get Lorrin. I knew if I didn't take a break, I was really going to lose it. I had never called them with such a request, and they had not watched Lorrin for any period of time before. I told them they could take turns watching her and that I needed some time—just a few days. Everyone agreed.

I have witnessed pain. Let me tell you about the pain that I was drowning in. Months before Lorrin's first birthday, I fell into a deep depression that continued for seven years.

I kept remembering what the neurologist told me about knowing Lorrin's true condition when she was one year old. That moment and those words played over and over in my mind. I didn't share them with anyone, but they became my mantra. "Go home and prepare for the worst!" the doctor from the Children's Hospital Los Angeles warned me. He told me that if she had not made any gains or improvement by her first birthday, she probably never would. His words were ingrained in my head. I'm sure he never thought about Lorrin or me again, but I heard his words every year. The depression would start in January, and by the time her birthday came around in March, I'd be reminded that she was one more year behind.

Lorrin taught me that there is so much that I will never understand. There is fate or destiny and sometimes there are just plain accidents that change our lives forever. People make choices every day that change the way we will live. God gave us free will. I believe we make agreements before we come to this earth and that sometimes we abide by those decisions and other times we make a different choice.

I believe that Lorrin and I have shared many lifetimes together. My undying love for her is from those lifetimes. I wonder, if she had been my worst enemy in our past lives, would I love her so much now? For that reason alone, I don't pass judgment on people. It is not for me to say what parents should do. I write my story to help share what I have done. I am not a sainted mother. I am human. I have made many mistakes. I have kicked and screamed the entire way. I want to tell the mothers who are listening, "You do not have to be perfect!" I wasn't and am not perfect. I did the best that I could do with the information that I had at the time. I write to offer suggestions and ideas about how I survived and enjoyed and came to love my gift, my daughter.

I became obsessed with pain, dying, healing, faith and the miracles in life. I studied how people heal, why some did and others didn't. I read book after book about miracles. I studied miracles. I needed to understand that I was not the only one in pain. I have never felt guilty for Lorrin and the vaccination. I know many parents feel guilt. Strangely, I never did. It was tough living in Orange County and later in Thousand Oaks, California, because it didn't put me in contact with many people who were suffering. Or, at least, that was my illusion. By reading other people's inspirational tales, I was motivated to make the best life I could for us both.

I felt compelled to understand pain and why people suffer. How did they overcome tragedy? I read books of suffering. I was so naïve. I struggled to understand loss, my loss. I compared my devastating feelings to others' experiences. To my surprise, I found that pain was everywhere. Unjust things happened every day. I wasn't special. I was another person suffering in this world. The recognition of the pain around me brought out an inner compassion— another of the many gifts Lorrin gave me.

I started to believe there was a greater picture, a reason this was happening to me. I refused to believe that all of this loss and suffering was for nothing. I knew that something great was to come of Lorrin and her existence. She survived too much. The stories I read made me feel strong. I could see how people inspired me with their stories of tragedy and their stories of survival. I wanted to believe that I too could make a difference.

Part of why I suffered was because I knew Lorrin was awake in her body. I knew she could feel. I knew she was in there. She had an ability to communicate with people in ways other than talking.

When Lorrin was just three months old, she appeared to a total stranger and talked to her in her dreams. I purchased something at the store. The next day, I went to return it, and the woman said, "Your daughter came to me in my dream last night."

I was surprised and interested. I asked the woman what she had said. She told me they were just talking. This was new territory for me.

Lorrin began communicating with many people in their dream state. I never understood how or why she picked the people she did. I think she went to all the people she loved, but only a few remembered.

I tried and tried to get her to communicate with me by using her eyes. I knew she was in there, and I could tell she understood me. I worked hard trying to motivate her to blink for "yes." She started to respond with some consistency. I asked her questions and encouraged her to respond so that others could witness this miracle. It made me feel happy to know that she was able to communicate, and I hoped she could do more of it. I had dreams of her making her own choices. I wanted the world to know that my baby was in there!

I was at my best friend Barbara's house, and we were talking. I was feeling particularly low about all that I had gone through with Lorrin and my failed marriage. I had bragged about Lorrin and how she had started to respond to me with her eyes. Barbara was patient and loving. She was Lorrin's godmother and was full of love for her.

I was disappointed in Lorrin's lack of participation while Barb was present. I had been bragging about Lorrin and her blinking for weeks. I tried to get Lorrin to blink and participate in our conversation. Lorrin just looked at us, seemingly uninterested. This went on all afternoon. I felt a bit embarrassed by the whole thing and started to second-guess myself. Maybe her communicating with me was just wishful thinking on my part. I spent so much time alone with Lorrin in environments that were foreign to my old world of socialization.

Then Barbara said, "Maybe you don't want her to talk, because if she did she could probably get you thrown in jail."

In that moment, it happened. Lorrin gave the most purposeful blink possible. She smashed her eyelids together as tight as she could. Barb and I fell over, holding our bellies, full of laughter. I had never been so proud.

Lorrin also enjoyed certain foods, and she always lit up when I read the Bible to her. So I read to her. This started a healing process for me. It gave me hope that she was capable of participating in life. It really helped me to understand that I could survive and focus on what Lorrin could do, instead of looking at all the obvious things she couldn't do. It helped my healing to bring things into her life that she enjoyed.

Chapter 23
~ Dolphin Experience ~
Seven Years Old

"I knew Lorrin lived a different life than my sister and me, but innocently, I only saw the cool toys and accessories, exciting vacations, and a permanent pass from homework. I felt special to have Lorrin in my life and remember bragging about her with my friends about all the cool stuff she could do even though she had so much to overcome. Having her as my cousin automatically taught me to see the person inside first. To treat everyone equally and on their own merit."

~ Mackenzie, Lorrin's cousin

In my research for therapies available to Lorrin, I heard about the mysterious healing qualities of dolphins. I had also read many articles describing miraculous events involving dolphins and children with disabilities. For a long time, putting together a trip for Lorrin was just an idea. But in 2000, Lorrin's physical therapist told me about a client who went to Island Dolphin Care, a non-profit organization for children located in Key Largo, Florida.

Lorrin's therapist thought dolphin therapy would be something that she would really enjoy. He had worked with Lorrin three times a week for eleven years. Her personality was blossoming with him. He spoke to her with respect and worked with her playfully and lovingly. He was the first healthy male role model in her life. He grew to love her, as most people did when they spent any amount of time with her.

Another one of his clients went to Florida and had a month of biofeedback. He felt that Lorrin would be the perfect candidate for this type of therapy. I researched the idea and decided to take Lorrin there. The protocol was four weeks of therapy, eight hours a day, five times a week. To motivate her to try her hardest, I scheduled a week at Island Dolphin Care to swim with the dolphins.

Tom and I were at the worst point in our relationship. We were just divorced. He was still healthy enough to make me miserable, and he did just that. He really believed that I had everything and that my life was easy. He was not interested in the truth and was not around to see all the drugs Lorrin was taking or to watch her in the hospital. Yet, somehow, I got Tom to agree that I would drive Lorrin to Florida and live there for a month. I hoped the experience would be physically helpful and emotionally motivating for her, and fun for both of us.

Deena Hoagland, L.C.S.W., C.H.T., Executive Director, and Island Dolphin Care Instructor, was amazingly supportive in working with me to ensure that our trip would be successful. She was patient and listened to Lorrin's special circumstances. Because of Lorrin's trach, Lorrin would not be able to submerge into the water. Deena had to come up with a plan that would allow Lorrin to play with the dolphins by sitting on the side of the deck. Deena bent over backwards to help us.

There were many obstacles that got in our way. For one, Lorrin became sick each time we tried to make the trip. We first planned to go in February, but we had to postpone it because she became too ill. Then, as the new date got closer, it seemed like everything started to fall apart again. Lorrin became gravely ill for no reason.

All of my efforts were put into planning this trip. I felt as though I was going to lose my mind. All of a sudden Lorrin was requiring six liters of oxygen. I took her to see a new pulmonary specialist at Cedars. He had never met Lorrin. For some reason, when we arrived, they denied our visit. I fell apart and started sobbing in the lobby; I explained to them that I was supposed to drive to Florida the following week and that I needed her to be seen by the specialist. Lorrin was sick again and without a diagnosis.

The thought occurred to me: "Am I being unrealistic by expecting Lorrin to make this trip? Maybe the trip is really about me and not her."

Once we finally made it in to the specialist's office, he took one look at Lorrin and said, "I don't know your daughter just by looking at her, but from her x-rays, I think she needs to be admitted to the hospital." I was scared now, and put her back into her wheelchair to walk her next door to the ER. I called Tom in tears while I was on the way. I was watching our trip slip away for the second time.

After six hours in the ER, Lorrin's stomach had filled with gas. A doctor told me that if we didn't release it, Lorrin would have to undergo an operation. It was possible she had an obstructed bowel. Even though I thought we were there for her lungs, once they took a look at her stomach, it became the priority.

What was I supposed to do? I felt confused about what was happening. I was here for a routine checkup, and now the doctors were freaking me out. Did we go home, sit, wait? Or would we beat the odds? What did these people know about Lorrin and her life mission anyway?

We finally worked out the stomach issue that had become a priority in the ER. Then the pediatric team came to assess Lorrin. They took one look at her x-ray and said, "If this was the picture of a healthy child's lungs, we would panic. But it is not, it is Lorrin's. Her lungs always look this bad."

I was relieved that Lorrin was not getting worse, but concerned that I had become clouded to her medical condition. I was so used to Lorrin having pneumonia, it was as though it were a cold. I was deadened to the severity of it. What I thought was a normal trip to the doctor became an eight-hour ER adventure. I was exhausted.

The next day, I loaded Lorrin up in the car to run an errand. The transmission blew in my van. I was sitting just outside of the driveway, and my transmission just gave way. This wouldn't have been such a shock if I hadn't just got it out of the shop a week before. I had just replaced the transmission. I drove a van with a wheelchair ramp, which made the van much heavier than intended. I had to replace brakes and tires every year from the excessive wear and tear. I had just gotten the van back from a complete rebuild.

I started to cry. I was melting. My nerves were shot, and I was pushed far beyond my reach. I tried to phone the body shop that had replaced my transmission. I must have sounded like a crazy woman. I was crying and couldn't breathe as I sat halfway out of the driveway. Lorrin sat next to me in her wheelchair and just started laughing at me. She was belly laughing.

I looked at her and told her it wasn't funny. For some reason, I felt as though she was causing my problems. She was on oxygen for no apparent reason, my transmission blew twice, and now she was laughing at me. I was so mad.

Something was nagging at me, telling me she didn't want to go to Florida for a month. I had the feeling she just wanted to swim with the dolphins. I called and cancelled the biofeedback and booked airline tickets to fly to Key Largo instead. As soon as I did that, Lorrin came off the oxygen and got well.

After a week of her being on oxygen, she was finally breathing on her own—with no explanation as to why she needed it in the first place. Her blood work looked fine and everything else checked out okay too.

We were going to swim with the dolphins! It seemed like she was telling me, in so many different ways, that she was not ready to drive across country, but she did want to have a dolphin experience.

I thought a lot about Lorrin laughing when the transmission went out for the second time in a week. Even though I knew she was not truly laughing at me, I was boiling with stress and anger. I had been preparing for months to take a cross-country drive and stay in Florida—all in Lorrin's best interest. I was doing everything I could to help her, but it just wasn't working out.

My dolphin diaries

Lorrin and I are in the air! I really didn't believe we were going to make this trip until we actually left this morning. Last night, when I kissed Lorrin and tucked her into bed, I wondered whether she was going to wake up with something that would delay our trip again. But, to my surprise, the trip is already going much better than I expected. What has changed from before? I feel like I have had a spiritual shift. It's not something I can actually express—rather, it's just something I feel and know.

The change happened last Wednesday when everything started to fall into place. I was awakened by the phone. It was the van rental agency—they were actually calling me to confirm my rental. Can you believe it? For once I didn't have to force it to happen!

Thursday, I was awakened by another phone call about Lorrin's medical equipment. I was told they were going to deliver it to our hotel room in Florida. Things were falling into place. I didn't start to pack until Friday afternoon, but I got it done. I'm not going to get too excited yet. I don't want to jinx this trip!

Flying is much easier than I expected. I am flying alone with Lorrin for the first time since Lorrin has had the trach. Her pediatrician recommended that he prescribe oxygen, just in case we got into the air and needed it. Lorrin has been wonderful, and I have everything I need. She is sitting nicely in the chair on the plane with the help of some pillows and blankets. We are only on the second leg of the flight and everything is going smoothly. Even the flight attendant was helpful. He came over and introduced himself to us. He told me that he was an EMT and I should let him know if I needed anything. I don't think I'll feel totally safe until we land safely on the ground.

I cannot explain the shift in Lorrin's health. I think we are connecting on a different level than we have before. She seems happy, and I love when she feels well. I know I could live happily forever this way. When Lorrin feels well, I am the happiest person on earth. I enjoy her so very much, especially during times like these. But it makes me wonder where I am when she is sick. It feels like a slap in the face or like the carpet is being pulled out from under me.

I think I am okay spiritually, but emotionally, I am scared and vulnerable. I wonder if I'll ever get used to it. When she was sick all the time, I was better adjusted to her situation. It is harder now that she is feeling better, because when she does get sick, I'm not always sure how bad it will get.

I know I have agreed to let her go when it is her time. I wonder when and how that will happen. I want that moment to be romantic. I want to be holding her. I want it to be peaceful. I don't want it to be scary or ugly. I want it the way I want it, but deep inside, I know better.

After the first swim:

Lorrin's physical therapist is the most amazing person I've ever met. I have never been around anyone who has treated my Lorrin so normally. He shares his every thought with her and talks to her at her level. Because he has such confidence in her, she works hard for him. He never has a bad day—or if he does, he never lets it show. Lorrin adores him. It brings such joy into my heart to see her so happy and content. I am brought to tears to watch them work together, to see her motivated, and to watch his patience. I have truly been shown today that it's okay to embrace all these unique and beautiful children. It's okay to love and laugh with them.

On the third day:

Deena told me that Lorrin was trying to hold her head up. Does that mean she's more motivated? She's also opening her hands to hold onto the rings and pull them off the dolphin's nose. Is this actual healing taking place? Being motivated is part of healing, isn't it?

I cannot think of another time when I've been so happy. Why is that? Is it because Lorrin and I have never been on vacation together before? Is it because being around such amazing animals as dolphins has created a natural high for both of us? Being in the water with those huge animals is really amazing. They love Lorrin and seem to really interact with her. I bet that's the answer. Being at Island Dolphin Care is like falling into the rabbit hole in Alice and Wonderland. Suddenly, everything is right. I fit in. I'm enjoying an activity that everyone wants to do. I'm staying at a fabulous resort. I wish I could bottle this on-top-of-the-world feeling and take it home with me! I'll have to figure out a way to make it last once we're back in California.

I met a man in Florida who brought his severely brain-injured son to swim with the dolphins. He told me he just wanted his son to experience life. What does "experience life" mean? For each person, the experience is different. For me, the experience of life was getting to Florida. I simply wanted to see Lorrin sit on the dock and enjoy the attention of the dolphins. The father of the brain-injured son said, "I just want to see the wind blow his hair."

What a beautiful thing to say. How many people can feel content just watching the wind blow? The biggest lesson I learned here: the smallest things can make the biggest difference.

I will always love that Lorrin and I made this trip. It was without a doubt one of our most powerful experiences we've had together. I can even say that all the pain I endured to get here was worth it. I can say that watching the wind blow in my daughter's hair has changed me.

Chapter 24

~ The Latest Court Events ~
Nine Years Old

Lorrin and I attended a conference with keynote Wayne Dyer. While we sat and waited, Wayne walked up, stopped, leaned over, and put his hand on Lorrin's wheelchair. He said, "I know you!" I told him that Lorrin understood everything and we had seen him speak a few times. He bent over and kissed her on the cheek. Every woman in the room of two thousand was jealous! I told Lorrin, "That is why you brush your teeth every day."

Being Lorrin's parent has brought many peculiar events and experiences to my life. On December 4, 2003, Tom was found dead in his home by his landlord. The coroner said he had died two weeks earlier. It was a traumatic and sad time. Tom was loved by many. Even through my struggles with Tom, I never doubted his love for Lorrin. I was living in peace for the first time since she was born. I had a court date to ask for a raise in order to purchase my first home. I was extremely nervous to be back at court. I was surprised at how nervous I was. I felt that familiar feeling of having my efforts to care for my daughter and keep her alive being weighed against money. I could never describe to the court how much work it took to be Lorrin's parent—the sacrifices I made to give her any semblance of a normal life. No amount of money could motivate me to do that. Only our love and soul connection could feed the dedication required to care for her. For me, there was no other choice.

As I waited in the court halls for my attorney, I was having, as I learned later, an ocular migraine. Part of my vision was blurred. I had been having that type of vision problems lately. I prayed to God it would go away. I worried that something would happen to me that would leave me unable to care for Lorrin. Or, worse, to be in a position that I need to be cared for.

Loye, my attorney and friend, came into my life when it was at its worst and took care of Lorrin's best interest. I knew immediately that Loye was good, and trust came right after that. I loved her. When she got to court, she walked up and hugged me. We went into the courtroom side by side and waited. We normally went to the family law courtroom, but the judge that Lorrin had seen since the beginning was now working in criminal court. She had kept only one case from her previous load, and that was ours.

So, we were on the criminal law floor, which was different than the family law floor. We sat waiting for the judge. I was there to ask for a raise, the first in seven years. I had never spoken with her. I only appeared in court and watched the attorneys do all the talking.

Since Tom had died, we were also requesting the guardianship for Lorrin's trust to be put back into my name. I had been doing Lorrin's accounting since she was born. Unfortunately, Tom forged my signature and took $53,000 out of her account, so the court had forced us to appoint a guardian for Lorrin's trust. Because of our inability to agree, we had to hire an attorney for Lorrin. Tom needed an attorney. I needed an attorney. Lorrin's accountant needed an attorney, and that happened to be Loye.

Today, the threat of Tom was gone, and even though I knew he could no longer attack me or cause me trouble, I still felt all of the nervousness and insecurity of being back in court. This was a place of great pain and hurt. My blood was pumping.

Now that our judge was in criminal court, I found myself in the company of a different type of people awaiting trial. As we waited patiently, criminals were escorted in wearing orange prison jumpers. Their hands and feet were shackled. They hobbled across to their seats. My innocent little girl in her wheelchair sat beside me. I was as surprised to see them as they were to see us.

The judge came out in her street clothes. She waved us towards her. My attorney stood up, and I followed her back into the judge's chambers, pushing Lorrin's wheelchair.

I told the judge all about Lorrin's latest achievements and her amazing life. I explained about Lorrin's adventures and her turnaround regarding her health. At one time, my attorney mentioned that we should probably leave so the others waiting could have their day in court. The judge said, "They are only going back to jail. They won't mind waiting."

As we were about to leave, I asked if we needed to discuss my raise and any of the other things we were in court about. My attorney said, "You just signed for it. It has all been approved." I was so naïve about what was going on. I never felt before that the judge knew or cared about me.

On the way home, I couldn't believe what had happened. I think it was the first time I had ever received any validation in court. After years of heartache with Lorrin's ongoing court hearings over money and Tom and my disagreements, I finally felt that I was heard and respected for the efforts and hard work that I had done.

Two years later I was back in court to complete another audit of my spending for Lorrin. I found myself in another unique experience. I was audited every two years. I must account for every dime I spend. This was the third audit.

For the first time we had a new judge. This went as smooth as ever. As we waited for our case to be heard, my attorney told me she had sat for this judge before. I asked her if she was going to be a judge. She said she had thought about it. It was then, I guess, I realized how accomplished she was. She is beautiful, brilliant, and well-respected.

Loye suggested we visit the previous judge, who was still in criminal law. She said, "I know she'd love to see Lorrin. Let's go see if she has a moment to visit."

I thought to myself, *What the hell*. All of us—my attorney, the attorney who is responsible for the accounting, Lorrin in her wheelchair, and me—all of us dressed in suits and heels, took the elevator to the next floor. We were now on the criminal court floor, not family law. What a difference a floor made. Different energy, different attorneys, and let's not forget the criminals. Oh, and the stares. I chuckled to myself as I wondered what they were thinking. Probably trying to figure out who the criminal was in our group. I'm sure they would've selected me.

We went into the courtroom, where we thought we could find our judge. We all walked in. The bailiff immediately asked us why we were there. My attorney told the bailiff we wanted to see the judge. He looked at us like we were crazy. He went to the phone and made a call. We all sat down. In this courtroom, people were in cuffs and wearing orange jump suits. There were cages for criminals and bulletproof glass protecting the judge and the seat for people who were testifying. It was as though we had stepped into another dimension. I became interested immediately and wanted to sit and listen to what was going on.

The phone rang and the bailiff picked it up. He couldn't hide the smile that came over his face. He looked in our direction and gave us the okay to go to the judge's chambers. My attorney, the accountant, Lorrin in her wheelchair, and I made our way back to the chambers. Chairs were pushed aside, trying to make a path for us. It was embarrassing and exciting. Lorrin's wheelchair was too big to fit through the small doors. The bailiff suggested we should go through the courtroom next to this one. So we followed him. Our entourage walked confidently into the next criminal courtroom as a trial was in progress. Pushing Lorrin's chair, I followed my attorney, and the accountant followed us. We totally disrupted the proceedings as we traipsed through to the judge's chambers.

The judge stood up, and she hugged me. Like old friends, we chatted about Lorrin's extraordinary life and her accomplishments. Her graceful presence lit up the room. It is hard for me to expect anything other than another out-of-the-ordinary adventure.

Chapter 25

~ Middle School ~
Eleven Years Old

For a few years, I drove Lorrin a hundred miles round trip to school. I had to take her suction, oxygen, meds, etc. One day while walking through the parking lot, I dropped her blanket, then her shoe fell off, then my purse dropped, then I rode over her oxygen tubing. All within a few feet. As I bent down for the fourth time, I looked around to see if anyone was watching and laughing at me. This must be a comedy show for someone!

There is a time in a child's life when he or she is obviously growing up. I believe middle school is one of those pivotal moments. When babies are born, we take note of their every advancement. At the age of five, new scholastic pressures of reading and writing consume every parent's thoughts and actions. Lorrin never made any of those gains. I was always fighting the school system, and Lorrin was always behind. Then came middle school. This is such a huge transition. I am quick to admit that I was not the normal middle-school parent. I was blown away by the attitudes of the teachers, the front office, the students, and quite frankly, the entire campus. I had no healthy child experiences to compare it with, so I had nothing to go on. I just continued doing what I do in my own way. Middle school started something like this.

We went to Lorrin's doctor for our annual school physical. Getting Lorrin in school required me to have tons of paperwork completed. Every medication had its individual prescription signed by the doctor. Every procedure had a prescription signed by the doctor. I was used to this and knew it was a huge pain in the butt. But it was part of what I needed to do to get Lorrin to school. Middle school.

I got to the appointment with her pediatrician so I could get the approval to enroll her in school. I waited in the room for the doctor to arrive.

I asked him immediately, "Can I bribe you?"

"No," he replied.

"With chocolate?"

His head suddenly turned toward me. I had his attention. I shared with him. "Every year you pull Lorrin out of school for the cold and flu season," I said. "It's really difficult for her socialization. She gets just a taste of school, and then she gets pulled until April. The staff doesn't take her too seriously because they know she'll only be there a few months. She misses almost the entire school year, which means she misses out on the subjects, friends and, she is, quite frankly, bored with me. Lorrin needs to be in school."

I offered a deal. It was my belief that I could make deals with her pediatrician. At least, I was going to try. "If I pull her out of school if she gets sick, will you agree to send her to school the entire year? This is important."

He looked at me, and I could see he was going to put up an argument. I reassured him that I would pull her out if she kept getting sick. It was normal protocol to pull children like Lorrin out of school during the cold and flu season. Lorrin was considered medically fragile and was bound to catch all the germs that were in the classroom. Pneumonia is what kills kids like my Lorrin. Most parents wouldn't consider sending a child-like Lorrin to school at all.

My next bribe was with Miss Lorrin. "Lorrin, it is up to you. If you get sick, Dr. Kundell is going to pull you out of school. You need to be well. You are in middle school now." She was listening and thinking.

Lorrin didn't miss one day of sixth grade due to illness. Not one day. It was the beginning of the best years of her life. I would also like to share that Dr. Kundell and Lorrin both enjoyed lots of chocolate.

The transition for Lorrin into sixth grade was huge. This step in her life meant she would not only be attending middle school, but she would be riding the bus. I had been driving Lorrin to school a hundred miles a day for the last four years.

Lorrin riding the bus to school was the first bit of freedom given to me since I'd become a parent. I was so excited. I was jumping up and down inside. I also had to jump through some major hoops to make this happen. Getting kids with special needs to school is a huge undertaking for everyone involved. The school principal, nurse, teacher, and therapist all put in a great deal of time to make sure she would be able to attend school and be safe while she did.

In the beginning, the school had plans to pair up Lorrin with what is known as a "para-educator" to take care of her needs, rather than a trained nurse. I was told there would indeed be a nurse on campus most of the time. This topic came up during Lorrin's Individualized Education Program meeting. An IEP is the school meeting which addresses the needs of children with special needs and puts the plan in writing.

"How much attention does Lorrin need to provide her a safe environment and equal opportunity for education?" I was always asked.

I used an unorthodox approach during all of Lorrin's IEPs. I would open the meeting by handing out a document that included the information I wanted to focus on. It always seemed redundant and time-wasting to go over the obvious information that everyone already knew. I wanted to get to the point of what I, as Lorrin's parent, felt her needs were. That way, if there was going to be an argument, we could get right to it.

For this particular meeting I took the floor for the first minutes. "One day Lorrin is going to die," I said. "I think we should all work smart and not have any regrets. This means that we need to give a great deal of thought to her health needs, especially since we are placing someone who is unqualified to be her caregiver. This person might possibly put Lorrin's life at risk. We need to have the right person."

I also told the school personnel that I respected their decision and was thankful for their help, but that I felt the para-educator in consideration was not qualified. I reminded them that Lorrin could only breathe though her trach, and in only a few minutes, she could suffocate and die.

Each of us in the room knew that should Lorrin's airway become blocked, she would likely die. I wanted them to understand how fragile Lorrin was.

The meeting continued on. My request for a nurse was heard and discarded. I said what I had needed to say.

Lorrin's first sleepover with her middle school friends

Lorrin and James Spicer

At Island Dolphin Care, making a new friend

Lorrin and her best friend, Sarah Rivera

At the Miss Pre-teen Pasadena Pageant

Getting horse kisses at equestrian therapy in Ojai

Lorrin and Nicolette, her canine companion

One of many hospital stays at Children's San Diego

Lorrin with Mom and James Spicer at Yosemite

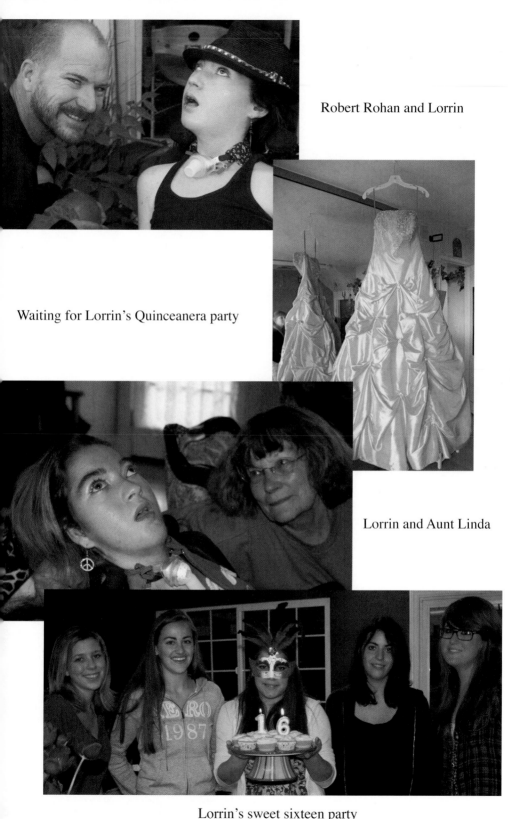

Robert Rohan and Lorrin

Waiting for Lorrin's Quinceanera party

Lorrin and Aunt Linda

Lorrin's sweet sixteen party

Debbie Hessler, Lorrin's nurse,
went to school with her each day

Lorrin's Quinceanera

Lorrin and Mom

Ed Rote and Lorrin at
her Quinceanera

Lorrin and her cousins, Clayton and MacKenzie Kero

Dancing at her eighth grade graduation dance

Lorrin and Aaron Fotheringham at The Abilities Expo

Meg Blackburn Losey, Lorrin, and Mom

Karissa Boyce, Karen, and Lorrin in Arizona

Lorrin with her cousins, Joshua Stuart,
Brittney Bayer, MacKenzie Kero,
Emilee Baumbgardner,
and Baylee Rascoe

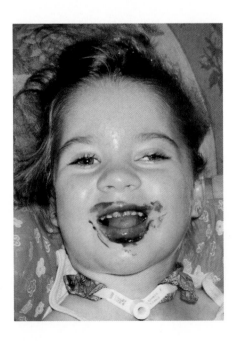

Eating chocolate

At the beach in Key Largo

Jr. Blind of America Camp

Emilee Baumgardner, Lorrin,
and Brittney Bayer

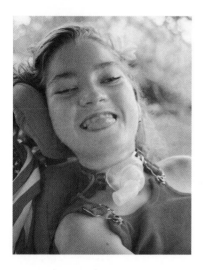

4th of July

Painted faces in Big Sur

Mom and Lorrin

Just being beautiful

Aunt Stephanie Baumgardner and Lorrin

The 9th Grade Homecoming Dance

The next priority was to have Lorrin attend one class with mainstream students. In my mind, that was the entire reason to attend middle school. An opportunity for Lorrin to make friends.

Later that day, I received a call from the school nurse. She told me the school decided to hire a full-time nurse for Lorrin. I had no idea how that decision would forever change Lorrin's life.

However, they had trouble finding a nurse. Lorrin didn't begin school until weeks after school had started. They finally hired a nurse and her name was Debbie. Until Debbie was fully trained, I lent the school Lorrin's nurse who had worked with her at home for five years. I also had to drive Lorrin to class until Debbie was fully trained and ready to ride the bus with her.

Not long after school began, I heard gossip that most of the staff didn't expect Lorrin to attend school regularly. She had a long history of being sick or being in the hospital with pneumonia, and consequently missing a lot of school.

I was determined to allow Lorrin to have the full life she deserved, to be away from me for a while, and to be with friends her own age. It certainly was not my intention to put her in harm's way, but it was hard for people to take us seriously.

For the first time in Lorrin's eleven years, she went to school the whole year through.

Although Lorrin did not miss a day of her sixth grade year due to illness, it was a bumpy first year of middle school. Debbie, Lorrin's nurse, was overwhelmed with Lorrin's medical needs. Lorrin was sleeping about half the day as she adjusted to being a full time student. Because of Lorrin's unique needs, she was in a county program for severely handicapped children. This program was located on the middle school campus. The middle school for regular kids and the county program each have a different principal and different days off. The two parts of the school act like two separate businesses.

This affected us in many ways. As a result of this, Lorrin's school picture did not make it into the yearbook. I was not invited nor allowed to bring Lorrin to the sixth grade registration event that took place for all the regular students. This was where the yearbook picture was taken and where students could purchase a yearbook.

The summer before she started middle school, I phoned the school and tried to go to registration, and I was told Lorrin was not required to attend. At the time, I thought nothing about it. I had no idea what this "registration" actually was. It was not until the last day of school that I realized Lorrin not only was not going to get a yearbook, but, to my surprise, her photograph was not in the yearbook, even though at the beginning of the year I'd made sure she'd had her picture taken.

For Lorrin to miss such a typical and special memory shocked me and left me heartbroken. As I did many times throughout the year, I marched myself right into the office. I searched for someone who could tell me why Lorrin's photo did not make it into the yearbook. After spending a lot of time standing in the front office with a ton of whisperers in the back room, I was sent to a counselor's office. It was apparently her job to manage the non-handicapped kids and their parents.

It was on that day I realized how much work needed to be done. I sat in front of her, almost in tears, telling her I couldn't understand why an entire class of special needs students had been omitted from the yearbook. What kind of message were we sending our youth when their photographs were not included in the yearbooks? Were we embarrassed of this class?

There were no good answers. I shook my head, wondering about Lorrin's classmates and their parents.

At Lorrin's next IEP, I included this on my list of subjects to be discussed and addressed. When I asked this question to the woman in charge of special education, her reply was simple. "Mrs. Kain, in fifteen years of doing this job, that question has never been asked."

It shocked and saddened me to know that our children who are unique don't get the same opportunities to become part of a simple thing called a yearbook.

It was a painful question that had only one simple and easy answer. Put all the students in the yearbook!

The next summer, a month before seventh grade, we attended registration. I had the date marked on my calendar. I called to make my appointment. When those sweet words came across the phone, "Mrs. Kain, Lorrin does not need to attend registration," I was ready. I knew exactly what to do. I told the woman to put me on hold because "NO" would not be an acceptable answer today.

She did exactly that. She put me on hold. But, a few minutes later, she was back. We were approved to attend the registration.

We went. The principal met us and walked us through the entire registration process. Lorrin slept through it all. I'm sure she did it on purpose. I held my head high and got her picture taken regardless. I knew full well she was asleep, and I could not blame her. We retook her photo later.

I believe that because of the fuss that I made that year, Lorrin's entire special ed class had a page in the yearbook. Lorrin was not in those photos, but her classmates were.

It was my conviction that Lorrin was part of this school. She had one mainstream class and she would not be ignored. When the time came for Lorrin to receive her yearbook, I was faced with a new challenge. I needed to figure out how I was going to get Lorrin to sign the other kids' yearbooks and how I was going to get them to want to sign hers. I knew there would be a handful of her best friends' signatures, but I wanted more for her. So, I bought stamps with Lorrin's name on it, one with her initials, and another with her name written in Chinese. I also bought some age-appropriate stickers that said "You're cool," "Too cool," "Best friends," etc. I placed all of Lorrin's stickers and stamps into a purple velvet bag that hung from her wheelchair, and she was set to sign yearbooks.

The highlight of the day was when a boy in Horticulture saw Lorrin coming to school with her yearbook and asked, "How is she going to get everyone to sign her book?" He then grabbed her book for her and took it around and asked their classmates to sign it. My heart melted when Lorrin came home and her nurse, Debbie, told me this news. How many thirteen-year-old boys would do that? Lorrin was forever a teacher.

Lorrin's wonderful nurse, Debbie, was always so available and kind. Her hands were full with Lorrin's care, but she made sure that Lorrin took out her yearbook, stamped her friends' books, and got signatures on hers. One student even went out of her way to go to Lorrin's class and get a stamp. At the end of the day, Lorrin's first yearbook was full of signatures similar to those in my own middle school yearbook.

Another funny thing that happened in sixth grade was the office getting to know me. I was used to going into the office and receiving the familiar look of horror on the faces that worked behind the counter. I would ask them questions like "When is the school dance?" They would reply, "The class that Lorrin is in doesn't go to the dances." I would pretend to be surprised. "Why, aren't they allowed to attend dance?" They would look at me with horror, then say, "I don't know. Let me check."

They would go into the back and be gone some time. They would return and tell me the dance would be Friday from three to six, and Lorrin was welcome to come.

Seventh grade was easier in many ways. Lorrin's nurse was used to all of her medical demands, and she and Lorrin had worked out their own way of communicating. Debbie was God-sent. She fell in love with Lorrin. She prayed for a long time, asking God to help her to better understand how Lorrin communicated.

Debbie had devised her own communication method. Lorrin would blink rapidly when she had something serious that she wanted to communicate to Debbie. They also had an entire toileting regime that they worked out together.

Debbie was patient and loving. As their friendship grew and she better understood Lorrin's preferences and medical needs, Debbie was able to relax and enjoy Lorrin. She learned to understand her personality and sense of humor.

One day Debbie returned after a school day with Lorrin. "Do you know Lorrin answers questions before I ask them?"

I giggled a bit and told her, "If I had told you that, you would've thought that I was crazy." That was something you had to experience to believe.

Lorrin also started coming to Debbie in her dreams and giving her all kinds of messages. She would laugh and ask Debbie, "Do you think my mom is crazy?"

She came to her another time and told her all the things she understood. She would show her math problems and talk about history with her. She would tell Debbie things like, "Debbie, when you're angry, people don't listen to you as well as they do when you're patient."

Time and time again, while we waited for the school bus to arrive, Debbie would share with me the dreams she had with Lorrin the night before.

Seventh grade started out on a much better note. Lorrin began her mainstream seventh grade Horticulture class at the beginning of the year with all the other students. I made sure of that. The school was on a trimester session. Many warned me that seventh and eighth graders were not as sweet as the sixth graders. In fact, I was told they were mean.

Debbie started Horticulture with Lorrin. After the first class, she came home and told me how nice the teacher was.

I had my hands full with what I thought I needed to do as a parent. I kept Lorrin dressed in the same styles as those in her peer group, I got her to school with the huge list of things she needed, and I loved her as much as I could.

I felt there was an emptiness in her life. Lorrin had no friends her own age. She spent a ton of time with my friends and me. Everybody loved her. But that wasn't enough. I started to pray to God that she would make friends of her own. As every parent does, I wanted my little girl to have a best friend.

Everything seemed to be going well at school. But right before Christmas, Debbie came home with some unsettling news. She didn't think the Horticulture class was working. The kids were really mean and Lorrin wasn't connecting socially as they had hoped.

I was a bit surprised. We hadn't discussed anything that would take my thoughts in this direction. Or maybe I just wasn't listening. I heard what Debbie was saying but I didn't want to accept it. I asked her to give it a few more weeks. Nothing about Lorrin had ever been easy.

I knew that I was expecting a great deal from Debbie. Her job was to keep Lorrin safe medically, not to be her social and emotional guard. But it was too late. Debbie had fallen in love with Lorrin and wanted the same thing I wanted—for Lorrin to have the best life possible. We were on the same page about that.

The first day of the second trimester in Horticulture, Mr. Saute, Lorrin's teacher, allowed Debbie to get up in front of the class and introduce Lorrin to all the students. Debbie explained to the other students that Lorrin was in a class for children who had special needs. She explained that Lorrin had experienced a bad reaction to her vaccination.

She went on to tell the class many things; Lorrin had seizures and took seizure medication. The seizure medication made it difficult for her to be in the sun for long periods of time because she was especially sensitive to sunlight and could get sunburnt. Sometimes Lorrin had seizures at night and needed to sleep during school. Lorrin loved the Disney Channel, and she loved to shop and eat chocolate. She loved to be read to and listen to music. But the most important thing Debbie said that day was, "Lorrin is totally comfortable with who she is."

The next thing that happened may seem simple but it may be the most amazing thing ever. Debbie asked if anyone had questions. A group of students raised their hands. They asked all kinds of questions. Can she walk? No. Can she talk? No. Can she see? Not too well. One boy raised his hand and asked, "Is she the worst disabled kid ever?" Debbie replied, "Maybe at this school." Debbie invited everyone from Horticulture to come and meet Lorrin's classmates.

It was on this day that Lorrin's life changed forever. Two separate groups of students came into Lorrin's class. They said hello to her and the rest of the kids. Every day for the next two years that she was in middle school, Lorrin had visitors before school, during both breaks, and during lunch.

Lorrin was lucky to have Mr. Saute, who proved to be an amazing teacher. Actually, it was more than luck—it was more like a blessing and a whole bunch of love. He tried very hard to get to know Lorrin. At times he would take it personally when Lorrin slept through class. He gave her as much love and attention as possible.

One day, I contacted Mr. Saute and asked him if I could have a party in his class. I knew Lorrin had stolen his heart when he told me that only once before had he allowed the class to have a party. He gave me permission to throw a pizza party for all the kids. I brought in soda and fifty homemade cupcakes, and had a large order of pizza delivered. I also brought in ten disposable cameras and passed them out to the class. I put a few of them on each desk and told the kids to take pictures of anything they wanted. It was a great party, and we all had fun taking pictures and eating pizza.

I had the pictures developed and put them into a scrapbook. I sent it to school with Lorrin so the kids could see themselves having fun. They sent a thank you note back, which inspired me to send a video camera to school. I asked the kids to record themselves while they planted plants around the campus. Then I sent a survey and asked the kids to vote on the songs they would like to hear in the background of their video. Of course, being middle school students, many of the songs chosen were not appropriate. Thankfully, Karissa, Lorrin's caregiver, helped me do a little research on the music they picked.

I edited the video and made thirty copies on DVDs. I included the pictures from the pizza party and the video that was taken with the music they picked. I sent one to each of Lorrin's classmates. I ended the DVD with a note of thanks to Mr. Saute and included Lorrin's website.

I knew that if one of Lorrin's classmates took the DVD home, they might listen and watch it with their parents and share Lorrin's message. I wanted people to talk about Lorrin and share their feelings about her. It took a great deal of work, but I felt that we were building wonderful relationships. This opportunity was the most precious gift we could ask for.

Lorrin had many other great accomplishments during her seventh grade year. Among those, she was voted vice-president of her Girl Scout troop and participated in the school musical. She also competed in the Miss Pre-Teen California Pageant with 240 neuro-typical teenagers. I spent the first couple years of middle school shaking my head in awe of the outgoing person she had become.

For eighth grade registration, we actually received an invitation in the mail. I arrived with Lorrin, and we saw about ten of Lorrin's friends during the process. Even a handful of boys came by to say a quick hello to Lorrin. I also recognized other parents I'd met. I was able to go to the necessary lines without feeling rejected, which was a new experience. What most people found a chore, I took as an opportunity. I gladly participated. It had become another milestone in Lorrin's amazing life.

On the first day of eighth grade, her friends encircled Lorrin. They stood around her and shared stories about their summer events. There was a brief moment when I wondered if they might forget about her during those three months of vacation. I had never been so happy to be wrong in my life. They came to Lorrin's class that day and visited her every day. A handful of those girls even applied to work in her class, and I know their lives will be changed forever.

Chapter 26

~ Allowing an Angel to be Present on the Bus ~ Eleven Years Old

When Lorrin was in middle school, it became apparent that she needed some expressive language. During her physical therapy, we made it a goal for her to learn how to give the finger—yes, the middle finger. After a few sessions, her curled up fingers just wouldn't work. So, we decided to do the "one eye." Lorrin would blink one eye with a smirk. She only did it to me and a few of her closest caregivers.

Lorrin's school nurse, Debbie, came home with her one day and told me about riding public transportation. The bus driver was upset about having to take time to secure Lorrin's wheelchair. The first time he pulled up, he told Debbie he didn't have room on the bus for the wheelchair. The second time, Debbie warned him that they weren't going to go away and had every intention of riding the bus. He moaned and groaned and cursed as he strapped down Lorrin's wheelchair. He did this right in front of Lorrin. He proclaimed that she was putting him out by riding the bus and making him stop to tie her down so that she would be safe. Debbie's reply was, "Get used to it. We'll be riding all year."

As she told me the story, I was angry and wanted to write him a letter to remind him that he is there to transport those who don't have transportation. How dare he embarrass my daughter and make her feel like a pain in the ass? I looked with sadness at my beautiful little girl. I got this feeling that she was not angry at all. Instead, she was blessing him the whole time. She never seemed to get sucked in to other's ego emotion. I believe she looked inside a person and sent them love. For all I know, he may have had larger problems weighing on him than I could imagine. He was lucky to get to be in her company. Maybe he would never know that she was sending him love.

So often we miss that moment of love. We get distracted or feel inconvenienced, and we miss the blessings sent our way.

Though I hoped for a peaceful outcome, the bus situation got worse. I ended up making a complaint to the city. The bus driver started driving around town with Lorrin not even strapped down.

Although Lorrin was my main concern, I sympathized with all individuals who are in wheelchairs relying on public transportation. I could only imagine how much guts it would take to get up, get dressed, and wait on the corner for the bus to pick them up, only to be treated with distain.

I ended up raising hell. The man was retrained. I didn't want him fired—I wanted him to do his job with compassion in his heart.

Chapter 27

~ *Beauty Pageant* ~
Twelve Years Old

"Don't curse the darkness light a candle."

~ *Ancient Chinese Proverb*

There have been many times in my life when one certain thing led to another and I ended up in the midst of a huge life event, wondering how I ever got there. This story goes just like that.

Lorrin had just started middle school. It was becoming clear to me that I was in a new ballgame. The social and emotional rules had changed. I had to be very careful how I dressed her. She was becoming her own girl; she liked rap music and loved making her own choices.

One Sunday morning at seven a.m., I was dragging myself downstairs to let the night nurse, Elizabeth, leave. I typically would be barely dressed, still tired from being up late watching TV or reading into the night, drinking wine. Elizabeth would typically be slow to leave. Once I would crawl into bed, I'd put my head next to Lorrin's. I would feel the air from her compressor flowing into her neck.

The compressor's purpose was to make sure Lorrin's lungs stayed moist. Having a hole in Lorrin's neck made her vulnerable to airborne germs. When people breathe through their nose, the nose hairs keep the lungs protected and help to keep the lungs moist. The compressor did this for Lorrin. It was not a ventilator, which helps you take breaths. Lorrin could breathe on her own.

Lorrin would usually be awake, and I would cuddle up to her. On this Sunday morning, Elizabeth told me that she had nicknamed Lorrin "Lo-K." She said it was a rapper name, kinda like J-Lo. Elizabeth was obviously a rap fan. I cracked up. I loved having a new name for Lorrin. She had many nicknames—Bubba, Bubblicious, Roarin' Lorrin, Brittney, and now Lo-K, one of my favorites.

Elizabeth was a bit quirky and not a woman of many words. She was a great nurse and friend to Lorrin. I love her dearly.

Lorrin has always loved fashion and shopping. She started picking out her clothes when she was about six years old. I had been at the Disney shop with her, trying to force her to wear yet another Tigger dress. She was very unhappy, and I had to realize that my girl was growing up.

One of the things I loved to do is shop with her. It was pretty easy. Lorrin would participate by blinking and/or giving thumbs up. She would give me a scowl when I was really off, and now that she was twelve-teen, she could give loads of attitude.

I enjoyed every moment with her as I watched her style change. She was quite trendy and always knew what she wanted. Her style was forever changing, and I was often surprised by what she picked. Always an interesting experience.

The first time I walked on the middle school campus, I realized that my cutie daughter had to be dressed in more of a grunge style. Most of what I saw on the campus I would consider a dark gray. No more bows and fluffy dresses. It was a time for jeans, cool tennies, lip-gloss, and glittery eyes. A bit of an adjustment, but I was on board.

Abercrombie and Fitch was the cool place to shop. It was also very expensive. Lorrin loved it. It was clear that the more Lorrin fit in with a fashion, the more acceptance and attention she got at school. Debbie, Lorrin's nurse who went to school with her every day, would tell me how many compliments Lorrin was getting from her peers. Sometimes when I was on campus, a group of girls would just come over and ask about Lorrin's hair or earrings. Lorrin had her hair weaved blond on top, which was her natural color, and black underneath.

Every girl's dream in middle school was to have their hair done fashionably. I knew that I was making some headway when we would get stopped on campus. My greatest wish was for her to have friends her own age.

My creative head got this really great idea. I started writing to places like Abercrombie and Fitch and Hollister Co., suggesting that they use Lorrin as a model. I'm not sure how or where I came up with this idea. I guess I was worried that the court would give me a hard time for Lorrin's expensive wardrobe, and I also believed that these companies who typically have perfect models should be using people who are unique in their advertisements. I also wrote Oprah and some other local magazines. I felt that Lorrin was doing a good thing being out in the community and should be embraced.

It was about this time I received an invitation for Lorrin to attend an event in Burbank. I called the number on the invite to figure out what it was, and they told me that someone had recommended Lorrin. I thought it may be a modeling opportunity. It didn't seem too far off for me to think one of my letters had been answered. For some reason, I thought it would be a good idea to attend.

Lorrin looked her cutest. She was into wearing hats at this time, and had a very cute pink hat with pink bling on the cap. She wore her favorite pink shoes and a tiny beaded white tee-shirt under a stylish white sweater with pale pink pants that would make any teenager proud. She couldn't have looked more stylish and cool. I got there early and found myself in a banquet room with about two thousand chairs in front of a stage. I sat up front with Lorrin. There were only about five other mother-daughter teams there. To say that we were standing out would be an understatement. I felt it. I was fully aware of how awkward this may get and kept taking deep breaths.

In no time there were about five hundred or so mother-daughter teams in the room. There was loads of chatter. All the girls were dressed in their best clothes. I was still unsure of what I had just gotten us into, but I tried to act as though we belonged.

Things were starting to kick off. A man got on stage and welcomed everyone. The first thing he did was ask that everyone who was there to participate get on one side of the room and all the mothers sit on the other side. My heart dropped. What? I was supposed to leave my girl in her wheelchair? She may need me to suction her. I was hoping I wouldn't be forced to leave her, but it looked like I would be asked to do so. I noticed as the other mothers stepped to one side without a thought. I felt as though I had no choice but to leave my twelve-year-old to sit with all these other girls. I reluctantly walked away. I was practically sweating as I walked to the back of the room.

I felt awkward. Lorrin was the only girl in the room who had a disability and a trach, who was non-verbal and so on. I also noticed that she was one of the cutest, in my opinion. I stood back. I felt as though a ton of eyes were on me. Yeah, this was normal. No biggie.

I was really regretting this. What was I thinking? I listened to the announcer as he talked. It took about five minutes before I realized this was a beauty pageant.

It was just about this time that Lorrin started to have a huge seizure in the front row. Her arms were stiff out in front of her and her hat was falling off. I stood there without instructions. I had no idea what to do. I walked up to the front row, half bent down and fixed her hat and waited for her to stop seizing. I asked her if she was okay, and she kinda scowled at me and blinked. I was thinking, "You are embarrassing me. I am not embarrassing you. I know I am your mother and you wish I wasn't next to you right now, but you're also having a grand mal."

I stepped back. Teenagers despise their moms at this age. Disabled teens are equally embarrassed and despise their moms.

Once the announcer said all that he had to say, I went to Lorrin. The room was full of young girls all excited about being a part of this pageant. This may be one of the strangest and most normal things a girl could do. I casually got Lorrin and pushed her wheelchair to the back of the room. The next step was to fill out an application and then wait in line to be interviewed. I was ready to leave *now*. I asked Lorrin if she wants to do this. She slammed her eyes shut. This told me yes, YES! I was still unsure of what or how we got involved in this. I was too embarrassed to just leave. Lorrin wanted to stay, so we did just that.

I waited in line with all the other girls standing beside their mothers. There was excitement in the air. The entire room was buzzing. We waited our turn. They invited us into an office where a man and a woman sat behind a desk. I can only imagine what they are thinking. I was thinking, "How did I get here?" I just want to leave. I could see the obvious.

I held my head up high and positioned Lorrin's wheelchair in front of the desk. I introduced us and explained that Lorrin communicated with her eyes—that she understood everything but was trapped in this body that didn't allow her to communicate quickly or freely. I shared what Lorrin's interests and hobbies were. I was feeling awkward and inept. I just moved forward.

We finished the interview and signed a form. We were free to leave. I was relieved. As we were walking, I asked Lorrin if she would be called to do the pageant. She quickly blinked.

I laughed to myself. I was happy to get the hell out of there. I shook my head as we left in the elevator with some other girls who were also contenders. I held my head up like this was no big deal to me and that I wasn't afraid. We left.

As life would have it, by Wednesday, Lorrin got a phone call that she had been accepted to participate in the Miss Preteen Pasadena Pageant—along with 240 other girls. I would like to mention that all were "able-bodied." Strangely enough, I was excited! We had been accepted. She had been accepted.

Lorrin just looked at me with a teenage girl's attitude, as if to say, "Duh, Mom. I knew I would be."

The pageant had many rules to follow. Lorrin had to get sponsored. This meant she had to raise $450. This was the cost to enter the pageant. She had to purchase a gown, sports attire, and two other casual outfits. She had to go to an event with all the other contestants, which was called something similar to "learning how to walk onstage in your dress shoes."

First things first, I started shopping for a gown for Lorrin. This was not an easy affair. It was January, and the event was in February. We were past the holiday dress season and too early for prom. We started desperately searching for a dress that would make Lorrin beautiful and match her wheelchair. This was extremely difficult. It had to be something fabulous! She had to look smashing.

The pageant talk was starting to stir up all kinds of gossip and opinions. I was getting the strangest feedback. Some people thought it was great. Those who knew Lorrin completely understood why she would be doing something like this. Then there were a few moms that seemed upset by us doing this. Some of the people I thought would be supportive gave me attitude. I felt that people were not happy that my Lorrin was doing this kind of thing. Yes, it was awkward, and I'm sure it made some feel uncomfortable.

But it happened and Lorrin was excited—just as excited as all the other girls. Lorrin was taking part in a beauty pageant. Who would have thought?

I was used to it. I expected the strange looks and attitudes that I got while shopping for a dress. It was very difficult for the shop staff to understand that I was shopping for a fancy dress not for myself but for my twelve-year-old daughter. A gown for a beauty pageant. I actually had to tell people over and over, "No, it is not for me. It is for her."

They kept showing me dresses, holding them up to me. I would take the dress and hold it up to Lorrin as we stood in front of the mirror. I would let Lorrin decide by blinking if she liked it. The looks that we got, I am sure, confused many. Eventually, we found an amazing red gown. It was absolutely beautiful. It matched her wheelchair. It was about the prettiest dress I have ever seen, and Lorrin lit up like she was Cinderella. It was outrageously expensive. I made Lorrin blink really hard a few times before I agreed to buy it. I warned her that I may go to jail when the judge saw just how much I spent on this dress. You better love it!

The next step was to go to the dress rehearsal, where the girls practiced walking in their dress shoes. I found myself caught up in the excitement. My next thought was that I was totally crazy. Then happy, then crazy. How does a mother protect her girl's heart? How did I hold my head up and go to this event when I was completely nervous and insecure about it myself? I was excited and horribly nervous. I was proud of Lorrin and afraid. I wanted to encourage her and protect her. This was one of the hardest things that I had to do.

I knew we would go back to the hospital again, probably for more dreaded surgeries. I knew that we would be rejected for as long as Lorrin lived. But to participate in a pageant with girls her age in which she would be the only one who was unique. I had no preparation for that. I had no time to even give it much thought until that morning. I was a nervous wreck.

I got up really early. I had Lorrin dressed in her cutest clothes—the only ones left that she wasn't wearing for the pageant. Lorrin sat tall in her wheelchair, and I held her shoes in my hands. The irony and the humor all in one. I drove to the event Saturday morning. The entire way I was grounding myself and asking for all the angels to help me stay calm.

I got there early, so when I was a bit lost it was not a problem. I saw all kinds of excited girls walking with their mothers, shoes in hand. Everyone wanted to be the prettiest, the most poised, and the most fashionable. I took another deep breath and got Lorrin out of the van. Lorrin sat in her wheelchair while I drove. Our accessible van had a hydraulic ramp that by the push of a button would open up and lower her down. We were quite a spectacle.

We walked into the crowded hotel lobby. I watched for signs directing us to where we needed to be. There were so many girls, I wasn't sure where the line began. I saw everyone walking toward a flight of stairs. My eyes darted around, looking for an elevator. I saw a few familiar faces and I smiled. The girls were really so self-involved, they didn't even notice us.

I tried to stay calm as I found our way to the front desk of the hotel and asked for an elevator.

The next thing that happened was quite possibly one of the most shocking and hurtful moments that I can remember. The young lady, who was about twenty and dressed in an ugly hotel uniform with her hair pulled back into a ponytail, and who was too busy to even look directly at me, said, "We don't have an elevator."

I asked her to repeat herself, and she did. I told her that it was against the law and asked to speak to the manager. I was still confident that there somehow had been a mistake and there must be way to access the downstairs, *where the rehearsal was!* I was getting a bit panicky. This young lady, whose head I now want to rip off, told me that she was the manager. I told her no, I wanted the person who was above her. I was here to take my daughter to this event, and I couldn't get there without an elevator. I wanted to talk to someone in charge.

This young woman couldn't care less about me or my daughter. In fact, none of the five people behind the counter cared that my daughter, who happened to be in a wheelchair and was here to attend an event that even normal girls get nervous about attending, could not get to where she needed to be.

I was getting really pissed now. I was not going away. The staff was starting to understand this. They asked me to sit over in a chair in the corner out of the way while they got someone to help me.

My worst nightmare had happened. I was sitting in a corner, staring at the wall, out of the way. I was accustomed to being put in the corner out of the way at restaurants and at social gatherings. Somehow, I was not prepared for this. I could hear hundreds of girls behind me. The room was starting to get quiet as they went downstairs. I was starting to crumble.

For some reason, this situation never crossed my mind. I couldn't for a moment understand how I had gotten into this predicament. I kept thinking to myself, this is a mistake, it's going to get fixed. How could they invite us to participate, fully knowing that Lorrin was in a wheelchair? How could they not remember the one girl who happened to be completely disabled? They invited her. Surely they must know. How could this happen?

The manager of the pageant came and sat in front of me. I could tell by the look on his face that there was no access to the event.

I was a mature adult. I was a mother. Brutal emotions overwhelmed me. Tears ran down my face. I wanted to be a mature adult, but I couldn't stop the tears from coming down. I looked at him and stated the obvious: "You guys called us and invited us. How could this happen?"

I am so pissed off and embarrassed for myself. Lorrin just sat there, acting much more mature than I was. She was calm and composed.

He looked at me and told me he would be right back.

I tried to wipe away my tears. I looked at Lorrin and I asked her how she could be so composed. I told her that I was sorry. I told her I was trying my hardest. I was so sorry. I asked her if she was upset. I told her that this was ripping my heart out. I couldn't protect her. I could barely breathe. I was trying my best to compose myself. I tried to call my best friend, but my call went to voicemail. I tried my hardest to get a link to any support or any words of hope. Voicemail again. I tried again. I was drowning. I couldn't breathe. I couldn't do this. Any kind of help or words of support would be greatly appreciated. I needed a lifeline.

The pageant manager returned and told me not to worry, they had a rehearsal tomorrow in Los Angeles and we could go to that one. The hotel there was completely accessible.

I looked at him, wanting to vomit. The morning's coffee was burning holes in my stomach. I wanted to crawl into a hole. How could this man possibly know that I had been up for hours getting Lorrin ready? To do this again tomorrow was completely mad. I had zero desire to do this again ever.

He could see that I was devastated.

"You have no idea how very difficult this is to do," I said and looked through his soul. I showed him the pain and disappointment in my eyes. I thanked him and left.

It was these random moments that tore me apart and left me feeling lifeless, worthless, and hopeless. It was hard to breathe again without wanting to scream. It was as if the universe was telling me, "You are an idiot. You don't belong. What are you doing?"

I cried all the way home. I tried my friend again and again, only to go to voicemail. I felt as though I was the biggest loser on the planet.

I looked at Lorrin and cried harder. I told her we were going to be okay. I was amazed of how she was not crying. Maybe she was even laughing at me. It was moments like these that made me feel as though I couldn't go on.

It is a mother's worst fear to be completely rejected while trying to stand tall for her child. Her uniquely abled child.

I held Lorrin's hand and explained to her that I was just not that strong. My feelings were really hurt and I was sorry. I should have known better. I would be better the next day and we would go back and she would do the dress rehearsal. *I promise you, Lorrin. We will do it!*

The next day, I was tired, numb, and waiting for the next insult. We showed up. We were now in a group that we would not be participating with and which we would never see again. I wasn't sure if this was a good thing or a bad thing. We were invisible. I tried not to have a cranky attitude and tried to smile and act as though we fit in. We went through the motions. The wind was out of my sails, but I went through the motions. Lorrin did it. We went home. We had to get ready for the pageant.

The pageant was an entire day's event. I had never done sports before with a child, but I'm guessing it is something pretty similar to this. Hurry up and wait. Go here and wait. Now wait.

I booked us a room at the hotel. The schedule was an eleven a.m. photo shoot. Lorrin would be wearing four different outfits. That may be easy for some girls. But to change Lorrin four times in a day was my worst nightmare. We got dressed in the room and went down for our pictures. We went back to the room for the next shoot. This was so much work. By two p.m., I was already exhausted. We had to travel to the pageant. I got there with Lorrin and her wardrobe. She would be wearing three different outfits on stage. The most important one for me was the gown. I decorated her wheelchair with flowers—her wheelchair was an extension of her.

I was so worried that Lorrin would not want me anywhere near her, I asked her physical therapist's daughter to push Lorrin on stage for the pageant. Amara was five years older than Lorrin. She was beautiful and one of the nicest people Lorrin ever met. She agreed to push Lorrin. Her mother brought her down to wait out the pageant. I was so grateful.

The funny thing about being disabled is that no one knows what to do with you. When we arrived at the pageant, they put all the girls in one room and put Lorrin in a room by herself. It immediately hurt my feelings. I wanted her to be just like the other girls. It felt so funny to be separated. It was painful. Yet, they did it to protect her. I think it would have been nice to be included in the excitement of getting ready with all the girls.

As the day went on, I became more and more exhausted. I dreaded the next step as much as I dreaded the dentist. I had no idea how Lorrin would be accepted and what the other girls would say and do. Amara did a great job on stage with Lorrin. She was confident and allowed Lorrin to do exactly what she came to do—be a twelve-year-old in a pageant with her peers.

When it came time for Lorrin to be in her gown, I felt very proud. I decorated her wheelchair with beautiful red and white flowers. Lorrin's hair and makeup was perfect. She had crystal beads threaded in her hair. She was stunning. We waited in the hall with the other girls. I felt a bit disconnected due to us having been separated. While waiting, a few of the girls waved to Lorrin and said hello. I told them she talked with her eyes and she was really exhausted.

Girls were running the halls laughing and being loud. They were being shushed as the staff tried to keep the halls quiet. A group of girls ran by and stopped to stare at Lorrin. You could tell these were the popular girls. They had obviously made a clique. The girls stopped right in front of Lorrin and started talking to her. They were going on and on about how beautiful she looked and how amazing her wheelchair was decorated. One of the girls said, "I want a wheelchair."

I was cracking up. It was the first time during the entire event that I felt as though Lorrin was observed and included. It was a nice feeling.

The pageant was twelve hours long that day. It was exhausting and draining. For the most part, the audience included family members of the girls who were participating. It was something that I never would have considered doing, nor would I do it again.

But it was also a time that we pushed the boundaries. We fought for Lorrin's right to be a young girl doing a normal event. Thanks to Amara for allowing Lorrin to stand on stage without her mother, Lorrin looked as beautiful as all the other contestants.

For a moment, I thought Lorrin was going to place. I had mixed feelings about going further with it. I was worn and beaten as the night grew to a close. Lorrin didn't get called, but I was just about the proudest parent in the house. Both Lorrin and Amara received a huge bouquet of red, long stemmed roses.

The curtains shut, and Lorrin went into the biggest grand mal seizure ever.

Chapter 28

~ Children's San Diego ~
Thirteen Years Old

Lorrin and Kelsy met while receiving their canine companion dogs. It was more a reunion than an initial meeting—it was as though we'd all been separated at birth—the dogs, the girls, us moms. Kelsy and her mom came to visit, and I bought the girls Top Gun *shirts and the movie. Just before the famous kissing scene, I paused and told the girls all about kissing. They rolled their eyes at me and listened intently.*

In May 2007, Lorrin was accepted to receive a Canine Companion. We spent two weeks in San Diego training to be certified to handle the dog. We were gifted a half Labrador, half Golden Retriever named Nicolette. She was absolutely a gem.

During the second week of training, Lorrin got sick. I took her to the ER. I knew after three days of two antibiotics that not only was she not getting better, she was getting worse. I was scared by the way she was breathing. It sounded like she had oatmeal in her lungs. I was crazy stressed out. She was too sick to continue training. I was also greatly concerned about us failing the certification and not being able to bring Nicolette home with us. Receiving a canine companion was the opportunity of a lifetime, and we had waited two years for this. I held off taking Lorrin back to the ER until we took the final exam with Nicolette. I took the test along with twelve other eager participants and then went straight to the ER.

I second-guessed myself the entire time I sat waiting in the ER to be seen by the doctors. Was she sicker than I'd thought? Was I overreacting? Typical feelings, teeter-tottering from how bad is this going to get to maybe I'm overreacting. By the time Lorrin was seen by a doctor, she required oxygen and her stomach was distended. Her belly looked like it was going to pop.

There is always a funny reaction in the ER. Doctors know that her case is extremely complicated. A good doctor will be open to suggestions from me. A not-so-good doctor will act like he or she knows everything.

This doctor took one look at Lorrin and asked me what I thought we should do. He then said we needed to be transported to the Children's Hospital of San Diego. We ended up staying there for two weeks. Lorrin was gravely ill.

I sat in a metal chair next to her bed in the ER, hunched over, consumed by the yellow liquid moving slowly through the tube. I could do nothing more than concentrate on the movement of the fluid. They said it would drain. So I got up again and made sure the urine from Lorrin's catheter was draining efficiently into the bag. I sat back down in the chair and stared at the floor as a mop swished by my feet. I smiled at the person mopping the floor, knowing how filthy the emergency room was, knowing that in any ER if something falls on the floor it is trash.

I felt like the carpet had been pulled out from under me. I watched her urine catheter, her IV, the oxygen, and her chest going up and down too rapidly for comfort and wondered if this would be the time she died. I knew that pneumonia was a killer for kids and adults like Lorrin. How quickly the fear and anxiety set in.

Being a parent of a child with special needs who is sick is like giving birth. Each time I go through it, I forget how horribly scary it is. If I felt that enormous fear and pain every day, I wouldn't survive. So I forget. It never goes away, but I can't stay in that emotional flood, I would drown in it.

I tried to stay calm. Tried to accept what I had no control over. Lorrin was going to be admitted with a hefty case of pneumonia. She was on fifty percent oxygen.

I hated being in the hospital with the dirty bathrooms, the horrible food, and the stares of strangers. The ER nurse was in tears after I shared our story with her. As touching as that was, it made me realize how screwed up our situation was. The balance between survival and succeeding, between death and hanging on by a thin thread was always delicate. The question was, to what lengths would we go to keep her alive?

My day had started at 6:30 a.m. Friday in the Canine Companions for Independence dorm room. It was now 4 a.m. on Saturday. I had been through two hospital emergency rooms, an ambulance transfer to CHSD, and admissions to a step down unit, meaning it's one step down from Intensive Care (ICU). I was exhausted. Lorrin had a fever. Her arms curled up around her face. She was having a crazy amount of diarrhea. The seriousness of her medical condition was scary. I didn't know how worried I should be.

I thought I would get a little respite when we got to our room. But questions needed to be asked and answered. I was used to being admitted to Cedars-Sinai, where everyone knew us. Here, we were new faces, a new case. Three of the five nurses fussing over Lorrin questioned me. I was barely awake, scared, and stressed.

The first battle was to get the nurses to use the diapers that Lorrin normally wore. I told them she would pee-out the ones they had. To have these strangers telling me how to diaper my daughter was trying. Like I never do it. I told them over and over, "I'm her caregiver. I know what will work."

I almost got into a fight with the nurse as she was weighing Lorrin. None of the nurses would listen to me. I'm not used to being treated like an outsider.

Lorrin immediately peed through their diaper, and they reluctantly agreed to let me get mine out of the car while they changed her bedding. This was going to be a long morning after a long night. Then a nurse told me that Lorrin's trach piece was too small and the hole in her neck was too large. I asked her if she had ever seen a tracheal diversion. She told me that they have tons of kids like Lorrin on the "pod." That was what they call the rooms across the hall. She told me that we would be in the pod for children with trachs, if they had an available room.

I told all the nurses and the respiratory therapist that it was crucial that they understood that Lorrin only breathed out of her neck. Not her nose or mouth. They acted like it was nothing. One nurse said, "Our doctor will fix you up tomorrow. Her trach setup isn't right."

Maybe I had been out of the hospital too long and didn't know the latest things that were done for kids like Lorrin. With these five nurses and a respiratory therapist against me, I felt like I didn't know what was going on with my daughter. I told the nurses that Lorrin needed some Ativan to calm her down. She was tight as a board, holding her arms up to her chin. She was coughing blood out of her trach. They said the doctor didn't order it, so therefore they couldn't give it.

I told them they needed to contact the doctor and get him to approve two milligrams of Ativan for her or she wouldn't calm down. There was no need for her to be tortured further. Fighting her body was not going to be helpful.

It was the strangest experience to have nurses act like I didn't know my daughter's needs. I was extremely tired and I knew that I wouldn't get any rest if Lorrin's body was going to be flailing out of control all night. She was coughing and choking herself with her arms clenched around her neck. I guess they thought this was normal. I showed them pictures of Lorrin and explained what she looks like at home.

This wasn't her typical behavior. She was overstressed and needed help to calm down. During the next hour she needed three diaper changes from excessive diarrhea. And I mean excessive. Her whole body was going crazy.

I knew from experience that they were going to ignore my request for Ativan. And I wasn't going to let her suffer needlessly. I told them to call the doctor. They told me he was resting. I told them that if they didn't get Lorrin Ativan, I would take her to another hospital. Why were they arguing about this? It was a huge scene.

The charge nurse came in after hearing the commotion in the wee hours of the night. Usually the floor is pretty silent at four a.m. I told her that it was not my intention to admit my daughter and not have her treated appropriately. How could Lorrin's body heal and rest when she was stressed to the point of practically suffocating herself with her arms wrapped around her neck, coughing up blood? Years ago I might not have been such a bitch. But by this time, I knew what was best for my daughter and I wouldn't let her suffer under anyone's watch.

The Ativan was given. Lorrin fell asleep. I slept for two hours.

The next day, when I could wrap my brain around what had happened, I realized the nurses thought it was normal for Lorrin to be all fisted up. When they saw her, they understood what I was trying to do. It was frustrating that in five minutes' time they thought they knew Lorrin better than I did.

It dawned on me that most kids like Lorrin are placed in homes, and the parents aren't usually the caretakers. But I was, and I knew what I was doing.

Our first visitor was the pediatrician from the night before—only hours ago. He was unhappy with my demand for Ativan and the overriding of his orders, and he said little to me that day. But clearly, Lorrin was calm and resting.

When the Ear, Nose and Throat (ENT) specialist came in, I was eager to learn any new ideas he might have for me. After the way the nurses talked to me, I felt guilty that I was not informed about recent trach diversions. Though Lorrin's type of diversion was rare, the respiratory therapist told me she'd treated many children with the same diversion.

I jumped up off my cot with my bad breath and a horrible case of bed hair to ask about the tracheal diversions he was overseeing here at CHSD. I was shocked to find that he was equally interested in Lorrin's diversion. He told me that he had only seen two in all of his practicing years. One patient died, never leaving the hospital after the diversion was placed.

I was half-pissed that I had been mistreated by the ignorant staff and half-gratified to have my confidence in my own capabilities and knowledge restored. I was teeter-tottering between anger and relief.

The ENT asked about my experience with Lorrin and the diversion, how it worked, and about the doctor who did it. For the first time at this hospital, I was being treated with respect. I conveyed that the staff had made me feel ignorant and negligent about my daughter's medical care. He confessed they had never have seen a diversion before.

The ENT doctor was fabulous. Thank God. He was the head of the ENT department at Rady Children's Hospital in San Diego. This is a gigantic hospital specializing in children. He seemed open for suggestions and he understood how sick Lorrin was. He was a kind and gentle man.

Lorrin needed assistance to help her breathe. We put her on a C-pap machine. It helped her take breaths. Lorrin's lungs were too congested to breathe on her own. Before we put her on the machine, I sat by Lorrin's side and asked her what she wanted to do. I held her hand and explained what was happening and allowed her to make the choice if she wanted to use the breathing machine. I asked her if she was done, and she told me that she wasn't. We had a very long conversation. I told Lorrin all about the things the hospital could do to help her. She responded by blinking for yes. To make sure I was on the right track, especially during serious conversations such as this one, I asked her to blink really hard. She knew I needed confirmation from her. I cried so hard that day. I wanted to be honest with her and wasn't sure of the choice she would make. I believed she had a good life with her new best friends and a canine companion dog waiting. On that day, Lorrin chose life.

During our two-week stay, the nurses got another chance to take care of Lorrin. They remembered how sick she was when she came in. They acknowledged Lorrin's normal state, her body tone, and awareness. If only they had listened, that horrendous admission night would have been so much less difficult. A wonderful thing happened the next day, Debbie called me to tell me that Lorrin came to her in her dreams and told her that the breathing machine was helping her and not to worry.

Chapter 29

~ *Big Sur - Sofanya* ~

While attending a Caroline Myss conference, Lorrin and I got into the elevator with a rather handsome young man in a suit. It is always awkward on the elevator with a disabled child. Lorrin looks at me and takes her arm and smacks him in the groin. He looks pitifully at the poor, disabled kid in the chair. Lorrin starts to belly laugh so hard her shoulders are shaking. Once we're off the elevator, I scolded her.

Big Sur has always been a place of healing for me. I have been drawn there since my first visit. There is something about the large redwoods overlooking the ocean that takes my breath away, it is magical and mystical. Spending time there has been invigorating and healing for me. When I leave I feel an inner peacefulness and know that everything will be okay. The beauty of the forest mends my heart.

In 2007 Lorrin and I camped at Big Sur, twice on our own with her canine companion Nicolette. There was a portrait studio where an artist named Sofanya painted portraits of the aura surrounding the subject. I wanted her to paint Lorrin.

Before beginning Lorrin's portrait, Sofanya sat for a few minutes meditating. She asked Lorrin and me to also take a moment and breathe with her. Then she began by spraying the canvas with water. She took small jars of liquid watercolors and dropped them onto the page. I watched like an excited child. I was not surprised that the colors she picked were violet, green, blue, some orange and yellow. The hues were brilliant and powerful. Sofanya tilted the page and the colors started to bleed together. She set the canvas to dry a bit before she started drawing with a white colored chalk pencil and charcoal.

She drew Lorrin's eyes. Lorrin sat on Sofanya's left side facing her. Lorrin smiled the entire time. I tried to explain to Sofanya that Lorrin rarely smiled so big and never kept smiling for such a long time. Sofanya drew her eyes perfectly, one eye a little off from the other. She sketched in her nose and mouth.

She started to draw images that magically emerged from the colors. Each image had meaning to me. She drew a dolphin over Lorrin's nose; a crescent moon; an owl; shooting stars; a heart with faces; angels; waves; a hawk and a Goddess. The images on the canvas all made sense to me except for one, the hawk. I told her that Lorrin had swum with the dolphins and long ago in a very intense meditation with Lorrin I was gifted an owl. The only thing that didn't really fit was the hawk. I understood the meaning of hawk medicine but it drew no special recognition for me. All the other animals in the portrait were on the left side of Lorrin's face. Sofanya told me the left represented the past and the right the future. The hawk was on her right.

Sofanya told me that she saw so many angels and guardians that she couldn't paint them all and that Lorrin communicated by singing angels. She was sent here to share her wisdom. At the top of the portrait there were dinosaurs, symbolizing the many years that Lorrin and I had been together. I wouldn't have believed her ability to draw so many of our powerful totems if I had not seen it.

Three hours into the drive home on a busy stretch of Pacific Coast Highway we passed Cambria. I love Cambria, and just driving through it made me smile. I was relaxed, listening to our iPod playing the music loud. Suddenly I felt like we were in a time warp. Out of the corner of my eye on the left side I saw a huge hawk. I took my foot off the gas petal as I watched this bird dive down to pick up some road kill that was on the opposite side of the street. I could see people standing and watching the hawk. It was as if time slowed for a moment. The hawk dove down towards the road. I took my foot off the gas. The hawk's huge wingspan grew as it came closer. It attempted to pick up a dead animal that was on the highway. My van was slowing with my foot still off the gas. There was oncoming traffic approaching fast, and I knew the bird didn't have much time. The huge bird lifted up a piece of the road kill off the pavement. Suddenly, instead of flying up like I expected, the hawk flew right in front of my car. The wingspan covered my entire grill. The impact jolted the van as we hit the hawk dead on and it landed on the ground. I felt like I had been struck by lightning.

I didn't know what to do. I kept driving for a mile or so afraid to look in my mirror. I was so freaked out. I immediately gave thanks to the bird and blessed it for giving its life as a message to me. I pulled over to get a grip on myself. Taking a hawk's feathers is illegal unless you are Native American. I thought to myself, *If there is a feather on my grill, I am keeping it.* I had no idea what to expect when I got out of my car.

There was nothing on my car. Part of me wanted to go back, but I was afraid that I would lose it if I did.

I phoned Sofanya when I got home to share my experience with her. She told me that my daughter was here to share her story. I am the messenger for Lorrin.

The hawk's sacrifice was a message to help empower me and remind me of this task.

I felt like my life was about to shift again to a higher vibrational level. What I was supposed to do was becoming clearer. The mystery of life and the hawk's message kept me speechless for hours. I will never forget that powerful message. It might not have reached me had it played out in another way, without the magnitude of the event. I'm dense. Messages need to whack me in the head. I always ask for big messages so they don't slip by me. This one was unmistakable.

The hawk's message is referred to in Jamie Sams and David Carson's *Medicine Cards* as the Messenger of the Sky. The hawk reminds you to pay attention! You are only as powerful as your capacity to perceive, receive, and use your abilities. The hawk is referred to as the messenger of the gods. Hawk medicine teaches you to be observant, to look at your surroundings. Observe the obvious in everything you do. Life is sending you signals.

Chapter 30

~ The Cute Question of the Day ~

Lorrin was a bit spoiled at middle school. I did my best to make sure she fit in with the cutest clothes, hair, and, of course, shoes. Her wheelchair always had cool stuff hanging off it. One day after Christmas, a girl ran up to Lorrin to show off her new shoes that were just like Lorrin's. She looked down only to see that Lorrin had the latest tennis shoes with skulls on them. I bought two pairs, on one foot Lorrin wore a black shoe with colored skulls and on the other wore a white shoe with black skulls. The girl looked down, took a breath, and added two new items to her wish list.

Being a parent of a child with special needs means you never really get a break, even when you sleep. Lorrin was always with me unless she was at school, and even then my cell phone was attached to my hand, waiting for the next emergency. When it rang my heart would sink, anticipating bad news if I saw that it was Debbie calling. But things were starting to change. I started to receive random calls from Debbie with questions that I had never been asked before. The teachers, school staff, and Lorrin's new friends were curious about Lorrin and how she did things. You might be surprised about the questions from the adults. They would ask, "Is Ms. Kain happy?" The kids had obvious questions for middle school students. "Was Debbie with her all the time? How did Lorrin bathe? Did she cry? What did she like to watch on TV?" Once the kids were able to ask as many questions as they needed to, they were able to accept Lorrin for who she was. One day, Debbie called with one question in particular that gave me an idea I had never had before. The question was, "Has Lorrin ever had a sleepover?" I had given up on the notion she might ever experience a sleepover, along with graduation, a wedding, and getting her driver's license. Only weeks before Lorrin was about to turn thirteen, they asked Debbie if Lorrin had gone to a sleepover.

Holding the phone tightly in my hand I asked Debbie if she thought that the girls would like to have a sleepover. Her reply to me was, "Yes, I think they would love that!"

Sarah Rivera was one of the girls who from the beginning took a great interest in Lorrin. She was quickly becoming Lorrin's best friend. Even at twelve years old, Sarah was a leader. Debbie talked to Sarah and together they started to plan Lorrin's first sleepover. Sarah was in charge of who was going to be invited and who wasn't. She told Debbie that a few of the girls weren't really Lorrin's friend and therefore were off the list.

She came up with five girls. There was much buzz around the classroom of the party plans. There was talk about what kinds of food they wanted to eat. What they wanted to do. One of the girls kept asking Debbie how long Lorrin was. She would come up and hold her hands over Lorrin as she sat in her wheelchair.

Finally Debbie asked her, "Why do you keep asking me about how long Lorrin is?"

"I am making her a blanket for her birthday," she said.

I threw myself into the party. I started shopping for a karaoke machine and an American Idol game. All the while, I was overjoyed and filled with love and gratitude for all the exciting adventures Lorrin was having. On the night of Lorrin's birthday, I had a chocolate fountain, bowls of Cheetos and Doritos, pizza, loads of drinks, sour candies, and sticks of gum everywhere. The agenda also included painting one another's nails, prank phone calls, watching movies, and taking pictures.

It was a bit awkward when the girls showed up for the party. I had never met any of them and I felt nervous. I tried to act really cool, like this happened all the time.

One mom brought two of the girls to the house. When she came in, I could tell by the look on her face that she was shocked by the magnitude of

Lorrin's disability. I can only imagine her daughter telling her, "Mom, I'm invited over for a sleepover at my new friend Lorrin's house. Oh, yeah, she's in a wheelchair."

It was clear as I stood in my kitchen that this mom was not at all prepared for what she saw. I felt as confused as she did. I never expected this to happen.

The day after the party, we woke up and scrapbooked the events from the night before. It was a lot of work, but everyone, including myself, enjoyed every moment. I have to give special credit to Lorrin's nurse, Debbie. She came over to be there when the girls arrived. I had never met them. Then Debbie returned the next day to help with making their scrapbooks. Each girl took home a book full of memories. The party would not have come together so well if it hadn't been for her love and extra effort. The best part was that Lorrin's friends saw her as just another middle school student. Her friends appreciated her and were able to see past the exterior and enjoy who she really was on the inside.

This started a pattern of sleepovers. We had sleepovers any time the girls asked. The evenings progressed to scary movies, Rock Band, Halo, toilet papering, gingerbread making that led into flour fights, scavenger hunts, and, sometimes, scary stories. All the girls would sleep together on the sofa, and the house would be a complete wreck.

I would wake up tired and happier than I could remember. I made them breakfast which included farm animal waffles, bacon, sausage, all kinds of juice, and scrambled eggs. They would giggle and laugh. I knew they'd been up all night and would be horrible when they got home.

Each time they left I'd find cell phones or socks all around the house. I loved those days, those very important days. I am forever grateful for the innocence and bravery of those girls.

One day in March, Lorrin was having a really rough time with her seizures. In December, she started having bouts of cluster seizure episodes. She would have one seizure after another. I could not stop them with Ativan. We changed to a new drug called Diastat, which was an anti-seizure drug that is given rectally and will, or I might say, should, knock her out for hours. After calling all over town to find a pharmacy that had it, I went to pick it up. I asked the pharmacist when I could administer a second dose to Lorrin.

He had not given me too much notice, but he immediately looked at me over his glasses straight in my eyes and with a firm voice said, "You go to the hospital."

I had felt frustrated all morning. Lorrin was having seizures that I couldn't stop, and I had to chase down a drug that no one had. One pharmacist told me that in the thirteen years that he had been a pharmacist, he had never dispensed it. And now the guy at the counter was telling me to check into the hospital if one dose of this stuff didn't work.

I already knew that one dose wouldn't work. Lorrin wasn't like other children. I didn't live in his world.

The topper to the day is that when I tried to pay him, he said that I had to wait in line. There were people in front of me. I stood there as he walked away. I was so confused. My daughter was home having uncontrolled seizures and her medication was filled, but I couldn't have it.

"Excuse me, sir," I called. "I need this medication because my daughter is in status seizures (meaning seizures that don't stop). I appreciate waiting my turn, but seeing how it's all ready to go, do you think maybe I can get this now?" I tried not to say the obvious and become the bitch that I know is inside of me, begging to come out. I smiled a fake smile and thanked him.

As I headed for my car, I realized that my life was different. I didn't live in their world. As I walked out of the store and saw all the Easter candy and garbage on the shelves, I was reminded that Easter was coming. I reminded myself to breathe. Just breathe.

During this dark time with Lorrin's health, she was still having powerful and joyful friendship experiences. On this particular day she was at school in the middle of one of her cluster seizure episodes that may have been due to puberty. Who knew?

Debbie, Lorrin's nurse, told Lorrin's best friend, Sarah, that she needed to get to the magnet attached to Lorrin's chair. Lorrin had a vagal implant. It was about the size of a pacemaker and had been implanted just under her left breast. The implant was connected to the vagal nerve in her neck. For some reason that is not completely understood, when the implant tickles the vagal nerve, it can help stop seizure activity.

The timing of the implant is set by the doctors and goes off every few minutes. When the magnet is swiped over the implant in her chest, it sets it off. So if Lorrin started to have a seizure, the protocol was to take the magnet and swipe it over her chest. The implant would go off and hopefully the seizure would decrease and/or stop.

So, Lorrin went into a seizure and Debbie was reaching for the magnet. Sarah said, "I need to learn how to use the magnet. I already know how to feed Lorrin, and I know how to get her wheelchair in and out of the van. I just need to learn how to use the magnet, because when I turn sixteen and get my license, Lorrin and I are going to the mall without you or Karen." Sarah was confident and had no idea the impact she was having on Debbie.

At the end of the day, I waited for Lorrin and would greet her with her canine companion Nicolette by my side as she got off the bus. I would get excited as soon as I heard the bus pull up to the house. This was the best part of my day. I longed to hear about all that took place at school.

This day I was rewarded with a seizure story and a story about friendship. As Debbie told me this story, we both cracked up and my heart felt big. I could only imagine Lorrin and Sarah at the mall. I saw it clearly in my head. "Sarah gets distracted and Lorrin is left sitting at the mall by herself; Sarah picks up some cute guy. They both are in trouble." I'm sure Lorrin had dreams of this day also. Debbie and I laughed as we talked about the overlooked obvious concerns about Lorrin and her airway. Suctioning had not come up. Did Sarah really know how medically fragile Lorrin was? She couldn't possibly know that everyone else who has had a tracheal diversion died within five years. She hated the grossness of snot. But maybe by the time she was sixteen and with some intense training, she could take Lorrin to the mall. What a thought.

I immediately went back to a vision of a security officer calling me. "Excuse me, Ms. Kain. I found your sixteen-year-old daughter in her wheelchair sitting by herself in front of Hot Dog on a Stick. Oh, yeah, she has a canine companion with her. That's how I found your number."

It would really be a dream come true to for Lorrin and me if she could go to the mall without a nurse. What a thought.

Another day, Debbie shared with me something cute that happened at school. Sarah, Lorrin's BFF (best friend forever), came into class and asked Debbie if she could have a moment with Lorrin. "I just need to talk to her alone."

Debbie stepped away. Sarah sat next to Lorrin on the floor while Lorrin lay in her bean bag. She got really close to her ear and started talking and talking.

Lorrin was blinking and listening intently. More talking and more blinking. Finally, after a few moments, Sarah had to get to class. She thanked Debbie, then said, "I'm sorry. I hope I didn't hurt your feelings. I just needed to talk to my best friend, Lorrin, in private."

School Dances

Lorrin has drawn many people into her life. She has been so lucky to have captured a beautiful and fun caretaker named Karissa. We met Karissa, a firefighter who happens to have a huge tattoo on her shoulder of a female firefighter in flames, when she was twenty-three. Did I mention that Karissa happens to be hot? Firefighter hot and sexy hot. The girls loved her. Karissa took Lorrin to school dances so Lorrin didn't have to be embarrassed by her mother.

Karissa does the mambo, the footloose dance, and the do-si-do. I have pictures of many dances in which Lorrin is in the middle of her BFFs dancing, encircled by ten to fifteen girls. They are all having fun.

Karissa has opened the door for the other kids to dance with Lorrin by setting the tone. It only takes one person to be the example. What a gift Karissa has been.

After one dance, Karissa told me a boy came up to Lorrin and gave her his hat. She had no idea who the boy was. He said hello to Lorrin by waving in front of her face. When they got home, we talked about it briefly and left it at that. What a sweet thing for a boy to come up to Lorrin like that. It was starting to happen more and more. Lorrin was such a flirt that I'm sure this made her feel great. It warmed my heart.

For their eighth grade graduation dance, I hosted a party. I invited all the girls to come over before the dance and get ready together. I had loads of food. By this time, I had a good idea about what the girls wanted to snack on. Karissa did hair and makeup. I had the counters filled with makeup and goodies for the finishing touches. I hired a cameraman named Chuck, who was quickly becoming a lifer in Lorrin's book. He has become a lifer in my heart as well. He filmed the girls and took pictures of the entire evening.

Karissa took the girls to the dance. On this night, something amazing happened. The girls danced with Karissa. Lorrin's group surrounded her. There were tons of streamers and decorations everywhere. This was another night I never thought would happen. "My Lorrin living long enough to go to her eighth grade graduation. My Lorrin dancing with her friends at eighth grade graduation. My Lorrin having friends. My Lorrin was about to make it to high school."

As Lorrin danced with her friends, the boy who gave her the hat at the previous dance joined her crowd. He was about six feet tall and wore a white shirt and black pants. He danced in front of Lorrin and with her. The other girls backed up and gave him some space.

Lorrin looked beautiful in her blue silky dress with her hair up and nails done. She had beads woven into her hair, and her makeup was perfect. He danced with my Lorrin. He held her hand and danced in front of her wheelchair all night long.

Later, when Karissa told me about the boy, I keep pushing for more information about him. His name was Ron Stone. She told me Ron knew Lorrin from when they were young. He'd met her horseback riding. I immediately know who she was talking about. I laughed out loud. He was the boy we met when Lorrin was about five years old. The story goes like this....

I found a place fifteen minutes away that would let Lorrin ride a horse with a rider. She didn't have to work, just ride. It was there we met Ron. Lorrin was so tiny and skinny. The man who was on top of this huge horse was about 300 pounds. I remember it took three of us to get Lorrin's tiny body, which had no head or trunk control, on this horse. Once she got on the horse, the man held her head up in his huge hands. Lorrin's legs would immediately relax from their otherwise bent state. She loved being on a horse. I felt that Lorrin was safe in this man's arms and walked around the dusty track taking pictures. There was so much dust and dirt I knew she'd get pneumonia in a week from this, but she was sure having fun right then.

After Lorrin rode, we hung out, watching other kids ride. I figured that Lorrin loved horses so much, it was a shame to take her home. We just hung out on the stands and watched the other kids take their turns. That is when Ron came up to Lorrin. He had the biggest brown eyes and beautiful skin with just a smattering of freckles on his rosy cheeks. He was so sweet and curious.

Lorrin's trach had been put in only months earlier, and we were still in the adjustment phase. It's basically a hole in her neck. I had a trach collar over it. Ron came up to her and was completely enamored by it. He kept telling me that he didn't know anyone with one of those. I asked him if he would like to see it, and he quickly leaned in closer as I pulled her trach collar away, allowing him to basically see inside her lungs, or as close as he could possibly get.

This had never happened before. When I explained things to other people, especially kids, they seemed to be okay with everything. Well, with Ron, it was a bit different. The more I explained, the more he asked. He kept repeating, "I don't know anyone with one of those."

I fell in love with him and his curiosity. He was adorable. I believe he rode often and actually helped brush the horses and clean the stables. He was filthy, covered in dust and dirt.

Someone wanted my attention, and I stepped away from Lorrin as Ron sat next to her. I was so worried that he'd put his dirty fingers right in her neck. Ever since Lorrin was trached, I worried that someone would put something down into her lungs. I knew that Ron didn't have a hurtful bone in his body, but the curiosity of a six-year-old boy trumps all.

I gave them both a bit of space and stood back and watched. He immediately seemed protective over Lorrin. It was a great day that I remember clearly. I told Karissa about my story. I told her I was sure that it was him. I could tell by the pictures that Karissa had taken as we uploaded them onto my computer that it was indeed Ron. Wow! Was he tall. I could see those big brown eyes.

I tried soon after that to contact him. I wanted to talk to him. On graduation day at Sequoia Middle School, I had two jobs: one, hold back the tears; two, find Ron Stone.

I found him. I tried not to frighten him. I didn't want to embarrass him, but I really wanted to meet him again. What did I say to a boy who danced with my daughter all night at the graduation dance? I was sure Lorrin was mortified, but I think I handled it well. I asked him if he'd take a picture with Lorrin. Then, I asked him where he'd met her.

Ron was completely unaffected by my excitement and nervousness. "I met her horseback riding," he said. "I was trying to keep the flies out of her trach."

I wanted to give him a great big hug and ask for his phone number. Where was his mother? I wanted to hug her too. It was so hard for me to just thank him and walk away. This young man had no idea how he'd just gifted me, Lorrin, and Karissa.

The summer before Lorrin was going to high school, I worked for weeks to get her an accessible computer to take with her. She had a switch that she held in her hand that activated the computer. All she had to do was hit the switch. Then she could navigate around the programs I had designed for her.

I had pictures of her summer events, our holidays, and her friends. I put up a page for her feelings, activities, and jokes. I spent an enormous amount of time and money on software to get this ready for school. I found myself in tears trying to master this program. I was not a speech and language expert. I used what I had learned at the conferences that I went to for guidance.

I so much wanted this for my Lorrin. I wanted her to communicate with others so she could show everyone how smart she was. I busted my butt to make that possible.

What I did not realize is that she didn't want to communicate via the computer. She wanted people to look in her eyes and take the time to understand her slightest gesture. She wanted people to see her soul. After a very frustrating summer of me hitting my head against the wall, I completed the program and she took it to school. She never used it.

I should have realized I was the one trying to force this to happen. It was my deal, not Lorrin's.

I tried everything I could to help her. Some things paid off and some didn't. I had to understand that my daughter had her agenda and I had my agenda. From that experience, when I set goals for her, I made sure she was on board. I think it can be difficult as a mother to separate the two.

Chapter 31

~ First Day of High School ~
Thirteen Years Old

Lorrin was a big flirt. I hired my nurse's husband Eric to play computer games with her. I came home and put the groceries on the counter. Eric was at the table with Lorrin in her chair, the switch to control the game in her hand. But her eyes were closed. "What's going on?" I asked. "She won't open her eyes," Eric replied. Lorrin looked out of the corner of her eye and giggled at me.

On the morning of Lorrin's first day of high school, I ran around like I always do. Too much to do, too little time to do it. I woke up at 6:30 and let the canine companion out, grabbed Lorrin's meds, and fed the dog. I started Lorrin's first of three breathing treatments while she was receiving something called a VEST treatment. The VEST treatment is a jacket similar to a life vest that attaches to a machine that shakes her for ten minutes. It's done twice. This machine has changed her life. It helps to keep her lungs clear. I, of course, put off getting it for years. I didn't want one more thing, or piece of equipment in my home.

Once I put the VEST on her and started the treatment, I hopped in bed with her. I lay back down for a moment. I put my hand in her jacket and used the vibration from the VEST as a snooze button. I tried to quiet my mind, to think good thoughts. It was my habit that before I put my feet on the floor I thought of the things in life that I was thankful for. I fell asleep for ten more minutes twice.

I could barely open my eyes; my body felt like I was dragging. I took the two ten minute snoozes and set the machine to run for an extra five minutes. My mind wasn't thinking. The machine stopped, I sighed in disappointment and wondered why I was so tired. I looked at my darling. I then realized it was Lorrin's first day to meet her new teacher at high school. I jumped out of bed. Now I realized how much that five minutes would cost me. I ran and turned on the oven, took her vest off, gave her her meds, fed her, bathed her, picked out clothes, got the cookies in the oven, dressed her, got the cookies out of the oven. I knew I was doing too much, but this was her first meeting at high school.

I wanted to dry and curl her hair. Her nurse came, as she always did, to take Lorrin to school. They rode the bus together to ensure that nothing happened medically on the way. Debbie could handle anything.

Debbie could tell immediately that I was running late. I told her I had to run the curling iron through Lorrin's hair. I told her the rattling that she hears in Lorrin's chest was stuck and I had suctioned her twice and couldn't get it. "You know Lorrin," I tell her.

I was now running around in my nightgown, getting the cookies—I know, I should have baked them last night. I should have, but I was too tired then. Sometimes I thought I ran on vapors of what was left in my body. I had been so tired recently. I had little energy to do anything, but today I was excited to be baking cookies for her new high school teacher.

I felt silly and knew that I was over doing. I sent the teacher a video that I had just edited which was played on the local cable channel yesterday. It was the first ability awareness week footage from Lorrin's school. I put my business card in it, hoping maybe he would watch it. It aired yesterday, and not one person except the producer called to say anything. I was cranky about that.

Debbie was used to me. I loved her. Thank God for her. I was barefoot and realized the bus was coming down the street. Lorrin had so many things to take to school, her blanket to lie on, her extra blanket, eight each of pads, diapers, chucks, and all her regular stuff. I told Debbie thanks for carrying the cookies. I couldn't even help Debbie and Lorrin to the bus because I wasn't dressed yet. I thanked them as I barely got them on their way.

I shut the door and hoped I didn't cry when I met her new teacher. How could he know how unlikely it was for Lorrin to be alive, *and going to high school!* It really was going to happen. I wanted to cry. I cannot imagine how we had come this far. WOW. My heart was full. I honor this day. Thank you.

I was teary-eyed the entire morning. A few hours later, my insurance company called to tell me that my two nights a week nursing care from eleven p.m. until seven a.m., had maxed out on benefits and denied for any more hours for the remaining year.

It was only May. It was the Friday before a three-day weekend. *Oh, by the way, Mrs. Kain, we don't think you need help.*

I was already emotional and tired and vulnerable. It was hard not to cry. I told them I would fight it and asked what my next step was. I would call my attorney next. She told me she would call me back.

How much could a single parent take? Thirteen years I had been doing this. No end in sight. How do I survive? My body hurt. I felt so tired. Did anyone care? I still had so much to do. I still needed to work on the court audit.

I took time to sit with my girlfriend and have coffee that morning. I would pay for that. I would have to work extra hard to catch up on all the paperwork, bills, and other crap on my list for today.

Now Blue Cross thought I wasn't worthy to have *two* nights a week of nursing care. Nice slap in the face. Validation, thank you.

I called my doctor, but he wasn't in. The insurance finally called me back. They realized I wasn't going to accept this bullshit. She would no longer say anything because she knew I had an attorney.

Don't shoot the messenger, she told me. I told her she was representing me. She was my Blue Cross support. I also said, "You could have called me Tuesday. Now I can do nothing but have a sucky weekend."

I knew I'd work this out. I knew I wasn't going to take this. But why did I have to fight this battle? F#@!!

I would be forty-six this year. I felt happy. I felt tired. One moment I thought I was good-looking for forty-six. The next I was feeling very old. My bones hurt, my face looked like I was eighty. I would have loved to have beautiful skin. It would be nice to have some kind of partner to spend time with. Someone who didn't think only about themselves. Someone kind.

I no longer longed for someone to share the rest of my life with. I had no patience for all the bullshit. I was very happy by myself. Everything else seemed like work. I liked the middle of the bed, the side, the bottom. I liked to do whatever I wanted whenever I wanted. I liked eating crackers and cheese for dinner, breakfast, and lunch. Cheese, cheese, more cheese. Cheese with anything is good.

So I cried on and off the rest of the day and ate cheese.

Chapter 32

~ In Between ~
Thirteen Years Old

One of the best things about Lorrin having friends was that they would hide her from me. At the skating rink, I would go get popcorn. When I turned around, all three of the girls were missing. As a parent of a child in a wheelchair, I got used to her being in the same place I'd left her. Sarah always put a twist on things.

Lorrin's friends from middle school all went to different high schools. Sarah kept in touch with her the most. She came over for sleepovers all the time. When we were lucky, we got to have her over for two nights at a time. She was truly a dream. She got into the car and sat next to Lorrin and started telling her all about the latest gadget (iPod, new cell phones, whatever) that she had brought over.

She told Lorrin in detail about her hand-held Guitar Hero. I looked over to Karissa, who was sitting beside me, and told her I was going to cry. She looked at me and said, "I know." My heart exploded with joy and love and compassion as I witnessed this amazing miracle in awe. They were truly friends.

I knew that high school would be fun, but having Karissa in our lives made this time for Lorrin and me absolutely magical. Early in summer, Karissa and I planned for the high school activities. We spent time looking at the school events calendar online to make sure we saved the dates for the school dances and football home games. I couldn't wait for the football games. I saw it as another way that Lorrin could become part of the social atmosphere and meet new people.

Karissa agreed to take her to the school dances and pep rallies on Friday afternoons.

Sarah, Lorrin, Karissa, and I went to the first football game. I was totally a dork mom, and upon arrival, I purchased all the Moorpark High wear that I could carry: seats, sweatshirts, hats, and a blanket. I was so excited to be part of a High School football experience. Lorrin and her BFF, Sarah, were not so impressed and were seriously embarrassed to be seen with us. I found this irritating—and yet refreshingly appropriate at the same time. I was so proud. My daughter was a proper teenager.

Because Lorrin was in her wheelchair, they had to sit at the top of the stadium in accessible seating. Karissa and I sat a few steps down. I could keep an eye on them by looking over my shoulder every five seconds. It made me nervous not being able to hear Lorrin breathing so I could make sure her airway was clear. Sarah has always been really great about telling me when she thought Lorrin needed help. I was relying on her. Not easy and not fair to Sarah, but what else could I do? On occasion Sarah has had to come to get me saying, "Karen, Lorrin is blue again." Not a normal BFF thing to do.

I tried to act calm and not make a scene. But we were at our *first ever football game!*

I took pictures the first quarter, completely embarrassing them. I stopped after a few scowls because I didn't want to spoil the evening for either girl. Sarah was pretty good about putting me into check when I was bordering on being an annoying mother.

Our middle school experience had taught me how to break down the barriers. High school seemed more welcoming to our needs, but I knew I still had much work to do. I was preparing for Lorrin to attend the dance.

Children who have disabilities similar to Lorrin's make up less than one percent of the population. The dynamics for Lorrin's high school went something like this: the severely disabled students were put into what was called a county school program. The demands of these disabled students were far greater than what the regular school district could manage. There were special funds allocated so that they could receive what was referred to as an "equal education." This county school happened to be on the same campus as the regular school. That made it a great deal easier when trying to participate with regular students. The schools were two separate entities. Some days that worked for us, and some days against us. I look at it as being similar to having Taco Bell and McDonald's side by side. Different businesses, different rules. What works for one didn't necessarily work for the other.

I was a little apprehensive about Lorrin going to the dance with Karissa. Her middle school dances had taken great effort. The first dance she went to wasn't exactly wheelchair accessible. The kids were not so hot. It took almost two years for Lorrin to make connections. Karissa was a huge part of that success. I was ready to take high school on, but fully admit my hackles were up a bit.

Lorrin was not getting information about the regular school programs, i.e., the dances and football games. Each week we would go online and look at the current events. Karissa was pivotal in this area. She was ready to take Lorrin to the dance—I just wanted to make sure the school had a heads up in hopes to eliminate any embarrassing and painful moments. I certainly didn't want them to get all dressed up and excited about going to a dance only to be turned away.

I phoned the office, asking to connect with a liaison that could help me bridge this gap between the schools. I did not get a return call. I always got confused about the relationship between the staff and students. Of course, I called back and demanded to speak to someone. I was not about to let another message go unrecognized. Time was passing quickly, and I knew that if Lorrin could start the year off right socially, it would be easier than coming in the middle of things. I finally got referred to one of the vice principals. I guess in high school there are many vice principals. This was a new experience for me.

After much explanation of my agenda to the assistant, I was asked to hold a minute. I was on hold thirty minutes. As I was holding I was sharing with Karissa how difficult it was to just get her to a dance. It was hard not to take it personally. It was hard to be a parent of a child who needed unique considerations to just get in the door of the dance. I didn't want to throw Karissa and Lorrin to the lions. I didn't know if the staff at the dance would have a problem with Karissa taking Lorrin to the dance. I wanted to set them up for success.

After thirty minutes on hold, I got to speak with the high school VP on the phone. I just wanted to introduce myself and let him know that I was available to help as much as I could with making Lorrin's high school experience a good one and to reassure him that Lorrin would be accompanied by a caregiver/nurse everywhere she went. I spoke with him for about fifteen minutes.

The minute we ended our conversation, the phone rang. It was Lorrin's teacher calling. It became clear to me that while I was on hold, the VP was calling Lorrin's teacher to find out why this parent of a child who was not even in his school system was calling him. In my mind, I thought I was helping, and he was trying his best to be polite, but I think people were just afraid of us.

I hung up the phone and told Karissa that this was the reason kids like Lorrin do not go to the dances. Craziness! I went through similar battles to get her an ASB card so she would be allowed into the school dances.

Lorrin did go to the high school dance. She met a group of her friends who were seniors and had a blast dancing all night long. Much gratitude to Karissa.

The next thing that happened, I wasn't quite ready for. Lorrin was invited to the next dance with her new friends. Wow! My Lorrin, who was never supposed to live long enough to attend high school, was invited to go to the dance and hang out with seniors. The Homecoming Dance, I might add.

In the next few weeks I found out what started as a simple dance was becoming a huge ordeal. When I was in high school, we went to the Homecoming game, and after that, the dance. Today, it's a big deal. Karissa was informed about the Homecoming Dance protocol. I had no idea there even was a protocol. She told me that I should be getting Lorrin a corsage, hair extensions, and hours of prep before the dance. I don't ever remember spending hours on my hair before anything.

The Friday before the dance, I got a phone call from Ariel, one of the girls who was a new friend and who Lorrin had been having lunch with. She called to invite Lorrin to the pre-party at one of the girls' houses. I was very confused at first, trying to understand how I would get Lorrin to the party. It was made very clear that I was not invited—the invitation was for Lorrin and Karissa.

It was a bit awkward and I would have been offended if I wasn't so excited. For the first time, I really didn't have a hand in this. It was just happening. Lorrin was making friends, senior girlfriends. What could I say to that?

The event was on! Karissa took Lorrin to the special lunchtime event to vote for the Homecoming Court. Lorrin didn't show any interest in voting for the girls. She was, however, eager to vote for the boys who were nominated for Homecoming King. Is it important to mention that the boy she voted for won? Friday was the pep rally, and Karissa took Lorrin to that also. Friday evening we all went to the game—Sarah too!

Saturday morning started early and we had so much to do. I picked up the corsage; Karissa spent hours making hair clips. This was after spending a fortune on hair extensions for her up do. Sarah had stayed the night and was happy to help Lorrin get ready for the dance. We all participated. Sarah and I drove around town getting everything we needed. We ran in and out of the flower shop and extra stops to pick up more hair gel. My heart was full of excitement and feelings of joy. Each time I looked at Sarah, I was reminded that my daughter had a true friend. I could not love her any more—that just would not be possible.

As the dance grew closer, I was really starting to freak out. I had so many emotions. I was happy, protective, worried, excited, and overwhelmed with joy. Was I doing the right thing by sending my girl to a homecoming dance? Would the kids be nice to her? I was joyful one moment and then fearful and unsure the next.

As I was bathing her, I asked Lorrin, "Do you want to go to the dance? Is this your deal or mine? Are you ready to do this?" She blinked yes, yes, yes. Okay, this was the right thing to do.

It was a regular event. Karissa and Lorrin went to the pre-party and Karissa ended up helping the girls with their up-dos. Lorrin danced all night long with all the girls. A group picture was taken. They had a blast. Both girls came home exhausted and fulfilled.

Chapter 33

~ What Else Can I Do? ~
Fourteen Years Old

Sarah's Poem Friendship

Friendship is something better than best
It beats homework and all the rest
Friendship is sharing
It's caring
It's giggles and laughs
It's candy, it's blasts
Friendship is . . .
Friendship? Best/Friends

The Ketogenetic Diet

I got a call from the dietitian at the Children's Hospital of Los Angeles (CHLA). She phoned to tell me that she had an open bed for Lorrin to start a special diet that sometimes helps to stop the seizures. I thought this might be the right thing to do. What else was there? I agreed to it.

This meant we would spend four nights at CHLA and starve Lorrin into ketosis. Ten percent of people who are in ketosis see their seizures stop. It has been known since 1921 that if you starve someone into ketosis, it changes their body chemistry. For some reason, this can stop seizures.

In the 1940s, Dilantin and Phenobarb came onboard as prescribed medications. Most medical time and energy is spent researching newer drugs and utilizing Phenobarb and Dilantin. Not much time was spent on using the diet—until the Abrams family had a son named "Charlie" who had intractable seizures. In Mr. Abrams' research, he found the diet. He and his family were the ones who got attention focused back onto making the diet available for families. This is an entire story in itself.

The main reason that we hadn't tried the diet before now was that Lorrin's doctor thought that Lorrin wasn't strong enough to be on the diet. His exact words were, "She is too weak. It would kill her." So I didn't push it. For the most part, since the time Lorrin was put into a coma when she was three, she has maintained some kind of control. I'd like to add here that Lorrin never really was in control—meaning "seizure free"—but she has done pretty well until now.

A year ago, a year before her menses, she started struggling with being in a state of status seizures for no reason. Sure, at times after an illness or excess use of antibiotics she would have periods of complete seizure chaos, but that would pass. She started having random times when she would be in status for no apparent reason. Something was changing. There was much discussion about hormone changes that can cause havoc at this age. Some doctors want to medicate and some want to leave alone. Some thought medicating them into a coma was okay, especially for kids like my Lorrin. Not me.

Journaling

I know I can be extremely pessimistic. Sorry, shit happens. I am fueled by my pessimism to write. I write my truth. I am and was a broken mother who has been through hell. It would be a lie if I wrote this book pretending to be a sainted mother. I never was. I am as screwed up as the next person. I am a survivor who had no rules. Maybe writing this helps me heal. Maybe it will help you heal. And just maybe I am full of shit.

Someone said to me recently that by sharing my spiritual journey, I was helping others. She also mentioned that I would be full of shit if I talked like I was totally at peace spiritually. That would also not be believable.

So here is the truth of my state of mind. I hate some days for many days. For long periods of time, I hate being alive. Sometimes my love of God and higher understand-

ing of life kicks in and saves me. I can see the light in many things. This last month or two have put me into a tailspin with my beliefs. I hate my life today. There is a good reason to believe that tomorrow may be the same. My daughter is having long episodes of uncontrolled seizures for days at a time. It is exhausting and I am frightened.

Today we are home. We have made it past Christmas. I hate Christmas. Did I mention that? Lorrin has been on the diet for eight days. For Christmas Eve, she had life-changing diarrhea for me to clean. Yes, I bathed her and changed her sheets. Merry Fucking Christmas! I am in a bad mood. So the day starts like that. I drop everything that I could possibly drop. My back is out. I don't want to be awake. Everyone is calling. Oh, Merry Christmas! I don't want to talk to anyone. Lorrin is barely out of a coma. She is dead asleep all day. I can't blame her—I am in a horrible mood. I know the more I feel like shit, the worse the day will go. It is cyclical. It just keeps going round and round. I feel like shit, I drop shit, I cut my finger, bruise my leg, and drop some more shit. I love my life. Lorrin looks like she hates me. I feel like I hate her. I wish I could get a glimmer of what she is thinking. I hate being a caregiver. I hate my life. I glance down to a Better Homes and Gardens Magazine and I see "15 ideas for Caregivers." I immediately glance back and see what it really says: "15 ideas for Gardeners." I really am crazy.

The day after Christmas, I feel too much like shit to be in a good mood. I am never going to leave my house. Yeah, that is it. I will stay home and never shower again. That is my new fantasy. I have been working with my therapist to dream a new dream. I cannot come up with one single dream. I have given up. I am too tired to dream. I cannot imagine anything that would be safe enough to focus on. Too much shit has happened. I can only see death. I see no future. Maybe Lorrin will shit all over everything again? That will be more my speed. It is hard to come up with anything better than that for today.

I am at the point that I tell Lorrin I am done. I don't have any more to give. I am done. When will she be done? How can she keep going? She is killing me. Does she care? How can she not know that I am dying inside? Is there a plan? I hate writing this book. I am a fraud. I am a loser. These words come easy. I can only think of horrible things about my past. I cannot think a single kind thought when it comes to me and this book, my life exchange. I cannot remember a time when things were good. It is hard to breathe. I will not shower. I will not leave the house. I am never going out again.

January 13, 2009

I took Lorrin to a new pulmonary doctor. Dr. Kundell referred him to me because I was not happy with the Children's Hospital of Los Angeles Pulmonary Team. Dr. Kundell told me in his office on Friday that putting Lorrin on a ventilator during the evening when she slept would help her. He said it matter-of-factly and then got called out of his office. When he stepped back in, I was in tears. We had started this diet because she was so out of it from the seizures. Now that she was on the diet, she wasn't having seizures but she was still totally out of it. Now he mentions the "V" word. I was starting to buckle. The tears were flowing. I can't remember the last time he saw me crying.

Dr. Kundell and I have worked together for fourteen years. I know he is connected to Lorrin. As I sat there, I imagined the next ten parents in the waiting area who were with their sick children, longing for his coveted attention. Dr. Kundell is a Development Specialist, meaning he treats children who have all types of special needs. Frankly, the man is brilliant. And he has put up with me all of these years.

I sat there, up against the wall on my familiar perch in his office. I had sat in there many times, going over endless medical questions that as a parent I was never prepared to discuss regarding my child. Now, we are talking about a vent. I told him that I did not want a vent.

"You just plug it in. It's not that big of a deal," he said lightheartedly.

I didn't buy it. I said nothing, but I know my face said it all anyway.

"Are these your boundaries?" he asked.

"Yes," I said.

He continued talking. I didn't hear anything he was saying. I wasn't available for his conversation any longer. I could only think about the vent. I could no longer hear anything. I was crippled. Everyone said that it wasn't a big deal. To me, a vent was death. *Death.* I needed to leave.

I couldn't write the next sentence without first sharing with you how much Dr. Kundell means to me. He had cared for Lorrin since she was a year old. We woke him up all hours of the night while in the ER. He had been a doctor and father to Lorrin. He had been the smartest, gentlest, funniest, kindest man I know. I am forever grateful for his care and support during the most difficult times in my life. We laughed together and cried together. He was one of the best people I have ever met.

He suggested that I see this pulmonary doctor. "You will love him. He won't be afraid of Lorrin."

I told him I would go see him. We talked about doing a sleep study for Lorrin. That would really give us the information we needed to properly assess what was happening at night. Lorrin had started to require oxygen at night, and this is a huge set back. She has not been on O-2 for nine years. We agreed to do a sleep study. I was still panicky about even the discussion of a vent.

Not knowing what to do, I took Lorrin to visit her class at the high school. I went there directly from Dr. Kundell's office. She had now been on home school for a month. My heart was heavy. Maybe if I took her to school to see everyone she will feel better. I would feel better. We get there, but it was awkward.

All these beautiful handmade cards from her classmates decorated the classroom. There was one that caught my eye immediately. It was the letter "L" in pink tissue. Cool. The other was a red devil from a boy named Kyle. *Hurry back. We miss you.* I loved the devil thing. I laughed, but I wanted to cry. This was hard. Lorrin was semi-conscious—that is our new word for her. She could barely open her eyes. Everyone was as nice as ever.

When Lorrin was too sick to attend school, I felt many strange and confusing feelings of inadequacy, among other emotions. Somehow, I felt as though I should be sending her to school. The next minute, I felt as though I should keep her home. Did I have control over this? I knew deep inside that I didn't, but a part of me felt guilty that she was missing school. Almost as if she had been in school, things would be normal and would return to the way they used to be.

The next moment I felt as though school wouldn't be fair for Lorrin, her nurse, or anyone else involved. The reality of the situation was gut-wrenchingly painful.

Strange the way my body works. My gut and insides knew. I knew it was almost time. I had always known that the end was just around the corner. I had been lucky to share the love that Lorrin had given. I had been so lucky to experience all the joy that she shared. I had stolen time and I know that. I had been grieving for months. There was safety in silence, and now the "vent" word was said aloud.

I longed for a partner to help me make this decision. I needed help. It was hard to be a single mom. The physical demands were always hard. Being isolated, getting to the store when your kid was sick, running errands now that Lorrin had been home for a month was crazy. Her time was limited. I didn't want to take her out for bullshit errands like the grocery store. Nothing compared to the feelings I had while being forced to make life and death decisions.

I was so blessed and felt so honored and appreciated so much that I could bounce my painful feelings regarding Lorrin's life and death decisions off Karissa and Debbie. I would have been lost without them.

It was funny because yesterday there was a moment when Lorrin looked really good. I thought, *I don't want to change anything. She may be coming back.* Maybe this was just another hiccup. I had a glimmer of hope that she would return to her old self. We all missed her. We all waited for her eyes to open.

Friday evening, I was home with Lorrin. Karissa was working the graveyard shift. I didn't have a nurse. I was trying to swallow what was going on. Lorrin started to have seizures. She was having the most seizure activity since starting the diet. Her breathing was rapid. I was watching. I was trying not to react. She was having so many seizures I remembered why we had gone on the diet. Her body was shaking non-stop.

I decided to give her some Ativan. I was afraid to give the normal dosage because her metabolism was so jacked up. I gave her one milligram instead of two. Now, let me remind you that one milligram of Ativan would put me out for eight hours, and, I am sorry to say, I was more than twice her weight.

I gave her the Ativan. She continued to breathe fast and have more seizures. I was feeling pulled and confused about what to do. I wasn't going to take her to the hospital. I didn't want to do any life-saving measures, but Lorrin was struggling to breathe.

I sat her in her wheelchair. I watched as her body moved up and down. She was hyperventilating. I got the oxygen and put it on her. She didn't calm down. I needed to do something, nothing, I didn't know. I felt mad. I felt scared.

A few hours passed and Lorrin was still going. I gave her all her treatments. Her body was stiff as a board and her chest was rising as high as it went and moving fast. Any normal person would have passed out. Doctors have looked at her and immediately taken a blood gas level when she did this.

The blood gas level was a test to see if she was actually getting enough oxygen. While we were in the hospital in December and Lorrin started this breathing, the neurologist took one look at her and said, "We need to get a blood gas level." My comment was always, "She does this all the time."

Then last week in the emergency room the doctor suggested it after watching her breathe for a few moments. I made the decision to put her into her bed and give her more Ativan. I was concerned she would die. She could die just from this crazy moment. Really? Was it going to end like this?

I suctioned her over and over. I could hear junk in her lungs but I was unable to get to it. I wanted to scream. It was still in the early hours of the evening, around ten p.m. I was bored with this behavior, trying not to get sucked into the drama of what was happening. I was now getting the severity of the situation. Was she going?

I wanted to be compassionate, but mostly I was tired and pissed off. By four a.m., I wanted her to die. I felt like I was in a torture chamber. I couldn't imagine how she must have felt. I didn't even know if she was in her body at all.

I was tired, scared, mad, and wounded. I tried to sleep. I felt bad if I didn't try to suction her airway, but each time I did, I got nothing. I worried I would injure her lungs when I went down too far. Fuck. That was all I could say. I felt like I was in a torture chamber of hell. I hated this. I was FUCKED. I thought about the feelings I had for a brief moment earlier when Lorrin was doing better. I had a glimpse of her getting well. I was going crazy, no really, crazy. Who wouldn't be?

The next day came and I felt like shit. I was tired and cranky, but I needed to get up and give Lorrin her treatments. God forbid, she might get sick or even die if I didn't get those breathing treatments and medications in her. Like anything mattered anyway. I was crazy at this point. I felt so un-human. I tried to keep it together, but who was I kidding? She could go on this way for years. I had so much to look forward to.

Did I mention I needed to change her diaper, bathe her, and mix up her formula? I didn't even know if she was in her body. Maybe she was out of her body somewhere. I hoped so. I hated her today. I hated everything today. I went back to bed.

Chapter 34

When I went out with Karissa and Sarah and the dog, we all tag-teamed getting things together. Karissa and I were both controlling, always making sure things were done, and Sarah just loved to help. One day while driving in the van, all of a sudden Lorrin fell out of her chair. The top half of her body was flipped over the wheelchair side. I slammed on the brakes, laughing terribly hard. Lorrin rolled her eyes, and we all jumped to set her straight. I told Karissa that I thought she had strapped her in, and, of course, Karissa replied, "I thought you strapped her in."

What an exhausting week. I had readings with Ed and Lisbeth—they are both psychics and channelers that I have worked with for years. The readings helped by opening up another source of intuition that gave me validation about my own intuitive feelings and messages that I got from Lorrin. I was starting to feel a little better and more balanced. Lorrin also had a great weekend. When Lorrin did well, I generally do better. My attorney came over with her husband, and we all had dinner. She was really amazed how alert Lorrin was. Me too!

For a brief moment, I actually contemplated sending her back to school. Oh, except for her rash. A rash usually doesn't make it on the list of things to worry about with Lorrin. But since she had come home from the hospital in December, she has had some kind of rash over her chest area. It first started around her belly button. Then it moved up around her trach and then turned into hives. One day she had hives and the next it appeared to be gone with no rhyme or reason.

I saw the pulmonary doctor and he suggested I try Cortaid, and if that didn't work, he gave me a prescribed antibiotic. The Cortaid did nothing. I picked up the antibiotic from the pharmacy and put that on her. In four hours, the rash around her neck was gone. Almost immediately, a rash under her bra started to present itself. It was bright red and looked like it hurt like hell. Lorrin was flinching in pain any time you touched it. It looked ridiculously bizarre. The rash took the shape of a bra. It eventually started blistering as though her skin were being burned off.

I felt horrible for her and took her immediately to see a dermatologist. He said frankly, it looked like a contact rash. He wrote another prescription. He told me that if this didn't work, she would have to start IV antibiotics. We talked briefly about the interactions with all the medication that Lorrin was normally on and the adverse reactions this may cause. I picked up the ointment on Monday and gave it to her twice.

Tuesday started out to be a shitty day. Lorrin started doing this wrenching spitting and seizure thing. Oh, yeah, and her stomach was hard as a rock and full of air. Another day in the life.

Did I mention that I was giving a presentation to the Kiwanis Club in Thousand Oaks? This one was to raise awareness for the Ability Awareness Week that was taking place in two months at Lorrin's old middle school. I was speaking about children who have special needs in our community. I had no nursing help and had to bring Lorrin to the presentation. Part of me felt guilty about bringing her and the other part of me thought this is an opportunity for people to see what parents actually have to go through. Life happens. If my daughter wasn't so messed up, she would be in school right now. Lead by example.

While having lunch before my presentation, it was becoming apparent to me that Lorrin was going to start another of her cluster seizure episodes. *Do I take her while she was having a seizure to the bathroom, which was not accessible and was located in the lobby behind the hostess station?* It was noon and the lobby was full of people waiting to be seated. Everyone in this room acted as though nothing was happening. *Or do I just give her medication that hopefully would calm her down and try to make my presentation?* I choose to leave her where she was. I got out one of her anti-seizure medications while I ate my lunch and started drawing it up. I was giving her Verset today. It came in an IV vial and was normally given through an IV. I had to draw it out with a syringe and needle. Using the needle, I attempted to draw up the medication, a procedure that I was very accustomed to doing. It somehow exploded and spilt everywhere.

I administered what was left of it by putting it up her nose. I gave my presentation as Lorrin sat passed out and drugged in her wheelchair.

By the time I got her home, she was having seizures again. I gave her two milligrams of Ativan. *When do I worry?* The next day, on Wednesday, I gave her another dose of Ativan. Wednesday evening, I slept with her, and the bed shook all night, her body convulsing, twitching, and shaking. Her mouth contorting and spitting. I wanted the seizures to stop. I felt crazy. I wanted to drug her, I didn't want to drug her. I told myself one more seizure and I was going to give her more Ativan. I knew that if I did, I would ruin her day. Prioritize: lunch date with Kathy or Ativan for Lorrin? I fell asleep. I woke up after maybe ten minutes with Lorrin having another seizure. I had already given Ativan on Tuesday and again on Wednesday.

I worried. Fear set in. I decided to get up and give her Ativan at seven a.m. She shook some more for the next hour, then she finally rested. I canceled my plans. I was home.

Great, I would get much done. Lorrin woke up five hours later with more seizures. They were on again, not stopping. I gave her more Ativan. I gave her Ativan three times on Thursday. The nurse came for the evening—the insurance was covering nursing expenses for three nights a week. I didn't even want to talk.

I went to bed. I told her to wake me if things got crazy.

The next morning, I came downstairs feeling like I had not slept at all, although I knew I got at least a few hours in. The nurse told me Lorrin started having seizures at 4 a.m. Fuck! That was all I can say.

It was my plan to work the Festival of Abilities at the Aquarium of the Pacific in Long Beach, and stay at the Westin Hotel this weekend. The festival of Human Abilities takes place every January at the Long Beach Aquarium of the Pacific. It is an annual event that celebrated the creative spirit of people with disabilities. There was wheelchair painting and dancing, live music, signing choirs, art demonstrations, storytelling, service dog demonstrations, and other creative performances featuring people who have disabilities.

Jim and Chris Rohan, who publish the *Disabled Dealer Magazine,* have a booth every year and part of their booth is an adaptive pinball machine. They are dear friends of mine. Their son Bobby Rohan is married to my best friend, Ellen. I met Ellen and her daughter, Melody, when Lorrin was just three months old. Years later, I met Bobby while line dancing. Ellen read the *Disabled Dealer Magazine*, which featured an article about Bobby, who happens to be a quadriplegic. Bobby is always in the news because he's always doing something amazing and inspiring. After Ellen read the article, she said she'd really like to meet him. I introduced them, they got married, and we are all family.

It is important that I make a note that Bobby tattooed Lorrin's name on his arm. He was very inspired by her and felt that if it weren't for Lorrin, he would have never met Ellen.

When Lorrin's health started to decline, we had a tattoo party. Lorrin, of course, thought it was cool. To date, Lorrin's name has been tattooed on three different people. Ellen was going to get a tattoo with Lorrin's name on it too, but was sick on that day and couldn't. I also need to mention that Ellen and Melody's names were tattooed on Bobby's arm first.

The first time Lorrin played pinball was at the Aquarium a few years earlier. Five of us all stood by and watched her with wide eyes and anxious hearts as I strapped the adaptive switch to Lorrin's tiny palm. With her limited eye sight and minimal hand movement and control, none of us had much hope of her actually playing the game appropriately. I have worked with Lorrin since she was two years old with adaptive switches. What I have learned is to just let her have some time to get to know and feel the switch in her hand and push when she is ready. It's impossible to understand how overwhelming it is to have a switch thrown in your hand, especially for someone who has never used one before, and expect you to play or use it correctly. These things take time.

Lorrin hit the switch. We all cheered in support. Then she hit it again. No one took their eyes off the pinball machine. In twenty minutes, Lorrin was playing pinball. She was not doing it perfectly, but we all were witnessing a cause and effect attempt made by her. I know I had tears in my eyes, and I think Jim and Chris did also. I knew on that day that I would buy Lorrin a pinball machine. I worked with the court and got that expense covered as one of Lorrin's therapy and social emotional necessities. It changed our lives in many ways. For me it was the joy of knowing that my daughter could play a game with her peers and be motivated to enjoy something independently.

My weekend plans just got put on hold, as I sent the nurse home and gave Lorrin some more Ativan. I was really planning on being at the Aquarium and having a weekend full of inspiring and fun activities while seeing my friends. I felt really shitty. My face felt swollen and my heart and stomach were heavy. I was exhausted, but now I had to get my head around what was happening.

I paged the neurologist. The fellow called me. A "fellow" is the highest level of training before they become a doctor. She was brief. She told me that she would call me back when she got to the hospital.

I waited. I won't be going back to bed. I needed coffee.

The fellow called back and told me that I needed to take her to the ER. I asked if there was anything I could do at home. She told me that she cannot assess my daughter over the phone and she warned me that the neurologist said she would probably take her off the Ketogenetic diet. I felt pissed. She hadn't even seen her and wanted to take her off the diet. I didn't want to go to the ER.

I questioned myself. I felt so tired. I felt scared. I hated this game that we played when Lorrin's seizures wouldn't stop. I could fake it for a while. I kept on with my day and acted like it would be okay. Now, on the fourth day, I felt fear. It wasn't the fear of death. That seemed easier right now. It was the fear of life. Of Lorrin continuing to live in this way, living in a physical condition that was worse than she'd ever been. Fear of staying at the hospital—I hated that place. Double torture, seizures and the hospital.

My inner gut instinct told me there must be something I was missing. I knew there wasn't one medical opinion that suggested the ointment I had been putting on Lorrin's rash could have anything to do with this seizure activity. I knew there was no cause and effect, but there had to be some rationale.

At least my heart was counting on some kind of sense and/or explanation to this madness. Too much to ask?

So I started phone calls to Lorrin's pediatrician and the hospital to get the latest lab results. I wanted to look at Lorrin's blood work to see if that had any information. I could read her blood results. I'd been doing this too long. The results weren't in yet. I talked to the pulmonary doctor's assistant. I knew that I was doctor hopping, but I didn't want to go back to CHLA.

I got the pulmonary doctor to phone me. He suggested I take Lorrin to his hospital and admit her to the Pediatric Intensive Care Unit. I had never been admitted there. I longed to stay home and didn't want to go. I also knew that this doctor was new to Lorrin and he had been taking a great deal of care in treating her. This was critical right now. I agreed to come.

I took a deep breath and accepted that this was how this day was going to be. I canceled my hotel reservations. Packed the car for who knew how many days. Lorrin continued to have seizures, even after her seven a.m. dose of Ativan. I was feeling panicked now.

I bathed her. I wanted her to look her best for the fight that was ahead. I needed to look my best. I needed to be in the best place I could be to deal with the long hours and sleepless nights that were ahead.

The first thing I would like to say is that the staff in the ICU in Tarzana were the nicest. The entire hospital experience was an enormous difference from the attitude I'd had at the last hospital stay. Wow, how refreshing to be treated with kindness. We were actually treated as though we were human. It could be really simple. That was all I had left right now—my humanness. My hope and dignity were not with me in this moment. No one could change my experience, or my life as it appeared right now.

To simply be kind. It really meant a great deal. My daughter was still alive and she was a soul who was doing important work. Maybe it didn't look like she had much value on the surface, but give her a moment. She would tug at your heartstrings. It was just her way.

After we settled in the ICU, the nurse said to me, "You are really cool! Most parents of kids similar to Lorrin are kinda nutty and pains in the asses. We were expecting the worst when we heard you were going to be admitted."

I get that. I told her it was because this lifestyle can make you nuts. I was isolated, tired, looked over, broken, single, and had too many wrinkles. I didn't have time to get my hair or nails done. God forbid a massage.

I also think the only reason that Lorrin was still alive was because I am a control freak. Being controlling was part of what made me a good caregiver. I could only control the surrounding environment, not what was happening to my child. I controlled what I could while my heart was being ripped out. The irony was that I loved the shit out of Lorrin and have sacrificed my existence to keep her comfortable.

I continued to feel puzzled and pleasantly amazed at how nice everyone was. Lorrin was admitted without any problems. The ICU staff was helpful and supportive. What a huge difference. The pulmonary doctor came in right after we got there. He told me that it was possible that Lorrin was at the end stages of her life.

In my gut, I know it to be true.

He had only treated Lorrin once before. He told me there was usually an insult that started a decline in health. I was trying as we talked to remember what happened that started this decline. I immediately remembered the horrible bout of pneumonia that Lorrin had after her thirteenth birthday. She was sick for weeks and almost died. It was now making sense to me that she hadn't really bounced back. She used to be the bounce-back kid.

We chatted a little about Lorrin's prognosis. We agreed to treat the seizures. I felt confused about her next steps. Were they heading towards life or towards death? I thought she might make it to her fifteenth birthday party, and now, after watching her body struggle, I wasn't sure.

The chaplain was sent to visit us. Now what could I say to that? She just showed up. I felt very confused. No one asked me if I wanted a visit from the chaplain. Was that offensive or sweet? How was I to take that? I wondered if the doctor had sent her because he was uncomfortable with my tears. I was not a blubbering baby, but my kid was messed up, and I was tired and confused. I was human underneath all my toughness.

I really wanted what was best for her. What was that? Does someone know? How did I make the next decisions? Someone tell me the rules. After four days of drug-induced coma at home from the Ativan, when do we intervene with a new direction? No pressure. Just watch your kid's body convulse out of control for a few days. No worries. I was a veteran at this, but things were just getting really concerning right now.

Did doctors really know what message it sent to a patient when they send for the chaplain? I am a person who would like to be asked, "I know you're upset and your child is really having difficulties. Can I call the chaplain for you? Would you like to call a friend? Would you like to ask more medical questions? Do we need a doctors' meeting?"

There are so many gray areas. Please, remember I was tired. I had been fighting this battle for four days before we got here, not counting the fifteen years prior to this.

I learned from the staff that the chaplain visits all new patients. When I heard that, I started laughing so hard. I told them about the things that had been running through my head. The last time a chaplain came to see Lorrin, she was expected to die. I had no idea this was hospital protocol. It would've been nice if that chaplain would've told me that. If I'd known it was protocol I would've been able to actually listen to what was being said, not staring into her eyes the whole time wondering if the doctor had sent her because I was crying or my kid was dying.

During my stay in ICU, I wondered what made this horrible admission a bit easier. Was it the staff? They had been very caring and kind. Was I a baby? Did I need my hand held? I think just knowing that the medical community had taken the time to treat my daughter with kindness was comforting. I felt as though we were being treated as though she were one in a million. Not the millionth medically-involved kid that had been admitted today. Lorrin was important. I was important.

Every time Lorrin woke up from the last dose of Ativan, she went into a seizure. We gave her more Ativan. The pit in my stomach was heavy. The writing was on the wall: "You're screwed!" I settled down for the evening. I found the spot for Nikki to toilet outside the cafeteria. Hospital food was always scary. Should I eat shitty food or no food? Choice, no choice.

I thought about what was happening. When she comes off the Ativan and goes right into a seizure, I knew I was in trouble. That had been happening for five days now. The hope that I had for any tiny bit of relief is minimal. It was like a feather in the wind, the tiniest amount of opportunity to give hope to. My entire body resisted Lorrin living in a constant seizure. I just couldn't get my brain around that kind of an existence for her. No way, no way in hell.

Saturday, she woke up, her eyes open, and I felt an enormous amount of relief. Within the next hour, she started having more seizures. I felt like my entire body sucked into the earth. The very pit of my soul ached. My heart went numb. My hope was gone. I couldn't live this way.

If this continues, I would give her too much Ativan and kill her. I was dying inside, watching her life crumble. Just last week, I was considering sending her back to school. It was the biggest mind screw. How could any mother be sane in these circumstances?

The doctors told me that if I gave her too much Ativan, she would die. But if I allowed her to have seizures, she would die. What a fine line. I always just envisioned her leaving her body because she stopped breathing from pneumonia or something, not having seizures 24/7 until her entire body just expired from the exhaustion of it all.

The night wound down. I was alone, the lights were dim. The ICU was slow. I didn't want to share this time with anyone. I try to lie down, play Scrabble on my iPhone until I can drift into a sleepless night. I tossed and turned. This song kept going off in my head. I wanted to hear it. The song was "Sailing" by Rod Stewart. I tried to get it out of my head but it kept going off in my mind. I finally downloaded it on my iPhone. I listened to it. The lyrics hit too close to home.

I listened to this song over and over. I cried harder and harder. I got up and held Lorrin. I sat up with her most of the night on the rocker. She was fourteen years old, but I still held her as though she were a baby. I rocked her and held her tight. I finally went to sleep at four in the morning.

The next day, I crawled into bed with Lorrin. I talked to her.

She woke up after days of Ativan that has been in her system to stop her body from shaking. She opened those beautiful blue eyes. My heart sank. I wondered if I would ever see her open her eyes again. Her long eyelashes were prettier than any sunset I had ever seen.

I talked to her. I asked her the same question that I had when she'd had her last pneumonia. "Lorrin, are you ready to go? Are you ready to leave your body?"

For the first time ever, she blinked hard and tight. I was relieved and sickened. I asked her again, and she replied with another confirmation of yes. I asked her twenty times in different ways. As I held her, my mind raced.

Chapter 35

~ *Hope* ~

Eric was working on the computer another time with Lorrin. I was working on other things and walked into the room. Lorrin was just sitting there. I asked what they were playing. Eric said that she was playing a game where she had to hit the targets. She had hit them all but one and she refused to hit the last target. She looked at me and then hit it. She smiled. She was rotten, my child!

What is hope? I had returned home from a visit in the ICU and had spoken to Lorrin's pediatric doctor. We talked about neurologists in general and shared thoughts that it would be nice if they could give parents some hope. Is it wrong to offer hope? Doctors and hope are not two words that work well together. Can we change that? Should we? With all that we know today, our mantras, vision boards, *The Secret*. How can we discount hope? Didn't Bernie Segal open that idea long ago when he wrote, *Love, Medicine and Miracles*? Is it inappropriate for doctors to allow room for hope?

So, what is hope? What do most of us hope for? We hope to be married, to have families, to win the lottery. Is hope real? Is it a fantasy? If we didn't have hope, would we even get out of bed?

I go for hope. I will live today in the mindset that there is so much hope. I hope for a day to embrace, love, and be loved. I hope that today I will not have to give Ativan. I have hope for us all. I have hope for world peace.

Today I have hope that my daughter's brain will not need to be knocked out and her eyes won't be dilated from excessive medications. I have hope that she will be peaceful today.

I start with myself. I have hope for life. Today.

I will wish you all hope.

Maybe I should focus on simple hopes and stay with that.

I now wish that I had been documenting these last weeks. I didn't because I have been so busy. I was going crazy trying to pull things together for Lorrin's Quinceañera. I was barely afloat. I was wading in the water.

James told me that I was like a duck, swimming smoothly on top and paddling like crazy underneath. Oh, my God. That was total bullshit. I was a swan! And truth be told, I was barely afloat. I was paddling endlessly more so than ever. I had not realized this until today.

James. What can I say about James? He was an angel sent from heaven. He and Karissa are carrying me. I kept asking Karissa, "Am I being weird? Am I okay? Cause you are acting weird, and I just didn't know if you are worried about me or if I am freaking out and I don't even realize it."

Karissa responded as usual: "I am feeling a heaviness in my heart and I know you are having a hard time also."

It was surreal. Lorrin needed my support right now. I didn't have time for do-overs. I wanted to do this with grace and dignity, but I also wanted to scream and cry. So many mixed emotions of fear— and also of hope for a future.

I wanted to write about Karissa and tell of her beauty. But this chapter is about James.

Earlier in the week, I told James that I needed a few days to not speak. I needed to take a break from us and not talk to him. He lives in England and I live in the US, and we had been talking two to three hours a day. We met a year ago for the first time when he came to visit his sister who lived across the street. He returned nine months after that. We spent some time together and really got to know each other. I think the first time we felt connected, but realized how far apart we were from each other. But this last trip something happened. He returned home a month ago. He had never made a pass at me and we had never even kissed. I wondered if he was attracted to me.

He said he didn't realize his feelings for me until he was leaving for the airport and then he couldn't stop talking about me. We have been on the phone every day since.

Wednesday evening, I was feeling so many crazy thoughts. Immensely happy that he was in my life and devastatingly sad that Lorrin was leaving. Not truly feeling guilty, but definitely feeling a strange dynamic of what was happening. I felt unstable and weak. I asked him to give us a few days without communication. Just to hear him say my name had been enough to get me through my thoughts of pain in the moment.

He is kind and gentle. He said, "Karen, of course, sweetheart. You just let me know what you need."

I felt like I couldn't breathe and wanted to cry. I didn't want this to be who James and Karen became. I wanted to keep a piece of me and my grieving separate. I couldn't stop thinking that this might become a love affair. We said good night gently. I didn't feel afraid—I had so many other things to think about.

I had so much to be angry about. We were just mature adults trying to make sense out of bad timing and chaos. I was starting to realize that I was feeling so much for him. He had been saying loving and kind words to me since the day that he confessed his feelings. Now I was dangerously close to falling madly for him.

I woke on Thursday and saw the phone next to me. I had an entirely new relationship with the phone for calls, the cell phone for texting, and my computer for emails. I tease James that I should take my computer out to dinner. It was my new companion. I had never been so attentive to phone calls. When I spoke with James, my world changed.

It was three p.m. and I was feeling a bit empowered that I had not grabbed the phone and called him. No, it wasn't hard, but I thought a lot about my feelings. I made my list of things I had to do for the party, which was now only weeks away. I wanted to go back to bed, but I seriously needed to get some things done. I had not left the house since before Christmas.

I got a nurse so I could meet with my attorney and pick up a margarita machine for the party. I got into my car and felt a very weird sensation. I felt as though I had been in a coma. I don't know for how long—a week, days, months. Life had been throwing me some curves and I was managing, but at what cost? My heart was racing, my skin gray. Lorrin looked like shit.

Usually driving in my mid-life crisis convertible cheered me up.

A few years ago, I had a blind date. I was so sick of driving around in my handicap van with a ramp, I bought a 350Z and a new pair of boots. I immediately felt happy. A sports car can cure a ton of shit. I felt great while I was driving it and I loved how fast it was.

I cracked up at the way other cars treated me. Remember, I had been driving an adaptive van with a ramp for ten years or so. I loved the way other drivers behaved. I had such a dichotomy to compare it with. Some drivers were nicer than they would have been towards me in the van, and other people try to race me. I just loved driving fast. I usually listened to country-western, but when I was in my car, I was into rock 'n roll. LOUD! It made me so happy.

I totally get that it was shallow. I was driving in my car, top down, music blaring. I was on my way to Vons to pick up more baby wipes for my kid who just had another attack of diarrhea.

Today I was running many errands. Big day out of the house for Karen. I found it frustrating that I couldn't connect to any music that suited me. I took a deep breath and felt this lost feeling.

I said to myself, over and over, "What the hell have I been doing? Who is this guy?" I had been making a total fool of myself. Writing all my deepest thoughts to him. Trusting him to keep them dear to his heart. Not for a moment would I ask for his heart. I only appreciated the time that had yet to be ruined by some stupid bullshit insecurity thing that may arise in me. I had been going on like nothing was happening while secretly spending hours emailing stuff that I didn't tell anyone. I was thinking to myself that I had truly lost my mind. I wanted to ask Karissa. I wanted to phone her but she was tired. I could only imagine how hard it was for her to live with me, her job, and deal with what was happening to Lorrin.

I was now walking the aisles looking for stuff at Bed Bath and Beyond and saying out loud to myself, "What the hell have I been doing?" I was really out of my mind. I thought that I had been coping but really I had gone MAD!

Oh, I had made a fool of myself. I wanted to go back and reread my emails to him. I was so embarrassed. I continued to think aloud and talk to myself. He still seemed to like me. I was so confused as to what was happening to my psyche. I was sure that I looked just fabulous walking around the store with only four hours sleep over the last two nights, talking aloud to myself as I shook my head.

I got a devilish grin every time I started thinking about why I was so crazy, was this love? His voice. Oh, my God, his voice. I smiled. What was I thinking, writing all that gibberish to him? I didn't want to be that person. Crazy.

Back to smiling again. Couldn't wait to talk to him. Still thinking of him, even though I was taking a break from talking to him.

I got my Margaritaville Machine. Ouch, $330. It was for the party. Concentrate on the party. Let's get to the party.

I was now driving fast—couldn't find a good rock 'n roll song and still thinking of him. Surely, this was much better than calling him. I was a goner. I was now desperately trying to find out where I could find a CD called *Dream Harder*. James kept telling me about it and how wonderful it was. He has different tastes in music than I do.

So I was a big girl, not calling him, spending the day looking for a CD to listen to the music he liked. I was at Best Buy now, which was not on my list of things to do in the hour I had to see my attorney.

As I walked into Best Buy, my iPhone vibrated. I got it out of my purse to read a Facebook request that said, "Sweetheart, would you mind if I put that you and I are in a relationship? It may stop unwanted female attention. Or I can change my picture?"

Now, this was the kind of stuff that he did that just drove me crazy. I was now laughing at Best Buy, searching for some CD from some band whose name I didn't even know.

I reply, "What on earth did you expect? Your picture is of you standing in front of your motorcycle in shorts, no shirt! If you want to put on your profile that you are taken, brilliant! If I can have you, fabulous!" Now I was really laughing. I was in a relationship with a man who lived in another country. It was Facebook-official.

Within minutes, I got an email from Facebook, asking me to approve that Jim Spicer was in a relationship with Karen Kain. Really? Never had I thought this would happen to me.

Oh, by the way, did I mention? My daughter was dying? I was planning a party for a hundred people and my whole family was coming out.

I was really going to lose my mind. Sheer comedy at this point. Still couldn't stop thinking of him. Damn. He was so under my skin.

I was really trying to stay focused as I drove to my attorney's office. I hadn't eaten and had very little sleep. I realized what was happening. I had lost four pounds this week. No one would be happier than me to lose ten pounds. This was going to be a long haul if I kept this up. I needed to take care of myself. I promised Lorrin. Sure, I had had a massage. Yesterday. It actually made me feel worse. Or maybe just reminded me that I was attached to a body. I couldn't say.

So many feelings were flying around. Right now my life was like a whirlwind. How could this be?

Life didn't get any weirder. The fact that I was forty-six and had just been asked to have a relationship with Jim Spicer, just makes for good writing. I can't deny how happy I felt to be in a relationship. No worries about the large mass of water between us.

How funny, the way we feel about the simplest acts. The power of Facebook. Encouraging James' relationship with me. How simple, how sweet. It was times like that I thought of the little things in life that could become huge at any given moment. It was like the tear as it rolled down your face. Something so small could mean so many things.

It was so beautiful to shed the first tear. I was a professional crier. I could go months on end without crying, so when I did cry, it could be overwhelming. I felt at times that if I cried, I would never stop. So I was afraid to cry. Karissa and I spoke of this just this week. Yes, we need to take care of ourselves. We need to ground ourselves. We need to cry. She said I was just holding it in for fear of what might happen if I felt, if I let go, if I cried.

I had become so accustomed to monitoring my feelings and the energy that was in my body, that when I knew that I was about to cry, I got a feeling, a sense of what my body was feeling. How was my body reacting? Where was the emotion coming from? Was it my emotion or someone else's? After fifteen years of communicating without words with Lorrin, I was very sensitive to people and their thoughts and emotions. I took note.

When my eyes welled up and became moist, I waited in anticipation of that first tear. The first sign of release, it was so poetic. I thought about it. It was so romantic.

I think that is why we love romantic movies so much. When actors cry, we watch and believe for that moment that it's really happening. We can imagine that we are them.

I often watch myself cry in the mirror. I've had years of practice. To actually feel the emotions that are surfacing is so moving. Tears of joy are all the better.

So I took on the day. I felt like a teenager. What was so bad about that? How wonderful was it to feel encouraged, loved at age forty-six.

Did I mention my daughter was dying?

Alas, I digress. Back to the trip to my attorney's office. We were in this small room. Loye and I laughed. I was safe with her. She was a rock for me. She was heaven-sent. She told me last time we saw each other that she wanted to talk at conferences about "When you fall in love with your clients," referring to me and Lorrin.

We could do business, my will, Lorrin's DNR, and laugh about the latest crazy things that she and her husband had done. I told her that I realized I wasn't in the right state of mind. I hadn't slept. I couldn't eat. I was trying to focus and be safe. I told her that I thought I should start smoking pot to help me sleep.

Loye shook her head. "No, I don't think so."

I was thinking to myself, *Maybe. I also told her that we were having a tattoo party next weekend.* "Do you want a tattoo?" I asked.

I told her about getting one of me with Lorrin on my back, both of us mermaids. Karissa was getting an angel with Lorrin's name on it. Bobby Rohan was getting Lorrin's name on his arm. We continued to laugh in her office. I loved chatting with her. She was brilliant. What an amazing lady.

She asked about my James. I lit up. He would come when it was time. When Lorrin left her body, I would leave town. I would go see him. I would take time to heal. I would be okay.

We said our goodbyes.

I took off to the department store, focusing on my driving, making sure that I was being safe. I knew I should be home, but my mind wouldn't sit still.

I was thinking about James, Karissa, Lorrin, and my family coming. Bring it on.

Back to thoughts of James. I was on a mission to find a long coat to wear to England that would keep me dry and warm. And I needed a pair of really hot boots. Maybe two pairs.

I shopped, and in my mind, I fantasized about a trip to England. A distraction from what was actually happening. I tried to act like all was normal. Yeah, planning a party for my daughter that could end up being her funeral.

Oh, God, maybe she wouldn't die. I would have to deal with that possibility also. The mind and the way it worked kept me constantly in a state of fear and full of endless scenarios. I had a shopping cart full of coats that I wanted to try on. Oh, how I could use Barbara now to help me. She had such a fashion eye. She was always up on everything. How did she find the time? I was pushing the cart and needed to go upstairs. There it was—the elevator.

An elevator means many things to many people. To me it has been my vehicle to get to the first and second floors at the malls. Today, it triggers me. I never take the elevator when I'm alone. Only when I am with Lorrin. I was going to cry. The reality of her not being with me was overwhelming. I was eager and scared. I grabbed the coats out of the cart and rode the escalator.

I was afraid I may have forgotten the price I was going to pay, living without my child. The price I paid these last fifteen years. The stares. Of course, no one ever wanted to get into the elevator with Lorrin. God forbid, they might feel something. Pity, disgrace, sadness. Everyone felt so safe. This won't happen to me. But it does. It happens every day. Kids end up compromised in wheelchairs and parents' lives are changed forever. Kids die!

I took the escalator and reminded myself that I was planning a future. I was going to live. I just might bungee jump. Travel the world. Have sex. Stay in hostels.

I wanted to travel with a single backpack, not the tons of luggage that I had to drag everywhere. I wanted to know the world and all that it had to offer.

Did I mention the sex thing? I wanted to sleep all day. I wanted to do nothing and be okay with it. I wanted to read great novels. I wanted to have a partner that I could talk to, make love to, and travel with. I wanted to cry until I vomited.

I bought two jackets. Next stop was Boot Barn. I needed some hot biker boots. James had a motorcycle. This was so sexy. He was a great driver, he told me. He had been riding for many years. The fact that it scared me to death made me want to do it. I wanted to be on the back of his bike. I wanted to live. I wanted to live without fear.

I told him the same thing each time—I was more afraid of falling off the bike and living than falling off and dying. That was a true statement. Being on the back of a motorcycle was the most profound feeling. I was so afraid that I could only think about falling off every moment. It kept me present with what was going on in that moment. There were many things that we did that helped to ground us, and be present riding a motorcycle must be right up at the top.

So I got two pairs of boots. One for riding on the back of his motorcycle. They happened to be Harley Davidson boots. They were totally hot, in my opinion. I found out later that James was a Kawasaki guy.

I loved that we had this to banter about. It was really all about how hot the boots were, not about who made them. The fact that we could go back and forth about it was just a benefit.

I bought another pair with a heel, but I could still walk in them. I couldn't wait to see him. I wanted to walk the rainy streets of England, holding his hand. He was tall, which was super sexy.

I had asked God for a partner. I thought I was very specific. I asked for someone who was funny, tall, smart, well-read, open emotionally, strong, open spiritually, liked to camp, and enjoyed nature.

Note to self: next time when asking for a cute boyfriend, be country-specific. Maybe this was complete divine intervention. I wasn't sure if James lived in the US and was close by that we would've had the time to get to know each other as we did. Over the last thirty days, we talked on the phone two to three hours a day. Crazy, I know. I hated talking on the phone. We talked until his phone battery went dead, then we texted, Facebooked, and emailed.

Once I got home, I tried on my jacket, thinking of when I'd get to see him in person. Kiss him. Oh, I couldn't wait. I was scared to death. I was so tired and couldn't eat, couldn't sleep. I watched a few Quentin Tarantino movies—James' favorite. I remembered they were violent. I watched some vampire movie that was horribly gross, and then Pulp Fiction.

He liked random guy stuff. I could see the reference to other countries to be somewhat of a concern to me. James was so gentle. He never made me feel stupid for my blatant ignorance of world history, geography, and culture. I could talk endlessly about needles, medications, hospitals and meditation. But where the hell was the UK?

One night I used Google Earth to see exactly where he lived. First, I was shocked about how much water was between us. James made reference to England as being a tiny island, but I didn't realize where exactly England, Scotland, and Ireland were. I told James that I was stalking him via Google. I assured him I also was checking out Russia. Boy, was it huge! I also had a huge interest in Greece, Egypt, and Italy. Who didn't want to go to Italy? *Could I possibly be attracted to him because he is far away, or foreign, maybe both?* Was that bad? How did relationships start? I really should be doing something useful, like taking care of Lorrin and cleaning the house. Or how about getting ready for the party?

The phone rang. I was confused why people love this Pulp Fiction movie. I couldn't believe how long it was. I thought it was over, and yet it played on.

My friend called and said, "Hey, Karen, I forgot about coming over tonight." I was in a daze. Who? What? What day was it? Oh, hi, Joe. I remembered he emailed me a note earlier and asked if he could stop by tonight. I read it like I did most of my mail. Probably at the time I was searching for a note from James. I remembered reading it and thinking that I would get back to him. I actually emailed him, knowing he smoked pot. I asked him if he thought that might help me. I told him of Lorrin's condition and how hard it had been for me to rest.

Now that he was calling me, talking to him reminded me of the coma I had been living in. I really was in a time warp. I was lost to what was going on in the outer world. Now that I had figured out who I was talking to and what day it was, and yes, I wanted him to come over. I was trying to act like I knew what I was doing. In my mind, I was thinking that I had been living in a bubble. I was obsessed with a guy who happened to be in a different country halfway around the world. I was in a time warp.

Joe was a friend from long ago. He was a really nice man. Very good looking. He worked on my house for almost a year. I saw him every day. My girlfriend told me that he was the hottest guy in high school, but I couldn't remember him. I loved chatting with him. He had a huge heart. I couldn't find myself attracted to him. Maybe because he was so close by, so available. Who knew how it worked? What was really important was that he brought me some medical marijuana. OMG, yeah, I asked for some pot. I was desperate. I needed something to help me sleep that wasn't going to send me into a coma and keep me from caring for Lorrin. I had never liked smoking pot. Yes, I tried it. So many of my friends loved it.

Joe was so nice he also brought me a pipe. He was a total gentleman. He only stayed an hour. I was excited and nervous. I couldn't wait to try it. My heart had been racing for weeks now. I could feel it fluttering out of my chest. Was I having a heart attack? Please don't revive me! That was all I can say about that. My chest was so heavy. I tried to finish *Pulp Fiction*. It kept going. My heart was hurting. I decided to run upstairs and smoke my pot.

I went upstairs, shut the bedroom door, open the window, and find my lighter. I had no idea how much was enough to start with. I tried a puff. I tried another. I didn't know how much people smoked. I was home alone. What was going to happen? I went downstairs and watched every step that I took. Wow, it felt really interesting. I was observing every breath I took. I felt kind of let down a little bit, gently.

I went into Lorrin's room to check on her. I told her, "Lorrin, I got stoned."

She was so over me. I was giggling to myself. Not the giggles, just chuckling to myself for trying it. I wondered why this was illegal.

I was relaxed. I was hoping now that I could go lie down and sleep. Rest my mind, rest my body, rest my soul. I hopped in bed. I felt her. I wanted to relax and I was relaxed. But now I wanted to call James. It was too early. He had no idea that I found something to smoke. I knew he smoked pot. It kind of worried me. I was desperate. I didn't want to go to the doctor and get a prescription that I wouldn't be able to take.

I was relaxing. Oh, I gotta call him. You would think after a month of calling James I would have memorized his phone number. No. I had to get my cell to get his number off it and called him from my home phone. We had 253 minutes left to my plan. I hopped into bed and the phone rang. He picked up. His voice was sexy, that morning voice. I could hear that he was happy to be awakened. He loved when I called him in the morning. I loved to know that he was all mine, in bed paying only attention to my words. His day was about to start. I could make or break his day by a gentle hello. It was my Friday, his Saturday morning. I woke him at seven a.m. Poor guy.

"Hello," he said in his groggy voice. I heard the sheets toss as he settled in to a comfortable position. One that we have both gotten used to, phone on cheek. I laughed and told him I got stoned.

"What?" he asked.

"I got stoned."

"With who?"

"By myself."

"Brilliant!"

I was so happy he was pleased. It's on! We chat about the crazy irony in life.

I could feel every cell in my body. I was feeling each breath. I felt peaceful. For the first time in I didn't know how long. My heart was not racing and I was relaxed.

We giggled. As much as I wanted to talk, I wanted him to speak. I wanted to hear everything he had to say.

"Karen, I am so happy for you. You need to relax."

We talked until his phone went dead. It was never enough. I wanted to talk more. I kept the phone nearby and waited for our next conversation.

He called me the next morning early and woke me up. He always told me that he loved my morning voice. I would never get out of bed.

We talked again about the night before. Then he said, "Karen."

My heart sank when he said my name.

He told me how he felt about me. About the day we met. About the time we had apart and how he thought about me. I wanted to cry. I had never heard this before from anyone in my entire life. We talked more about our first thoughts of each other. I loved to hear it. Tell me again.

Of course, the phone went dead. Now I felt so good. Even though I had only gotten about four hours sleep, I couldn't sleep or concentrate. I ran upstairs and smoked a little bit more. I was probably smoking one-tenth of what a normal person would. That was perfect for me. I needed to sleep. I went back downstairs and got into bed with Lorrin. I felt her. The world slowed for a moment. I was really in a huge place of peace. I lay next to Lorrin, on my back. I closed my eyes and felt the wind coming through the curtains. I dozed for a moment, and then something started to happen. Each breath took me deeper. I could feel layers falling off me. I was sinking into sleep—or a dream state. I loved it. *Oh, no, don't think, go back to relaxing.*

I heard Lorrin's voice. "Mom, relax. This is what I'm telling you about. Mom, relax, be free."

I saw all these images come to me. The sun, a feeling of enlightenment, came over me. I felt clarity. This huge energy enveloped me. My body was light. If I had a better gist of what really happened, maybe I could describe it more clearly. I can only try to share how I felt. For the first time in probably fifteen years, I felt free. I felt present. I felt beautiful. Then it happened; I felt this enormous veil breaking. I immediately felt all the pain, anger, and frustration lift from my body. For the last fifteen years, I've had to put on knight's armor. Armor for the battle. The battle to help Lorrin, take care of her. The battle against doctors, hospitals, medical equipment, lawyers, teachers, strangers and their stares, and comments, not to mention Lorrin's father Tom and my family dynamics. The battle to make the right decisions. To stay up late, caring for her, when I'm dying inside. The battle to keep up a pace of health care that no single person could possibly endure. In one moment the armor fell off my broken body. WOW! Then I saw, heard, and smelled a vision. I got a message or felt it, I don't know. I heard, "James and I are going to write books together. James has to be at the party. He will forever be depressed and feel a great loss if he doesn't come and be part of a very powerful time in my life. James needs to be there. You will write together. He will come."

I knew in that moment that James was the one. He had been telling me time and again how he felt about time. He told me the very first time he phoned from England, "I just feel that if I don't come back and get to know you, I will be making a mistake of a lifetime." He told me his fingers were shaking and he had not eaten and was nervous.

Then he asked, "Would you be open to having coffee with me and seeing if we could get to know each other?"

He had met Lorrin and knew enough about me to know my baggage, or at least the obvious baggage. He could never know of my guarded heart and eternal disappointment in my failed marriages. He could see how hard it would be to be a mother of a child with enormous physical challenges. He could see my broken heart I thought was hidden.

My eyes opened. I felt this huge wave of elation. James was the man for me. I was falling in love. I could trust him. He had melted my heart. I had to let him in. It had happened. We were in love.

I called him. I wanted to share my new clarity. I found my cell phone to get the number from and grab the home phone to make the call. An unfamiliar voice came on and said that my minutes had been used up. I laughed. We talked for 253 minutes in twenty hours. Who does this? I totally trust the timing of this. I needed time to think.

So I emailed him. I wrote him another two-page emotional dump. I started with something like this, "James, our relationship has changed. You need to be here for the party." I told him I was out of minutes and to please follow his inner compass and find out what he knew was true in his heart. "I know you are afraid, James, but please follow what is inside your heart."

I am so blown away. It made so much sense. We would write books together. We were meant to be together. I knew he would be here. I knew it would work. I had no worries. Everything was going to be perfect. Wow! How did Lorrin do this?

Chapter 36

~ *Quinceañera* ~
Fifteen Years Old

During the last year of Lorrin's life, it was clear that she wasn't going to make it to twenty-one. We always had people at the house and often there would be some type of drinking going on. I would put my finger in my drink and tap it on Lorrin's tongue. She didn't like rum, but she loved red wine and tequila. When I put tequila on her tongue, she smiled. James called her a drunk. Lorrin winked a rotten wink at him, and we all laughed.

In parts of Latin America and elsewhere in communities of immigrants from Latin America, a *Quinceañera* is the celebration of a girl's fifteenth birthday. This birthday is celebrated differently from any other birthday, as it marks the transition from childhood to young womanhood. The celebration, however, varies significantly across countries, with celebrations in some countries taking on, for example, more religious overtones than in others.

In January, when Lorrin told me she was ready to leave her body, I knew she meant it. I was full of conflicting emotions. It didn't take me long to do what I always do and plan something that would make us both happy. Lorrin was to turn fifteen in three months. We had talked about it for some time: "A Quinceañera Celebration." Lorrin loved parties. She loved the attention. In this case, I have to say it had much to do about the grandiose dress.

I had always known and tried to prepare for the simple fact that Lorrin's body would not last as long as mine. The last two years were showing me her health was failing. It was a horrible moment when we all sat in the kitchen and Debbie said, "Lorrin doesn't smile anymore." My head turned to her and I understood this simple, obvious truth.

I knew it, everyone could simply see it, but it was never given a voice. Those innocent words cut me into pieces. My mind raced. I needed to support Lorrin. What was I to do? Keep pushing her? Send her to school each day so I could get a break? What was the right thing to do? Questions filled my head. If I kept pushing, would she push herself? Was it fair to ask more of her? Was she really done?

I needed and wanted to do this stage of her life gracefully. The writing was on the wall now with Lorrin's earlier confirmation. I could only do one thing— create a distraction. Get Lorrin to her fifteenth birthday party. Get her excited and motivated to live. In my head, that meant one thing: get her the biggest dress she could imagine.

I'm not sure if I was actually afraid to focus on her leaving her body. I was, on some levels, already ready. Her failing health was taking its toll on my health. Like her first seizure, I somehow knew it was meant to be. When it happened, I felt calmness inside me, a soul knowing the truth. The problem is the body. When my soul hears something that is right on, I can identify with it. It is as though I learn information I have never heard before, but I know it's true. It is getting the ego, body, and mind on board to support what is already taking place that is difficult.

My body wanted to push back. My body shook inside and fear overwhelmed me. My spirit jumped in and grounded me, giving me the strength and wisdom to go forward. My body wanted to push through with force. The same old familiar fight, wisdom verses force. Force jumped in and kept me paddling, and then wisdom got me to shore. I hoped to be able to combine my wisdom and acceptance with the force of a huge party to comfort and distract my human heart.

Karissa, Lorrin's caregiver, friend and live-in roomie was a huge help at this time. She was both resourceful and fun. We started to go online and researched just what a Quinceañera was about. We looked up dresses on the Internet. We found stores that sold the coveted dress. I was quickly learning the enormous cost. It was as though I was planning a wedding. I had no idea what I was in for. The other side to this was that I knew Lorrin would not be having a wedding, and this was my moment to celebrate her in a way that would be rewarding for both of us.

I called my attorney Loye and asked her, "How much money can I spend on a fifteenth birthday party without going to jail?"

Loye was sent to me by angels. Our relationship was far beyond client-attorney. She was also a witness to Lorrin's failing health. She could feel Lorrin slipping. She was intuitive and in touch with Lorrin in a beautiful way. She was not only my legal representation, she was and still is family.

Loye told me to have the best party I could, and she would cover me in court if I was questioned. She loved and understood Lorrin and the power of her. I was in complete respect of Loye and knew that if I was off, she would quickly get me back on track. I hung up the phone feeling safe. I was about to have a huge celebration of Lorrin's life, a celebration of my baby coming into womanhood.

Lorrin had a way of always getting what she wanted. Karissa and I spent hours looking at dresses on the Internet. We put Lorrin in her wheelchair and all sat at the table together, marking websites of our favorites. I was having a particularly difficult time getting a dress that I liked and Lorrin also liked. I couldn't get a response from her. Karissa also had her favorites. I fell in love with a dress that was lavender. I kept showing it to Lorrin over and over. I thought it was perfect.

Lorrin was not so impressed. Also at this time, Lorrin's health wasn't too good. She was sleeping a large part of the day and required oxygen constantly. The oxygen was just another reminder of what was happening to Lorrin. The physical reminder was depressing for to me to accept and also a pain in the ass to drag around. Lorrin had not required oxygen since she was five years old. This was such an obvious set back.

Lorrin was also a teenager. She wanted to be left alone in her room and listen to music and watch the Disney channel. She also spent more time sleeping. Her physical therapist kept telling me that she was a typical teen and it was just a phase. I felt that it was much more. I don't think he and I ever really agreed about the end stages of Lorrin's life.

I was getting very concerned about dragging Lorrin all over town to shop for a dress under her physical limitations. I thought it would be too much for her. We also needed a dress and we needed it quickly. Her birthday was in March, it was January, and we had much work to do. A funny thing happened. I had a dream. In my dream, I saw this vision of a coral-colored dress. It was similar to a princess Disney dress. It was huge. Much larger than the dresses I had been looking at online. It was nowhere near the one that my heart was set on.

I woke up the next day and told Karissa, "It's a coral color. The dress is huge." I went back online and looked at some local wedding shops. I called Sarah and asked if she would like to join us. Of course, that was a silly question.

We picked up Sarah and went straight to the first shop I saw online. It was the closest. It was a bridal shop. We went in and I said, "Bring me everything you have in a coral color." She brought three dresses. One was beautiful and straight, and the other two were quite large gowns. Loads of beads and sequins. To no surprise, Lorrin blinked at the most expensive one.

Karissa, Sarah, and I went into the large dressing room. We took Lorrin out of her wheelchair and laid her down on the ground. We proceeded to take this $800 dollar gown and put it on her gently. This is no easy task. It took all three of us. We laughed as we rolled around on the ground pulling and pushing at Lorrin's fragile body.

I laughed and gave Lorrin a hard time every time she would stretch her body or move in a way that was not so helpful to getting her into this dress. It was silly. I knew immediately that this was the gown for her. I had seen it in my dream. Lorrin had showed me as she always has done and waited for me to catch up to her. We laughed hard in the dressing room, all of us breaking into a sweat. It was clear this was her dress. What a beauty!

The woman who ran the shop could not have been sweeter. We quickly started trying on tiaras. Sarah was really enjoying this. Sarah is Peruvian. Her father always wanted Sarah to have a Quinceañera. Up until this time, she was dead against it. I could see her opening her mind up to it a bit while picking out Lorrin's dress. It is always about the dress.

Job well done. It was meant to be. We purchased Lorrin's dress. I knew from here on, the party was going to be a success. We went to have sushi and laughed together as we planned our party.

We got home with this huge dress in hand. What were we to do with it? I kept feeling as though my family, Karissa, Lorrin, and me needed to keep the carrot out in front of us. Otherwise, our home would become intense. We were in a fifty/fifty mode. Karissa and I could obviously see what was happening to Lorrin's body. She was on oxygen. We would take her blood pressure and see her heart rate going really high and then low. She was also starting to have moments where she would gasp for breath. It was crazy. I was trying to keep my head straight and accept what was happening, all the while having no idea of what to expect. I have never seen anyone actually physically die. I was trying to prepare myself and still be a mother.

Karissa and I would get really caught up in death talk. The next minute we would be talking about the party. Our greatest fears were that Lorrin would not make it to the party. I knew from all that Lorrin taught me, I had no control. I'm not sure if it was my idea or Karissa's, but somehow we decided to hang the dress in the middle of Lorrin's room. It was huge and needed much space. It was beautiful, and just by looking at it, made me feel hopeful. I would imagine Lorrin swallowed up in this amazing gown. It was a fantasy dress.

At the time, Karissa was dating a wonderful guy named Jason. I believe he was six-foot-four, and I think it was he who put the hook in the ceiling in the middle of Lorrin's room, which provided a great distraction for everyone in Lorrin's life. I told her night nurses that I realized it was in the way, but it was going to hang there until Lorrin put it on for her party. Lorrin was spending a lot of time in her room hooked up to oxygen. She had been out of school for a few months now and I wanted to keep her mind full of beautiful thoughts.

I was out one evening, and I returned home to find a huge "15" stuck on Lorrin's ceiling. It was just above where her head lay on her pillow. Karissa and Jason made it with my scrapbooking supplies. It was about three feet by three feet. It was pink and red with the word "strength" on it. It stays above her bed today. I still sleep in her room when I am home. It brings back such mixed emotions. The word *strength* means so much to me. In life, it is the simple things that can somehow sustain hope. I will never know how hard it was for Karissa to be part of our lives. I had no choice, but she did, and I am so in awe of her bravery and willingness to share that time with me and my girl. And all my love to Jason, always.

Now that the dress was taken care of, I knew exactly what to do. Throwing parties was easy for me. I invited everyone in her life that was important. Her doctors, acupuncturist, therapist, stock brokers, attorney, teachers, classmates, all of her friends from middle school and high school, canine companion friends, and my friends. We had about a hundred people show up. We had three margarita machines, a dance floor, and the best cupcakes made from the Chocolatine in Thousand Oaks.

My friends Hugo and Sabrina, who own the Chocolatine, had served chocolate to Lorrin many times. The Chocolatine was our favorite place to grab lunch and eat chocolate. We met there all the time with Lorrin's favorite people.

When Lorrin and I arrived, Hugo called his wife Sabrina, and asked her to come from home to make Lorrin's chocolate mousse. Lorrin was unable to eat anything cold and didn't like chunks. So mousse was her obvious favorite.

I told Hugo not to worry, Lorrin could try something new today. His response was, "If Sabrina knows that you were here and I did not call her, I will be sleeping on the sofa tonight!"

I ordered a hundred cupcakes for the party. Sabrina made a tiara on each and every one. They were perfect, beautiful, and delicious!

Everyone pitched in to make the party a success. Lorrin had wanted her hair dyed black for the party for many weeks. Karissa didn't like the idea at all. I didn't either. Lorrin was so pale, and we were both worried that she would look horrible with black hair. Lorrin was a natural blond and she had lovely hair. I was also worried about how I viewed Lorrin in her last days. Could I watch her die with black hair? It was too much for me. My dark thoughts haunted me constantly.

My new boyfriend James put it all into perspective one day. He simply said, "If she was an able-bodied teen, she would just go out and do it herself!"

Those words hit home to me. I had gotten so caught up in the party and my thoughts, my feelings, my own needs. I needed to realize it was really Lorrin's party, and I had to give her what she wanted. So I made the appointment to have her hair dyed black. At first it was a bit hard to get used to. Lorrin's blue eyes and white skin were beautiful. She looked a bit like Snow White. Most importantly, Lorrin was happy. That was all that mattered.

Karissa spent hours trying Lorrin's hair in different up dos. Lorrin had a tiara and beautiful earrings. She had her tennis shoes that she would start the party with and her big girl shoes that she would change into. This would represent her going from a girl to a woman. Her godmother was going to present her with a Rosary, and my sister, Stephanie, would present a Bible. I was going to honor Dr. Kundell in front of everyone and thank him for caring so diligently for Lorrin and putting up with me.

There was so much going on at this time in our lives, I could spend pages telling you about it. Maybe another time or another book. But what I want to tell you is that my Lorrin was about to have the party of her life. On that day, Karissa spent hours putting her hair up. The photographer, Mary, came early and took pictures all day long. The moment that stays in my mind is of Lorrin lying across the bed. Her hair is as beautiful as a princess'. Karissa and I worked together to get her dress on. Karissa had gotten Lorrin these plastic gels to go inside her dress. Lorrin had lost nine pounds off her tiny frame. She was painfully skinny. Karissa always supported Lorrin's womanhood. Karissa put the gels onto Lorrin's bare chest to help fill out and hold up her dress. In that moment, a beautiful and simple thing happened. Lorrin smiled the biggest smile she could make. It was at that moment that Lorrin was truly a young woman.

Karissa and I laughed so hard. To no one's surprise, my girl wanted to be just like every other girl.

Lorrin never complained. She never cried and gave only those who knew her an attitude of love. This plain and simple moment was not to be looked over. My baby, who had survived this body through endless seizures, hellish operations, and rejected countless times by her community, wanted the same thing other girls at the age of fifteen wanted. She wanted breasts. She just wanted to be like every other girl. She wanted to have the physical experience of being a woman.

This may not have been such a huge moment for me if Lorrin had not smiled. She hadn't smiled like that in such a long time. I will always remember that moment and give Lorrin the respect that she deserves for living in her body that disappointed her in so many ways. She is my hero.

When I look back at pictures, I wish I would have given more care and attention to what I was wearing. I had not picked out an outfit and thought I would be able to try something on the day of the party and make it work. I was not my best. But again, the party was not about me. It was Lorrin's celebration.

Her best friends arrived early and came into her room. Sarah had a vase of purple tulips in her hand. People were showing up and the party was starting to kick off. It seemed to me that everything was going perfectly. Food was being served and drinks were being blended. We had a virgin Margarita machine for the young ones. Everyone seemed to be having fun.

The second huge moment of the day happened when I got my hands on the microphone and roasted Dr. Kundell and thanked Loye and Larry, Lorrin's attorney and longtime physical therapist. Lorrin put on her big girl shoes and she was gifted her Rosary and Bible. Miss Sarah Rivera planned to give something special to Lorrin.

I don't remember what all was said, but I stood back in my James' arms and watched in awe as Sarah Rivera, a fifteen-year-old young lady, stood up in front of about a hundred guests and read this poem:

Lorrin,
You are the peanut to my butter
You are the remote to my halo
The guitar to my hero
The blue in my sky
The Dirt on my ground
And the color in my world
Lorrin
You are my everything...

I am sure there was not a dry eye in the house. Sarah's mother came up to me after that and hugged me and said, "Thank you for showing me who my daughter is." I was so numb that day for so many different reasons. I hugged her tightly and told her I had nothing to do with this. Sarah is just amazing.

Lorrin was surrounded by her friends and everybody danced on the dance floor, circled around her. We danced that night and stayed up late. I knew by looking at Lorrin that she worked hard to stay alert. A smile was hard to come by, and I secretly wished she were better able to enjoy the party. She did what she came here to do. She allowed people to come together in love and celebrate life and know that it is sacred.

Chapter 37

~Father Joe and the Witch Doctor~
Fifteen Years Old

"But even strong women need an arm to lean on now and then."

~ *J.D. Robb and Nora Roberts in Glory in Death*

I was lying in bed when the phone rang. It was my dear psychic friend, Lisbeth. She told me how wonderful it was to be at the party. Her husband, Matt, made a connection with Lorrin. Lorrin reached out for his hand. What a simple and powerful gesture. He was also in a wheelchair and understood the effort it took Lorrin to make such a small but large motion.

Lisbeth told me that Lorrin shared with her that she wanted to have her last rites given.

I am not Catholic, nor have I attended church much. I had an idea of last rites and what that meant. Lorrin received her last rites when she was three years old. It wasn't planned and happened in Cedars-Sinai ICU.

I respected Lisbeth and knew when I didn't listen, Lorrin would find someone who would. I was not surprised that Lorrin wanted her last rites. She and I both love ceremony.

My dear friend, Vicki, referred me to Father Joe. He was a Franciscan Monk. I met with him and asked him if he would consider giving Lorrin her last rites. Father Joe was working out of the same Catholic Church where Lorrin's Brownie meetings were held.

I invited Vicki, Lorrin's school nurse Debbie, my boyfriend James, Karissa, and my friend Victoria. Father Joe was perfect. He anointed Lorrin and said some prayers. Debbie sang Lorrin's favorite song. It was beautiful and peaceful. The entire ceremony left me happy and confused. It was the right thing to do. I fell in love with Father Joe and his kindness that day. It was perfect.

The next part may seem a bit weird. I also asked a dear friend of mine named Sonya to also give Lorrin her last rites. She is a healer and longtime prayer-giver to Lorrin. For the sake of drama, I will call her a witch doctor because I cannot logically explain her gifts and want to respect her privacy. I have known her about ten years. She has given me all the time in the world and supports me emotionally and spiritually. For me, it was a natural next step to ask Sonya to bless Lorrin.

James, Karissa, Lorrin, and I showed up at Sonya's home. Lorrin was dressed in white. Sonya was dressed in white. She had her rainbow necklace around her neck. We laid Lorrin down on a white sheet. I had brought flowers and gave them to Sonya. We all knelt next to Lorrin and Sonya read many prayers. She laid her hands on Lorrin. She blessed her and anointed her. It was lovely and sacred. It was a powerful moment for all of us. It was private and beautiful.

Chapter 38

~ *Letting Go* ~

"It is during our darkest moments that we must focus to see the light."

~Aristotle Onassis

Lorrin had been teaching me a whole new level of pain, patience, and frustration. Her tiny body held on tight to life. I felt like I was dying with her. I walked in and out of her room watching, waiting for her to take her last breath. Watching and waiting. Waiting and watching.

She spent the next day in bed, struggling for air. Her nostrils flared as she took her next breath. Her oxygen levels went to 79% and 80%. They should be at 100%. She can range from 95% all the way down to 80% and below in a day. I felt as though I was being tortured. How could there be a divine creator who kept watch on my pain as I watched my daughter go through her last stages of life? I was sure I had done all I could for her. Still, I wondered how much more will be required. My body was exhausted from stress. My chest hurt and I felt the weight of her breathing. I wondered how much more I can endure before I really do lose my mind.

December 16, 2009

Hospice came for the first time yesterday. Lorrin's pediatrician didn't seem too keen on it. I wasn't sure about it with all I was going through, I just felt exhaustion and confusion. Death and children, there really is no place for the two together. What happens to parents, during the process of watching children die, is true madness. There is no sense or promise in life when your child is catastrophically ill. There were so many days when I'd wake up and could see no future at all. It was hard to stand, move, or much less function.

People would talk and I'd watch their mouths moving, not even caring what they were saying. I was supposed to "carry on," but I could not care less. I fantasized about taking Xanax for days to numb my pain, but I knew I had to function. Everyone was still having simple-minded conversations. They don't understand my pain. My child was ill. I was losing my life. How could anything else exist?

How could God be present? He must know the pain I was in. How could he not care? I was not feeling so safe with the divine creator. I wondered if we made it all up to comfort ourselves. It certainly felt like it.

Months ago, Lorrin wanted to purchase a bunch of stones and rocks. We shopped at my favorite store in Thousand Oaks, The Hummingbird and The Honey Bee. Lorrin picked out $300 in stones. Even though her body was weak, she held each one and blinked. She wanted to put her energy into the rocks and give them to her closest loved ones when she died.

I had no rules for her death. I had only my intuition of what was right for us. I loved this idea and I knew her friends would be grateful when they received her energetically charged gifts. Each time I saw them on her bed, I was reminded that she was trying to prepare us all. She was protecting us from the hard fall we would have when she was gone.

She had been sleeping with these stones now for months. I knew a time would come when this bed would be empty. Nothing would replace her beautiful, loving energy that I had been so lucky to have for fifteen years.

Today my chest felt so heavy, like bricks were holding me down. I wanted to crawl. I couldn't bear to stand. I was so exhausted. I knew more than anyone that this meant nothing. I would keep struggling and suffering. Acting like I was writing to help people. I was just breathing because my body kept going. My mind, spirit, and any hope left in me was gone. Just existence. I hated every person who called me. Oh yeah, to top it off, it was Christmas.

I was in therapy, feeling like I had hit a wall. Even the therapist said I had every reason to be depressed. Even after all the spiritual work I had done, I was drowning. You'd think I'd quit eating, but I could muster enough energy to fill myself full of crap food that only makes me fatter. I was old, and felt alone, watching my daughter have another one of her episodes.

A few weeks ago, Lorrin was having so many seizures that I was sure it was the end, my greatest fear was that she may go on forever. I watched her body shake and shake until I could take no more and I drugged her, acting like it didn't bother me anymore. Keeping myself busy, looking up people on Facebook and numbing any thought process out with a bottle of wine. Sitting on my sofa watching Lorrin breathe.

When she woke up shaking, I waited as long as I could before I drugged her again. The moments ticked by, life happened. I was not in it. I could only act like I was living. My heart ached for change, completion.

This time, she could be done. It seemed she was barely breathing. I set up a romantic saga in my head of how the moment of her death would look. I was sure it was coming. I started to grieve. Since Thanksgiving I could feel her slipping away. I saw her in my meditations, floating away like a balloon. When I talked to her via meditations, I heard that she was tired. I encouraged her to let go. I would be okay. I waited. I walked out of the room.

The grief was hitting me. I tried so hard to accept what was happening. I was trying to be strong and my body felt like I couldn't walk. Getting up was too much. I was forced to care for Lorrin; otherwise I would be in bed in the fetal position. I fantasized about being left alone and not moving for days.

She was still alive, but I could only grieve. I wished I could enjoy this time with her, but I cannot reach her. I was angry with her for making me suffer so. I begged her to let go. She just stared at the wall. Was she in there? Did she have a plan? What the fuck was it? What made me so hopeless?

The night rolled on and my night nurse came. I was having a hard time talking. I looked past her. I wanted to crawl. Could no one see what was happening to me? I was only existing. It hurt to breathe. I was done for the day. I wanted to go upstairs, but I cannot walk. I took the dog out for her last toilet for the evening. She was depressed too. I made it upstairs and crawled in bed, I couldn't breathe, I didn't want to breathe.

I got under the covers. I didn't know what to do. There was no concept or any slight idea of survival or hope for me. I couldn't think a positive thought. I only knew that tomorrow I would wake up feeling probably more horrible than I did today. Maybe Lorrin would die. Or worse, she would live.

I started to cry. I couldn't remember the last time I cried. Not really hard like I knew I could. I was like a snowball—the momentum started and I cried harder and harder. I had so much grief in me I felt as though I was being turned inside out.

I hated this. It seemed that all I felt really meant nothing. I begged for mercy on my soul, on Lorrin's life, on my existence. I pleaded for relief. I knew this familiar feeling of despair. I had not cried like this for maybe ten years. As much as I wanted this to be a cleansing, I knew there were more nights like this in me. I could cry for ten years and nothing would change.

Life would still suck tomorrow. I had done good things. I was a good person who lived a life in hell. If I'd had any energy, I would puke. I fantasized about not waking up in the morning, frustratingly I knew I wasn't done.

I wanted to die with her. Could I live without her? Would I be able to enjoy my life again?

The next day came. I slept as late as I could. Dragging my feet down the stairs. Lorrin was still having seizures. I tried to talk to her. To meditate. What did she want from me? How could I manage my broken heart? My lonely future.

I felt death surrounding me. What would I do without Lorrin? It would be like waking up on Mars. Nothing would be familiar. Lorrin had taken over my entire life.

Everyone looked at me like I was doing the impossible. It was impossible—it was killing me. My spirit was gone. I couldn't imagine what life would be without her demanding all my time and energy. I longed for reprieve but couldn't imagine what that meant.

I spent time fantasizing about her death and trying to make myself a vision for the future. I was so focused on surviving without her that when I came back to reality, I needed to refocus on dealing with her if she lived. Where was the balance? Why did the phone keep ringing? I wished people would leave me alone.

My aunt, who came for the second time in a month, sat by my side. James had returned to England due to Visa restrictions. We originally planned for him to spend Christmas with his family and return for the New Year. Things were strangely falling into place. My aunt held space for me to grieve, the house was peaceful. Lorrin was home, where she needed to be. I walked through my home in a fog knowing the time was close.

I sat in a chair next to Lorrin's bed. The oxygen was hooked up, and her fifteen-year-old body was draped across my lap. I held Lorrin in my arms as though she were a two-month-old baby. Her chest heaved up and down, gasping for each breath. Her face was gray. Her heart was no longer beating but was just a low purr. The hospice worker came by earlier and told me she could no longer get a blood pressure reading.

I was so glad that I decided to call Sarah over to see her. She thought it would be good to tell Lorrin's other friends. I was nervous, they were so young and after all it was Christmas for everyone else. Only hours earlier, six of us were in Lorrin's bed, laughing as our hearts broke, all of us afraid of this moment. Everyone that got close to Lorrin knew she wouldn't live forever, but they took the chance to have their hearts touched by her angelic presence.

I was jolted back to reality by Lorrin's deep breaths. I knew this time it was really over. Her eyes gazed at me. I had waited and anticipated this moment since she was injured at six weeks old. I was tired. I was afraid. My worst fear was here now. My baby was dying.

I had waited to be free of her constant care needs. She really was ready to leave. The last months had been full of fear and anticipation of what it would be like. Who would I be if I wasn't Lorrin's mother?

With all my strength, I lifted Lorrin's head with my left hand and sat her on my knee. She never had head or trunk control, but now her body was practically collapsing as her head was cradled in my hand. I looked at her body, amazed at her strength. Her jaw dropped as she gasped for air. Then I saw it. A very strange thing happened to her face. I was afraid. I saw something scary shift in her entire body. I knew her spirit had left.

I closed my eyes and prayed to my angels for help. I asked my guides for strength. I wanted to do this. I needed to be strong. I thanked Lorrin for allowing me to be present as she drew her penultimate breath.

I opened my eyes. My aunt was in the room with me. "Did you see that?" she asked.

I shook my head. I put Lorrin down and sat her up. It was eleven p.m. I was so afraid she would die on my nephew's birthday, which was only an hour away. Silly, the thoughts that went through my mind.

I laid her body in bed. Kissed her. I grabbed the holy water that sat on her altar and anointed her third eye, her heart, and the top of her head. I did the same with sandalwood oil. I burned sage and blessed her, and then I went through the entire house.

The candles had been burning for days on her altar. I walked out of the room. I knew that she was gone but her body still worked—her body that worked hard for fifteen years to serve me and all the people that Lorrin had come into contact with.

I walked out. I was okay. I poured a glass of wine and sat with my Aunt Linda. She didn't drink, but she poured herself a glass. I loved her. I was glad I wasn't alone. I walked back into the room. Lorrin's chest was still moving. The color of her skin was greyish blue. I walked back into the kitchen, full of fear that I might have to continue this vigil tomorrow when I wake.

My worst fear now was that she might live, not die as I had prepared myself for. I sat down. Time was a blur. I walked back into her room. I knew immediately she was gone. My baby was gone.

Chapter 39

~ *Sweet Sixteen* ~

"Today would have been the birthday of the most amazing woman I've ever met. Lorrin was my inspiration for so many things. Today I vow to wear pink and eat chocolate in memory of the girl I'll never forget."

~ Brittney, Lorrin's cousin

Lorrin died December 22, 2009. It was now March, 2010. It had always been my intention to handle Lorrin's life with grace and dignity. Today, I felt lost without direction or example of how to move forward. How did I exist? How did I know what the right action truly was?

I broke up with James the day before Lorrin's service in January. Later, I found out that Karissa and Sarah both broke up with their boyfriends as well. I had no idea that they were as lost as I was. We didn't speak of this at the time. I'm not sure why. We were all just trying to survive like fish out of water. It is strange how one little girl who had no physical abilities could capture so many hearts.

James and I managed to repair our relationship, saying our misunderstandings were due to the enormous amount of stress we both were under. Then, as fate would have it, I broke it off with him in a mad rage only weeks after the service. I had no trust in any single person. I had done this alone. I had been cheated on, lied to, and stolen from. Taken advantage of by so many people that I thought were friends. I had been married and divorced three times.

Two weeks after Lorrin's death, her website has had 2,000 hits. Every day, complete strangers contacted me and complimented my strength and on the love and courage I exuded. Life is complicated. There was so much pain and loss of trust in the relationships in my life.

The people who stood by me during those unbearable, painful times were not those whom I thought would be there. I guess that is common knowledge to parents who have gone through the death of a child. People say and do the strangest things, especially when children die. What is done is done. Forgive, accept what is, and get on with life.

My dear friend, Stacy, came to my home numerous times and called me every day for weeks, maybe even a month or so after Lorrin died. She also knew the pain of burying a child. She told me that grieving is something you do alone.

I wake up every day and work through what may be grief, relief, sadness, and hope. There are many other feelings that come on a daily basis, but they are too many to mention. I continue to communicate with Lorrin daily. She is beside me always. I feel her and hear her.

The strangest thing is that when I feel her presence, she is in a perfect body. Now that she is on the other side, her skinny, crooked and bent up arms that I loved so much are free moving and perfectly able as they hold me. It is something I am trying to get used to. I am happy for her and her new perfect body, although I feel sadness for me and the lifetime of memories I have of those crooked arms I grew to love so much. Another weird part of her death and me learning to let go of my child.

Every holiday that passes feels foreign. When spring came and the tulips and lilies started to bloom, it dawned on me that Easter must be coming. What did that mean now? Easter? It used to be filled with plans of coloring eggs, a new Easter dress, fun party-type crafts that I would send to school. I loved taking the time to send each student in Lorrin's class something fun. I enjoyed making gift bags and cakes and snacks. I loved participating in small ways, celebrating the season and my role as Lorrin's mother. Joyful memories of Lorrin. Now what was ahead to celebrate? Everything seems so meaningless. I am too old to be making a fuss of this now. The days roll into one. Strange.

Spring reminds me it is on its way with the beautiful flowers and the birth of baby ducks and chicks. I remember when Lorrin was born there were baby ducks in the little pond by our home in Orange County. It suddenly dawns on me that Lorrin's birthday is only weeks away. I am not sure what to do about it. It will not be the first birthday I spend grieving and drowning in loss and pain. I grieved so many of her earlier birthdays. I remember when she was one year old, she was an entire year behind in all of her infant gains. When she turned two, even though I loved her completely, it was a landmark of her being two years behind in childhood gains. This went on for many, many years. Every year there was a great joy of celebrating her life and a sense of loss from the parenting experience that I thought I was going to have. The experience I hoped I was going to have. No one has talked to me about her birthday yet. The awkward silence awaits.

It would have been Lorrin's sweet sixteenth birthday. I was truly amazed that she made it to fifteen years old. I was able to love her in her body for an amazing fifteen and a half years. I got to have her on this planet longer than anyone anticipated.

I sat on the sofa enjoying a glass of wine. The moments in the evening were all mine now. I didn't have to do anything at all. No jumping up and down to suction, change diapers, give medication. Just Nicolette, Lorrin's canine, and me. We were doing our nightly ritual watching Craig Ferguson on the television. I put a blanket up on the sofa in an attempt to help intercept all the hair Nicolette sheds. I always felt so bad for Nikki. She had been a great dog, friend, and companion. Her work was done. I knew she was suffering from the loss of Lorrin's presence also. We both felt a huge hole in our hearts. Her big brown eyes looked at me with such sadness. I wanted to cry. She looked away and put her head down and took a deep breath. We sat together, both feeling confusion and loss.

I pulled out my laptop, feeling socially safe enough to see what others were doing in their lives. It became a nightly ritual. I tried not to make too many posts. I was too depressed as a newly grieving mother. What did people expect from me? Should I have been cheerful and push on in life? Should I have mentioned the pain that was eating me alive? So I just surfed what others were doing on their Facebook pages. For now I would live through them.

I had a post on my wall. It was from Sarah. "Hey, I have a proposition for you. Let's have a sleepover for Lorrin's birthday. I get the spot on her bed because she's holding it for me."

Only days before—minutes before—I was feeling low. I prayed for a bit of help. A sign. Some kind of gift or message to help me along. Something to reassure me that I was going to be okay. I could never have imagined this. Wow! Sarah wanted to spend time with me celebrating Lorrin's birthday! I never would have asked that of her. It really was an amazing gift. I didn't know the "rules," but I was sure this wasn't the normal situation.

Was this okay? What would their parents think? A sleepover? I had given up the thought of ever having the girls to my home again. What an amazing idea! My heart filled up. Tears pooled in my eyes and started to roll down my cheeks so that I could no longer read what was written. I felt so much gratitude. I was so blessed.

I replied to her and told her to make a list of who she wanted to invite. I shared with her that I would make sure we had sour candies, pizza, Doritos, and pumpkin deliciousness stuff. Sarah didn't like chocolate, which I found hard to believe. I always had to have plenty of chocolate for Lorrin at the sleepovers, and something special for Sarah. Pumpkin was one of her favorites. Over the years, I've made pumpkin bread, pumpkin muffins, pumpkin cake, and her favorite, pumpkin pie. I ordered loads of pie mix to ensure that I would have it on hand for her visits. I loved making Sarah and all the girls feel special.

My heart swelled. I couldn't believe these girls still wanted to spend time with me. A huge part of my healing and happiness as Lorrin's mother had been having the opportunity to experience regular events like sleepovers with Lorrin's friends. I was grieving Lorrin every day, in a totally different way than most parents would, I'm sure. I knew she was going to die. I had been grieving the loss of experiencing a normal child since she was injured. To think that I might celebrate her sixteenth birthday with her best friends was a beautiful thing. I wasn't sure anyone else would have thought of that. I knew just how special Sarah was. I knew how amazing all of Lorrin's friends were.

Sarah loved to take over and plan the slumber events. I told her that it was her party and let her make all the decisions. She was in charge and decided who would be invited. We agreed that I would pick her up three hours before the party. We needed time to go to the grocery store and then to Blockbuster to rent a few scary movies.

Sarah was the one who planned Lorrin's very first sleepover when she was thirteen! Sarah is an angel. When Lorrin was eleven, I prayed and prayed that she would have age-appropriate friends. Sarah was Lorrin's best friend. Because of her bravery, Lorrin lived a life full of love and had the opportunity to experience real friendship. What more could a teenager ask? Sarah brought Lorrin's world to her. Sarah was Lorrin's very best friend and soul mate.

On the day of the party, I was cleaning the house and it hit me. I was going to have a birthday party for my dead daughter. I tried to breathe through my pain and joy. The bittersweet was becoming a familiar feeling. I thought to myself, *Go forward. Just go forward!*

In the beginning, after Lorrin died, I was relieved to not have to wake up every day wondering if this would be the day that she died. Next was the relief of not having to care for her broken body. The last year of her life she lost nine pounds and had three diarrhea-quality bowel movements a day.

My girlfriend, Stacy, reminded me that grieving means that each day you carry heaviness around with you. It was weight that you couldn't detach. It followed your every move, your every thought. It was a burden, a pain, that kept you from smiling totally, from breathing in fully, and that took away the happiest thoughts. First the grief. Then maybe life could follow.

I was a bit nervous to see Sarah. She was so mature for her age. I wasn't sure what to expect from her and the girls. They were the bravest people I have ever met. I pulled up to Sarah's house and was immediately reminded of how Sarah was forever changing. She had grown into a beautiful young lady. Her short dress showed off her great legs. I remembered a time when she never would have been caught dead in a dress. She was so beautiful. Her hair was straight. Her make-up was on. She had been carrying a purse for a while now, but it still shocked me to see how quickly she was changing. How fast she was growing up.

My Lorrin was her age. I always think for a second what Lorrin would have been like in a healthy body.

Sarah was so beautiful—she was going to break hearts.

She popped in the car as only a teenager can. The world seemed so light. She had tales about the boys she was interested in. What her peers were doing. We always talked about how she was doing at school. We decided to go to the grocery store first.

Sarah told me about her plans for the party. She knew exactly what she wanted to buy. I told her that we should buy some hairy buffalo wings! We giggled as we remembered a sleepover a year ago. I had picked up Sarah and we bought her favorite buffalo wings at her local grocery store. When we ate them, they were full of hair. It was disgusting. She told me that she hadn't eaten them since. I told her we had to get some! We cracked up.

Sarah grabbed the grocery cart. She was assertive and confident. She started off by telling me that we had to get a certain kind of cookie. We went directly to the bakery section. She picked out what I would never purchase. A container of sugar cookies topped with more sugar. They looked completely disgusting.

"Grab two!" I said.

We grabbed brownie bites, and I searched for hairy wings. I couldn't find them. She told me what aisles I needed to go down and what aisles I didn't. She had planned out exactly in her mind how this was going to go. I asked her about spicy Cheetos, and she told me that no one eats those anymore. I asked about Pringles. Sarah said, "No." I had no idea what the kids ate.

I asked her if she wanted our traditional farm animal waffles for breakfast. She said yes. Sausage or bacon? Bacon. We buy one root beer, one cola, one lemonade, and one grape juice. I told Sarah to pick out four trashy magazines, meaning those with celebrity gossip and teen articles. The girls spent hours looking through them.

Since Lorrin had died, I stopped the subscriptions that used to come to the house.

I realized as we are checking out that it would be tough to fit all this in my sports car. Sarah said that we needed some toilet paper. I knew immediately what she was talking about. They wanted to toilet paper a house, of course. I told her that they can paper if they clean up. She didn't like that idea.

We barely managed to shove the groceries into my car. I suggested we go to the ninety-nine cent store to get some knick knacks to decorate the house. I follow behind Sarah inside the store. The aisles are so small and packed full of what I would consider crap. I pointed out some things, but she said no. I saw some feather boas and grabbed seven. We found the most hideous masks. They were Marx Brother-esque, except these glasses had large pink noses and they lit up.

It is easy to see why they were at the ninety-nine cent store. The glasses had scars and marks all over them. They were just horrible enough to get a laugh. Some of the glasses had buttons on the bottom of the noses that light up when they were turned on. We also found some Mardi Gras masks. These were much cuter.

My plan was to distract people from the obvious sadness they might feel when they walked into my home for the first time. I hadn't met two of the parents of the girls who were coming. I could only imagine what they were thinking after hearing: "Mom, I'm going to Lorrin's sixteenth birthday party. Oh, and she is dead!"

I love Sarah so much. We were driving, and I asked her all about her new boyfriend. She was so full of life. I know that if my Lorrin was alive, living a normal teenage experience, she would probably struggle sharing so much with me. Mothers are always the least trusted at this age. But Sarah felt safe sharing with me. I was overjoyed and filled with love. Before we pulled into the driveway, I asked her if she was okay to go into the house. She hadn't been in our home since Lorrin's death. She said yes. She told me how much she missed Lorrin. She mentioned that she could really use her right now. I agreed with her. I put my hand on her leg, wanting to connect with her. I knew that right now we could both burst into tears. But today was a celebration. We were here to have fun. I reassured her that Lorrin was with us both, and she was so excited about the party.

We were rushing around the kitchen and getting everything ready. It amazed me how responsible Sarah was. She just acted like she was an adult setting up the kitchen. She was fifteen. Sarah baked cupcakes. We purchased candles numbered "1" and "6" to light a "16" on top of the cupcakes. Sarah had no idea of the love and excitement that I had just spending time with her. She is an angel. All the girls are my angels.

I asked Sarah if she thought the altar that I set up for Lorrin next to the dining room table was going to be hard for the girls to see. Should I move it? Sarah went over to it. In the mix was my favorite picture of Lorrin and Sarah, along with three candles burning, a huge picture of Lorrin, a dried rose, Lorrin's peace ring, and two five-inch crystal angels. I have a cross with a butterfly necklace made out of rose quartz draped across it. There were two other heart crystals on the cabinet. And then there were Lorrin's ashes. They were still in the box that they came in. I hadn't found the perfect urn yet. I would. But for now, they were in a box with a tacky blue velvety bag covering it.

Sarah immediately saw the box and picked up the container. I asked her if I should move the ashes. Strange, that I was asking a fifteen-year-old what to do. Where are the rules in death? She said no. She picked up the ashes and started to open them. Her hands were on the box as her eyes dart over to mine. She was asking permission as she opened the container. "Can I see them?"

I somehow wasn't prepared for this. I wasn't afraid. I told Sarah that sometimes I put them in my sports car and drove around with them. We laughed. I hadn't told anyone this.

She was very curious. I allowed her to look as I continued to pick up and get the table ready for the girls' arrival. I let her do what she wanted. She had never given me any reason to censor her before. Why would I do so now? I acted as though I wasn't paying too much attention, giving her space. But my eyes were on her. I was thinking twenty different thoughts.

Sarah asked about the texture of what was inside the bag. I told her maybe they were Lorrin's bones and things burned down. Not exactly sure what to say. I offered what I knew. She lost interest fast.

I suggested that maybe we'd get the girls together and scatter her ashes. That wasn't planned; it just seemed to make sense at the time. She put the ashes back. I felt her curiosity and bravery. I love her. More than I can write.

We got back to setting the tables with all of the crap food that we purchased. The rest of the girls would be here soon.

The doorbell rang and two of the girls came over together. I knew the mom and gave her kind of a look, as though I was just as surprised as she was for having the party. She asked how I was doing. I told her good. I thought I was good. I was good sometimes and I was bad sometimes. That must be normal.

I shared with her that good things are happening to me. I spoke last week at Cedars-Sinai to a group of doctors, residents, and nurses about palliative care. That felt good. I also just spoke at an ELNEC conference for bereavement to a large group of doctors and nurses. It was a strange thing to be proud of, talking about my experience as a mother who had lost her child. But I cannot change what happened. I can only make the best situation out of it. If I can help someone by sharing my experience, then that's what I will do.

The girls started running around the house and looking in Lorrin's room. I had kept everything the same. I distracted them and tried to get them to wear the masks that we purchased. I got them wrapped up in the boas. This would at least make people laugh as they walked in the door. Parents were probably more afraid than the kids.

It was awkward, to say the least. I tried to keep things moving. I shifted through the rough patches as best I could. I wasn't trying to avoid the experience, just allow it to be safe. I watched the girls and followed suit. I encouraged them to make themselves at home and do what they wanted. They knew the house rules. Once you had been over and knew where things were, you had to help yourself.

The next time the doorbell rang, I encouraged the girls to answer it with their silly masks. The girls laughed and ran in to grab a mask for themselves. They slid on the floors with their socks. The music was blaring and the girls were laughing. Everything was normal. Except, for one small thing.

Miss Lorrin was missing.

Everyone felt it. No one said anything.

One of the mothers stayed and talked for a long time. She was wonderful. She told me her daughter has a really hard time with scary movies and that she might want to come home when we put the movie on. I made sure the kids knew they could go home whenever they wanted. Of course, the movies that we got at Blockbuster were disgusting and scary and gross, in my opinion. The girls loved them! At least, most of them. I kept my eye on them. It was nice to see the girls had their own opinions and were able to talk to their parents about it. The peer pressure at that age was tough.

Lorrin's nurse, Debbie, who had taken Lorrin to school every day for four years, came over. She was such a blessing. If it weren't for Debbie, Lorrin would never have met Sarah. Then there was Rosa, Lorrin's caretaker the last eight months of her life, who also came over. I loved these ladies. They looked at me and asked, "How are you doing it?" I could only reply that this night was going to be tough no matter what I did. To be able to celebrate it with Lorrin's best friends was a gift that I thought I would never have. I was going to go through this anyway, so why not make the most of it!

Sarah was in control of the evening. She wanted to sing "Happy Birthday" to Lorrin. Debbie looked mortified. She wasn't sure she could get through this. I didn't know what to say. I wasn't going to stop Sarah from doing what she has obviously planned for some time. Debbie walked out of the room. I was cracking up, watching this all take place.

Sarah got the candles lit. I grabbed my camera and took pictures of Lorrin's sweet sixteen birthday cupcakes. They sang "Happy Birthday."

A very weird feeling came over me. I wasn't prepared for this. Who could be?

Debbie stayed in Lorrin's room until the girls were done and on to the next thing. I knew it is rough. Even though I was very happy for what was taking place, my heart was also breaking.

We sat at the counter and the girls took turns playing their favorite music. There was much talk about boys. The girls were now more into love songs. Even though some of them were rap songs, the words were about sex, love, loss, and heartbreak.

Sarah offered to paint everyone's nails. Each girl waited her turn. Sarah painted Debbie's nails. She did a great job. She was completely in control. Everything was going how Sarah had planned. She had obviously thought a great deal about this night. I really had no idea what to expect. She offered to paint Rosa's nails. As she was painting, I could see that Rosa was falling apart. Sarah wasn't paying much attention. I told Rosa to stop it. Rosa was a mess. It cracked me up a bit to see Debbie and Rosa. They were taking such a hard hit emotionally. I realized that I was in this home every day. They were getting hit with the feeling of the home without Lorrin in it and all the emotions that the party was bringing out. I didn't know how I was coping. I just was. I woke up every day in my home that was empty.

For the first time in a long time, I got a knee-jerk reaction to draw up Lorrin's medication for the evening. It hit me. I hadn't had that feeling in a while. It must have been the girls. It was as though Lorrin was actually here. I knew that she was, in spirit. It was a strange thing to experience.

Rosa looked at me with those dark puppy eyes. I knew she was going to lose it. She told me over and over how amazing Sarah was. *I know*, I tell her.

Rosa loved her nails. They were painted with spots and flowers, as though Rosa were fifteen years old. Super cute. I could tell Rosa was going to leave. I hugged her and teased her and told her to get a grip. Her nails were wet as she fanned them. She told the girls good night. She looked at me for a quick second and ran for the door. I ran after her. I told her I loved her, and before she was out the door, she was bawling. I told her that it was going to be okay. She was gone before I could hug her. I shut the door and walked back into the kitchen.

Sarah was now on to Kelsey's nails.

There were times during the night I found the girls in the living room, just sitting. I could see that Taylor was struggling. I sat beside her and hugged her. I told her how much I loved her. I told her it was okay to cry.

The girls had been brave since this whole thing started with Lorrin's decline in health. I was sure on some level they never knew what they were in for, being Lorrin's friend. I didn't want to bring the party down, but I did want to allow them to share and express themselves. Taylor seemed to bounce back quickly.

I let them hang out and go through Lorrin's things. They were curious. As the night moved on, Debbie left. She told me that I was amazing and that she didn't know how I did it. *I don't know*, I tell her.

The girls got ready for the scary movies. I had two girls who didn't want to watch the scary movie and three who did. I put on Juno in Lorrin's room and got Nicolette on the bed to join and distract them from being in Lorrin's room. I had no idea about the feelings they were having. They seemed fine but who knew? We watched the movies in separate rooms and everybody seemed okay. When the movies ended, the girls were restless.

I knew what was coming next. "To toilet paper or not to toilet paper?" The girls were so good. I wanted them to remember this night as the most fun party ever. They were old enough now, and I knew they had been sneaking out in the evenings. One of the girls told me that her dad drove them. I no longer have the handicap van, so that was out of the question. I donated it to Rosa's family. She had a nephew who was in a wheelchair and on a ventilator. They had no way to transport him. So I gave the van to them. It never dawned on me that I could need it for a TP session.

I told the girls they all had to be dressed. No short night shirts and wearing a bra was a must. I told them they had fifteen minutes, they wanted thirty.

We settle for twenty-five. I started the timer. They were giggling and ran out of the house.

In about five minutes, the girls ran back into the house. They told me that while they were papering, a man came out of the house and chased them. They were all screaming and carrying on. I was relieved they were back. I was glad the TP event was completed.

The simple things in life.

The girls were so happy and scared, but excited.

It was getting late and I didn't want to hover over them. I wanted them to have their space. I went upstairs. I wanted to cry. I was so pleased how the night went. I felt so blessed. It was a crazy life. It was a beautiful life. I kept one ear to the door and made sure they were all in for the night. I could hear them giggle and chat. They watched some silly movie on HBO. I fell into a place of deep sleep and gratitude.

I woke up to the familiar slumber party ruins. Popcorn and half-filled cups of soda and water everywhere. All the girls slept on the sofa. I didn't know how they did it. Backpacks and purses and cell phones all over the floor. I started the traditional breakfast—farm animal waffles, bacon, eggs, milk, and orange juice.

Taylor walked around, talking, and started to videotape the house with her phone. She talked about how great the farm animal waffles were and how spoiled Lorrin had been. She videotaped Lorrin's altar and talked about her ashes. At some point, someone tied up Lorrin's ashes with a pink boa. It couldn't have been more appropriate.

I am exhausted. I knew this would be the last sleepover. I knew that I would have to move on from here. The girls would grow up and move on also. In some grand way, I felt as though we had made history. This might possibly be the first sleepover in honor of a dead, medically-fragile sixteen-year-old.

My Lorrin, how she continues to change lives.

Prayer for Love and Co-Creation

I call in divine light to surround me and my child. As I look into my child's eyes I see the depth of her soul. They are a window to heaven. I am witness to the magnificent love and light that is my child. We are mirrors. The love and light that I see in you, my child, is the love and light that is also in me. We are one.

I ask for divine guidance to forge on my individual path in co-creation with my spirit. This is my soul's journey. I ask for divine guidance for you to forge on your individual path in co-creation with your spirit, honoring your soul's journey. I ask for divine guidance as our spirits form union. Our alignment as one is as true as two ends of an infinity loop. We come together for the highest good and co-create our souls' purpose.

I call in divine white energy to be channeled to and through us. I invoke Archangel Michael to surround us both with white light and release any cords of energy that no longer serve us. I release and disconnect with those who cannot be witness to the miracle that is to occur. I release those who we were unable to reach in love and light.

I am the parent. I am the teacher. My child, while you are in this body, you are the student. You, who chose to become physical. I choose to embrace this perfect being of light and love. I ask for divine guidance to instruct this physical body, allowing use of all that is available to be a fluid vessel of total perfection of love and light.

I take care of myself first so that I can be witness to your miracle. I create the first image of total wellness. I feel the feeling first. I want it for myself. I want it for you.

My child, you are not a sacrificial soul. You are here to teach by enjoying life. You are love. You are empowered as a unique soul. Your spirit is total power. I call upon our spirit guides to help with this co-creation of love, light, and perfection in optimal health. This is a pairing relationship, a co-creation of paths uniting to complete our journey. There is no block. There is only choice and accountability.

We align our energies to one of perfection, wellness and one with spirit. As spirit manifests itself, this child becomes free. I am humbled and filled with appreciation. Who am I not to witness this miracle? Who am I not to see this energy manifest itself? Who decides we are not worthy to see when this is what we have been given in the first place?

As so it is…

My Favorite Resources

3ELove: www.3elove.com

456 Boler Rd Bionics: www.456bolerroad.com

Able Pathways Media: www.ablepathwaysmedia.com

Adaptive Pinball: ucandocentral.com

Adventures in Autism: adventuresinautism.blogspot.com

Ainsley's Angels of America: www.ainsleysangels.org

Age of Autism: www.ageofautism.com

Anne Dachel: www.annedachel.com

AutismOne: autismone.org

Autism Aid: www.autismaid.org

Autism is Medical: www.meetup.com/Autism-is-medical/

Autism in Long Beach: autisminlongbeach.org

Autism Research Institute: www.autism.com

Axis Dance Company: axisdance.org

Beds By George: bedsbygeorge.com

Canine Companions for Independence: www.cci.org

Christopher Voelker Studio: www.voelkerstudio.com

Cityzen The Band: cityzenband.com

Civin Media Relations: www.civinmediarelations.com

C.O.R.E. Wellness Center: www.corecenters.info

Colours Wheelchair: www.colourswheelchair.com

Deedles Photography:
deedlesphotography.wix.com/deedles-photography

Disability Today Network:
www.disabilitytodaynetwork.com/spoken-perceptions

Disabled Life Media: www.disabledlifemedia.com

Disabled Ministries: www.disabilitiesministries.com

Diverse City Entertainment: www.diversecityentertainment.net

Ed Rote: humminghoney.com

Elizabeth Birt Centre for Autism Law and Advocacy: www.ebcala.org

Extreme Abilities: www.extremeabilities.com

Full Ability Apparel: fullability.com/index.php/t-shirts

Gaia Health: www.gaia-health.com

Generation Rescue: www.generationrescue.org

Handicap This: handicapthis.com

Island Dolphin Care: www.islanddolphincare.org

Junior Blind of America: www.juniorblind.org

Keesago: www.keesago.com

KickStarter: www.kickstarter.com/projects/1365110527/collision-0

Kim Stagliano: www.kimstagliano.com

Kyle Pease Inspirational Speaker: www.kylepease.org

Lorrin's World: www.Lorrinsworld.com

Linderman Unleashed:

radio.naturalnews.com/Archive-LindermanUnleashed.asp

Libby Kimbrough: Libby.Kimbrough@facebook.com

Meg Blackburn Losey: www.spiritlite.com

Megan Assaf Wombs for Wisdom: www.wombsforwisdom.com

Michelle Francine: www.iinnersilence.com

National Autism Association: nationalautismassociation.org

National Vaccine Information Center: www.nvic.org

Natural News Radio: radio.naturalnews.com

Paintings by Michael Jr., Inc: paintingsbymichaeljr.com

Pushrim Life After Spinal Cord Injury: www.pushrim.com

Regarding Caroline: regardingcaroline.com

Robert j. Krakow Law Office: rkrakow@krakowlawfirm.com

SafeMinds: www.safeminds.org

Shut Up About Your Perfect Kid: www.shutupabout.com

Sniffle Buddies: snifflebuddies.com

Surfers for Autism: www.surfersforautism.org

Surfers for Healing: wwwsurfershealing.org

Talk About Curing Autism: www.tacanow.org

Team Long Brothers: www.teamlongbrothers.org

The Abilities Expo: www.abilitiesexpo.com

The Autism File: www.autismfile.com

The Bolen Report: www.bolenreport.com

The Canary Party: www.canaryparty.org

The Horse Boy World: www.horseboyworld.com

The Hummingbird & The Honey Bee: humminghoney.com

The Misuta Project: www.youtube.com/user/1jactivist

The Push Girls: www.sundancechannel.com/series/push-girls

The Puzzling Piece: www.thepuzzlingpiece.com

The Refusers: therefusers.com

The Sears Family: askdrsears.com

The Walk & Roll Foundation: walkandrollfoundation.org

Tommy Hollenstein Art: www.tommyhollenstein.com

Triumph Foundation: www.triumph-foundation.org

United States Power Soccer Association: www.powersoccerusa.net

Vaxtruth: vaxtruth.org

Wish Upon A Teen: www.wishuponateen.org

Dwayne Zot: zotartz.com